Time and Work

T0265196

The concept of time is a crucial filter through which we understand any events or phenomena; nothing exists outside of time. It not only conditions the question of 'when' but also influences the 'what, how and why' of our ideas about management. And yet management scholars have rarely considered this 'temporal lens' in understanding how time affects employees at work, or the organizations for which they work.

This two-volume set provides a fresh, temporal perspective on some of the most important and thriving areas in management research today. Volume 1 considers how time impacts the individual, and includes chapters on identity, emotion, motivation, stress and creativity. Volume 2 considers time in context with the organization, exploring a temporal understanding of leadership, HRM, entrepreneurship, teams and cross-cultural issues.

There is an overall concern with the practical implications of understanding individuals and organizations within the most relevant timeframes, while the two volumes provide an actionable research agenda for the future. This is a highly significant contribution to management theory and research, and will be important reading for all students and researchers of organizational behavior, organizational psychology, occupational psychology, business and management and HRM.

Abbie J. Shipp is Assistant Professor of Management at Texas Christian University, USA. Her research focuses on the psychological experience of time at work including: the trajectory of work experiences over time, how time is spent on work tasks, and how individuals think about the past/present/future.

Yitzhak Fried is Professor of Organizational Behavior and Human Resources at Syracuse University, USA. His research focus is on the contribution of context in the areas of job and office design, work stress, time in the workplace, performance appraisal, diversity at work, and cross-culture. He is a Fellow in the American Psychological Association, Society of Industrial and Organizational Psychology and Society of Organizational Behavior.

Current Issues in Work and Organizational Psychology
Series Editor: Arnold B. Bakker

Current Issues in Work and Organizational Psychology is a series of edited books that reflect the state-of-the-art areas of current and emerging interest in the psychological study of employees, workplaces and organizations.

Each volume is tightly focused on a particular topic and consists of seven to ten chapters contributed by international experts. The editors of individual volumes are leading figures in their areas and provide an introductory overview.

Example topics include: digital media at work, work and the family, workaholism, modern job design, positive occupational health and individualized deals.

A Day in the Life of a Happy Worker
Edited by Arnold B. Bakker and Kevin Daniels

The Psychology of Digital Media at Work
Edited by Daantje Derks and Arnold B. Bakker

New Frontiers in Work and Family Research
Edited by Joseph G. Grzywacz and Evangelia Demerouti

Time and Work, Volume 1: How time impacts individuals
Edited by Abbie J. Shipp and Yitzhak Fried

Time and Work, Volume 2: How time impacts groups, organizations and methodological choices
Edited by Abbie J. Shipp and Yitzhak Fried

Time and Work

How time impacts groups,
organizations and
methodological choices

Volume 2

Edited by
Abbie J. Shipp and Yitzhak Fried

Psychology Press
Taylor & Francis Group
LONDON AND NEW YORK

First published 2014
by Psychology Press
2 Park Square, Milton Park, Abingdon, Oxon, OX14 4RN

and by Psychology Press
711 Third Avenue, New York, NY 10017

Routledge is an imprint of the Taylor & Francis Group, an informa business

First issued in paperback 2016

British Library Cataloguing-in-Publication Data
A catalogue record for this book is available from the British Library

Library of Congress Cataloging-in-Publication Data

    Time and work / [edited by] Abbie J. Shipp & Yitzhak Fried.
      pages cm
  1. Hours of labor. 2. Time management. 3. Labor time. 4. Time—
Psychological aspects. I. Shipp, Abbie J. II. Fried, Yitzhak.
    HD5106.T55 2014
    331.2—dc23
    2013033782

ISBN13: 978-1-84872-134-0 (hbk)
ISBN13: 978-1-138-68469-0 (pbk)

Typeset in Times
by Apex CoVantage, LLC

This book is dedicated to Jeff Edwards and Al Bluedorn, who shaped and encouraged my earliest musings about time. And to Brad and Carter Shipp, who have filled my lifetime with love and laughter. – A. J. S.

To my beloved family, my wife, Dahlia, my daughter, Meital, and my son, Tomer. – Y. F.

Contents

Contributing authors

David Chan, Behavioral Sciences Institute, Singapore Management University, Singapore

Brandon Crosby, Department of Psychology, University of Maryland, College Park, Maryland

David V. Day, Management and Organizations, University of Western Australia Business School, Perth, Australia

Lauren D'Innocenzo, Management Department, University of Connecticut, Storrs, Connecticut

Yitzhak Fried, Whitman School of Management, Syracuse University, Syracuse, New York

C. Ashley Fulmer, Department of Psychology, National University of Singapore, Singapore

Michele J. Gelfand, Department of Psychology, University of Maryland, College Park, Maryland

Brett Anitra Gilbert, Rutgers Business School, Rutgers University, Piscataway, New Jersey

Donald Hale, Jr., Darla Moore School of Business, University of South Carolina, Columbia, South Carolina

Michael R. Kukenberger, School of Management and Labor Relations, Rutgers University, Piscataway, New Jersey

John E. Mathieu, Management Department, University of Connecticut, Storrs, Connecticut

Robert E. Ployhart, Darla Moore School of Business, University of South Carolina, Columbia, South Carolina

Abbie J. Shipp, Neeley School of Business, Texas Christian University, Fort Worth, Texas

Scott F. Turner, Darla Moore School of Business, University of South Carolina, Columbia, South Carolina

1 Time research in management

How time impacts groups, organizations and methodological choices

Yitzhak Fried and Abbie J. Shipp

As noted in the introduction to Volume 1, we created this two-volume book to bring together research on time and organizational management in a purposeful way, allowing experts in each field to become "temporal ambassadors" to their respective content areas. In Volume 1, *How Time Impacts Individuals*, the chapters focused primarily on individual-level issues related to time and work. In contrast, in the current volume, the chapters address primarily group-, organization-, and national-level topics related to time. In addition we included a chapter on methodological implications for temporal research.

The two volumes' consideration of temporal issues at multiple levels (individuals, groups, organizations, and national cultures) provides a rich platform for future research, as discussed in the different chapters. Moreover, the multilevel analysis of temporal context (which is especially apparent in this volume) raises additional conceptual and methodological questions that should be addressed in future research.

Concerning conceptual issues, an interesting question is how do characteristics of time at one level affect temporal issues at another level? Thus, for example, how does the development of organizational routines over time (Turner, this volume) affect leader-follower relationships (e.g., how quickly these relationships develop; Day, this volume)? The picture may be mixed: evolvement of higher organizational routines may, on one hand, slow the evolvement of creative, "out of the box" leader-member exchange relationships, but, on the other hand, may provide the predictability and support for quicker development of trustworthy relationships between leaders and followers. Another conceptual time-related issue pertains to the effect of the underlying temporal dimensions of national cultures (Fulmer, Crosby, & Gelfand, this volume) on individuals' accommodations and reactions to these cultures. Here again the picture may be mixed, contingent on the level of exposure of individuals to different cultural dimensions during their career. In our global economy, individuals who are routinely exposed to multiple cultures during their career are likely to develop multiple time perspectives that can be internalized and successfully applied in different cultural contexts. On the other hand, those who work mainly within one culture are likely to internalize the time perspective of this particular culture, resulting in less flexibility in adjusting to other cultural perspectives when required.

The foregoing two examples refer to the effect of macro-level phenomena on micro- or meso-level temporal phenomena. However, the effect can also occur in the reverse direction, such that, for example, dynamic changes at the individual or team levels may affect the dynamic changes at the organizational level (Ployhart & Hale, this volume). To illustrate, one strong and prevalent source of stress and strain is work-family conflict, in which the pressure to spend increasingly more time at work adversely affects family life (Sonnentag, Pundt, & Albrecht, 2014). Over time, work-family conflict leads to increased levels of stress and strain (ibid.). The increasingly adverse effect of work-family conflict can be expected to affect organizational human resource policies and practices, including their temporal characteristics (Ployhart & Hale, this volume). For example, in recruiting potential applicants who value work-family balance (e.g., generation Y) organizations may find it useful to initially emphasize both its expectations for employees to commit themselves to high work quality, and the organization's commitment to work-family balance through supportive human resources (HR) policies and practices such as availability of child care facilities, flexible work arrangements, or work from home. At later stages organizations may find it useful to shift to more specific information about the job tasks and the work environment (cf. Ployhart & Hale, 2014). In this particular example, individuals' increased concerns about the effect of work-family imbalance over time affect the organizational recruiting policies and practices over time.

However, one key take-away from the collection of chapters as a whole is that we clearly need research to explore how temporal phenomena at different levels (micro, meso, macro) influence one another. Further, we need more research on how these cross-level relationships affect organizational outcomes. Such ideas are complex but promising as researchers continue to uncover the multilevel and temporal aspects of these topics.

Beyond the impact of time on groups, organizations, and cultures, this volume also addresses the importance of time in methodological choices. Methodologically, future research on temporal issues will benefit from incorporating both quantitative and qualitative analyses. Significant advances in the power of statistical methods should enable researchers to rely more on quantitative methods in exploring temporal theoretical issues (Chan, this volume; Kozlowski, Chao, Grand, Braun, & Kuljanin, 2013). However, the complexity of temporal research also supports the value of pursuing qualitative analysis such as interviews or case studies (e.g., Orlikowski & Yates, 2002). The benefit of such qualitative methods is not only in supporting and deepening the knowledge generated from quantitative studies, but also in potentially providing new substantive directions for research on temporal issues.

Overview of chapters

As we indicated in our introduction to Volume 1, the chapters in the two volumes were written by authors from different parts of the world, including North America, Europe, Australia, and Asia, representing a diversity of views on research on time in work contexts. We now provide some detail on each chapter in this volume.

In Chapter 2, Mathieu, Kukenberger, and D'Innocenzo analyze three approaches to studying temporal influences on team functioning. Specifically, time represents a historical context within which teams operate. Second, time is considered as a developmental marker signaling teams' movement from birth to death. Third, time is considered as a cyclical phenomenon in which teams perform different activities at different periods of performance activities. These three approaches independently and collectively indicate that teams are doing different things at different times, and thus that different processes (e.g., planning, execution, interpersonal dynamics) have differential effects on work accomplishment at different times. The authors further discuss some methodological issues that researchers should consider when pursuing temporal research designs, including predictor-criterion time lags and aggregation periods. They conclude with theoretical, research, and applied implications of systematically incorporating time in research on teams.

In Chapter 3, Day focuses on leadership in the context of time. The author analyzes the influence of time in four key areas of leadership research and theory: (a) leader behavior concerning the appropriate level of time lag between actions and effects and related measurement implications; (b) leader emergence with regard to how followers' perceptions form and change over time; (c) leader-follower relationships concerning how quickly or slowly these relationships develop and change over time; and (d) leader development – how leaders acquire and develop leadership capacity and capabilities over time. The author further discusses the value of intensive longitudinal data with an appropriate number of measurements and appropriate intervals between measurements.

In Chapter 4, Fulmer, Crosby, and Gelfand focus on cross-cultural perspectives and time. The authors focus on several issues associated with cross-cultural and temporal dimensions. They first introduce and discuss a number of important temporal dimensions that vary across cultures, including time as a silent language; past, present, and future orientation; event time and clock time; pace of life and time as a cultural metaphor. They then discuss antecedents that may explain why people perceive and approach time differently across cultures. These antecedents include variables that are inherent within a culture, such as values, religion, social structure, and language, as well as variables that are related to the environment, such as natural climate and social and economic conditions. This is followed by an elaborated discussion on the effect of cross-cultural differences in temporal orientation on micro- and macro-related outcomes. Concerning the micro level, the authors analyze how these differences affect individuals' psychological, behavioral, and health outcomes, as well as negotiation, teamwork, and job performance. Concerning the macro level, the authors discuss the effect of these differences on human resource management, strategic planning, marketing, and the economic development of countries. Finally, the authors discuss the measurement challenges in examining temporal differences in the cross-cultural context, and directions for future research at the intersection of culture and time.

In Chapter 5, Ployhart and Hale discuss how incorporating time into the field of human resources would improve the rigor of HR theories, research, and practice. The authors first review the HR field at both the micro and macro levels, indicating the lack of systematic incorporation of time in HR-related theory and research. The authors then provide a framework comprising the key principles of time, duration, timing, and temporal dynamics, which they use to make specific recommendations for incorporating time into the theory, design, and analysis of HR practices and resources. The authors analyze how key HR practices (recruitment, selection, training and development, compensation, and strategic human resources) may be changed if their temporal framework were adopted.

In Chapter 6, Gilbert focuses on the context of time in the area of entrepreneurship. The chapter specifically aims to enhance understanding of when entrepreneurial endeavors are undertaken, the activities involved, how long they endure, and how they are experienced. More specifically, the author suggests that individual entrepreneurship is fluid, in the sense that it occurs under unique timing considerations. The constantly evolving nature of the person-environment fit produces different contexts that can affect individuals' readiness for entrepreneurship over time. Changes in individual knowledge, experience, and social networks affect the likelihood that individuals will pursue entrepreneurial endeavors at certain points in time. From a more macro perspective, the firm's use of available resources at present determines how long that firm will survive into the future. It is therefore important to consider a firm's founding, its current stage, and the decisions that are made as the venture moves forward to understand new venture performance. Concerning the issue of time and industry emergence, the length of time between inventions, initial commercialization, and mass market entry may provide significant information about the likelihood of success for entrepreneurial endeavors and the emergence of an industry. Future research is discussed concerning the influence of time on entrepreneurs, new ventures, and new industry emergence.

In Chapter 7, Turner analyzes how temporal perspectives contribute to the emergence and consequences of the important phenomenon of organizational routines, which are significant in explaining the stability versus dynamism of organizations' behaviors, and their efficiency and effectiveness. More specifically, the chapter focuses on: (a) temporal antecedents of routines, including time as signal, resource, and state of mind; (b) the effect of time on the performance outcomes of routines, concerning both time as an outcome (e.g., how much time is required to perform a routine) and the effect of time on the impact of routines (e.g., how realization of value from routines can change over time); and (c) how routines evolve over time. The author further discusses the methods scholars have used to study temporal issues in routines, and in conclusion offers suggestions for how future research can further incorporate temporal perspectives to enhance our understanding of organizational routines and their effects.

In the eighth and final chapter, Chan discusses important methodological issues in the research of time. Specifically, the author focuses on the conceptual bases for methodological choices in studies on time, as they relate to the constructs of subjective and objective time, and to the temporal characteristics of time duration, number of time points and the intervals between them, time lag between events, time perspective and temporal depth, time urgency, and polychronicity. This is followed by an analysis of design, measurement, and data analysis issues. Concerning design issues, the author focuses on three key design issues: nature of the longitudinal change or time construct under study, descriptive versus explanatory goals in the study of the temporal phenomenon, and observational versus experimental intervention approaches to examine the temporal phenomenon. This is followed by an analysis of measurement issues, including specification of timescales for longitudinal change and time constructs, dimensionality of time constructs, and measurement invariance of responses and changes in construct dimensionality over time. Then data analysis issues are addressed, including assumptions of data analytical models, analysis of reliability and errors, and aggregation of observations across time. The chapter ends with a list of strategic issues for researchers to consider in order to develop the conceptual and methodological bases for the study on time.

Conclusion

Just as Volume 1 offered a number of ideas and suggestions for future research on time for individual-level aspects of work, so too do the chapters in this volume create numerous directions for future research at higher levels of analysis. Such innovative perspectives on topics such as leadership, culture, and human resources, as well as conceptual views of methodological choices, provide extant research with a number of recommendations for future work at the intersection of time and work. We hope that both volumes will serve as a basis for future research aimed at enriching our knowledge and understanding of the role of temporal issues at work.

References

Kozlowski, S. W., Chao, G. T., Grand, J. A., Braun, M. T., & Kuljanin, G. (2013). Advancing multilevel research design: Capturing the dynamics of emergence. *Organizational Research Methods, 16,* 581–615.

Orlikowski, W. J., & Yates, J. (2002). It's about time: Temporal structuring in organizations. *Organization Science, 13*, 684–700.

Sonnentag, S., Pundt, A., & Albrecht, A. (2014). Temporal perspectives on job stress. In A. J. Shipp & Y. Fried (Eds.), *Time and Work: How Time Impacts Individuals (Vol. 1).* London: Psychology Press.

2 Time and teams

*John E. Mathieu, Michael R. Kukenberger
and Lauren D'Innocenzo*

Open up the sporting papers of any newspaper and conventional wisdom will convey that teams take time to develop, great teams deliver in crunch time, and how you practice is how you play; or, in the words of Casey Stengel, "The team has come along slow but fast." The scholarly literature is no different as the concept of time is ubiquitous in the study and application of teamwork. It is widely accepted that teams are dynamic entities that have a past, present, and future (McGrath, Arrow, & Berdahl, 2000). Ilgen, Hollenbeck, Johnson, and Jundt (2005, p. 519) observed, "Conceptually, team researchers have converged on a view of teams as complex, adaptive, dynamic systems. They exist in context as they perform across time. Over time and contexts, teams and their members continually cycle and recycle." Similarly, Gully (2000, p. 35) emphasized that "to fully understand work teams, researchers must investigate how team dynamics develop and change over time."

Mitchell and James (2001, p. 545) argued, "We believe that the management discipline needs to seriously consider issues of time, especially when events occur, in both theory and methods." We submit that this is especially true for the study of work teams. Time comes in many different forms that have different yet related implications for teams. Several theories of temporal team dynamics have been advanced over the years (e.g., Gersick, 1988; Marks, Mathieu, & Zaccaro, 2001; Waller, 1999). More generally, Ancona, Okhuysen, and Perlow (2001) reviewed the management literature and argued that time is generally conceived of in three forms: 1) clock time; 2) developmental or growth patterns; and 3) performance cycles or episodes. "Clock-based time depicts a continuum as linear – infinitely divisible into objective, quantifiable units such that the units are homogenous, uniform, regular, precise, deterministic, and measurable" (Ancona et al., 2001, p. 514). Linear time unfolds as history, and therefore also subsumes other historical features and events to constitute a context that evolves and changes over time. In contrast, theories of team development suggest that teams qualitatively evolve over time as they move through various stages toward maturity. Examples of this paradigm include Tuckman's (1965) forming-storming-norming-performing-adjourning framework, Gersick's (1988) punctuated equilibrium conception, Morgan, Salas, and Glickman's (1993) team evolution and maturation approach, and Kozlowski, Gully, Nason, and Smith's (1999) theory of team compilation.

Cyclical theories of team functioning suggests that events unfold in a recurring fashion over time in cycles or episodes as related to performance. Episodic time-based theories include McGrath's (1991) Time, Interaction, and Performance, Ancona and Chong's (1996) theory of entrainment, Waller's (1999) theory of group adaptation to nonroutine events, and Marks et al.'s (2001) recurring phase model of team processes.

Figure 2.1 depicts a modern-day version of the classic input-process-outcomes team effectiveness framework adapted from Mathieu, Maynard, Rapp, and Gilson (2008). As shown by the solid line running at the bottom of the figure, developmental processes unfold over time as teams mature. Also depicted are feedback loops, which represent the more cyclical or episodic processes. We should note that such feedback actually occurs as teams transition from one episode to another, not within episodes as such depictions are sometimes thought to imply. The solid line from outcomes to subsequent mediators, within Figure 2.1, suggests that feedback of this type is likely to be quite influential, while the dashed line suggests that outcome and process influences on subsequent inputs would likely be less potent. This follows from the fact that team states are likely to be readily influenced by their progress over time, and teams may readily adopt different processes as a function of outcomes. Alternatively, the influence of team outcomes or mediators on subsequent member composition, team structure, organizational contextual factors, or other inputs is likely to be less immediate or malleable. Finally, naturally everything depicted in Figure 2.1 unfolds in a larger historical context that includes the influences of previous performances, competitive pressures, the advent of new technologies, changing employee and customer expectations, and so forth.

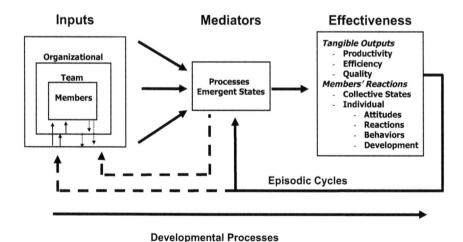

Figure 2.1 Modern-day team effectiveness framework.

In this chapter we outline three ways in which time has important implications for team functioning. First, we consider how time represents a *historical context* within which teams operate. Second, we consider time as a *developmental marker* signaling how teams move through a life cycle from birth to death. And third, we consider time as related to *cyclical phenomena* as teams perform different activities at different periods of performance episodes. We then consider the theoretical, research, and applied implications of taking time to consider time more seriously in teams research and application.

Time as historical context

Johns (2006) noted that all organizational behavior occurs in context and therefore is subject to influences that exist in any given historical period. Certainly teams have existed throughout history, but most management scholars and applied psychologists trace the dawn of team research back to the Hawthorne studies of the 1930–40s (Sundstrom, McIntyre, Halfhill, & Richards, 2000). Soon after the dawn of the industrial revolution, the Western Electric Company began a series of engineering psychology experiments in its Chicago Hawthorne plant. The legacy of the Hawthorne studies is that the engineering interventions did not have the anticipated effects, and that work group and interpersonal relations played an unexpected large role in performance outcomes. Whereas what exactly was, and was not, demonstrated at Hawthorne has been the subject of lengthy debates (cf. Bramel & Friend, 1982; Sonnenfeld, 1985), what is clear is that the work sparked the human relations movement. Teams were at the center of the human relations movement, and attention shifted from a purely scientific management/ engineering orientation toward the optimization of work environments, to a more comprehensive one that incorporated interpersonal relations and work groups. This shift roughly coincided with the rise of the labor movement in the United States and elsewhere, placing additional emphasis on employees' welfare. The time was right to understand team dynamics and effectiveness. The ramifications of the human relations movement and related later drivers such as Kurt Lewin's (1945) work on group dynamics were that factors such as group morale, norms, and interpersonal interactions came to the forefront of work group research. These factors occupied both researchers' and practitioners' attention and were seen as critical drivers of both team effectiveness and members' personal welfare.

Events surrounding World War II brought about a different emphasis for team research. Whereas large organizations focused on scientific management principles in the production of war material resources (Sundstrom et al., 2000), innovations in war fighting placed an emphasis on small teams operating with technology. Tank platoons and bomber squadrons illustrated the interface between teams and technological innovations, and how members needed to work closely with one another, not only to optimize their own team's performance but also to coordinate their actions with those of other teams to optimize effectiveness of the entire system. In so doing, these developments spawned *the sociotechnical systems* emphasis wherein team effectiveness was considered not solely in terms of scientific management or human relations principles but also as a joint function of the synergy between technology and interpersonal teamwork. Sociotechnical system principles were later observed in the context of Trist and Bamforth's (1951) chronicle of the frustrations associated with the longwall method of coal extraction, and in their conclusion that the social consequences of work arrangements need to be considered. Their conclusions also highlighted the importance of team members' competencies, cross-training, and backup behaviors, and issues concerning decision-making, authority, and responsibility. This sociotechnical system theme was also considered in other industries such as textiles (Rice, 1953) and has been manifest in different ways through to today. In so doing, the technological imperative has often placed premiums on different team competencies and processes.

Organizational designs of the late 1950s to the early 1970s, while emphasizing employee participation, did not tend to feature teams. While some interesting team-based designs were attempted, typically in Greenfield sites (cf. Sundstrom et al., 2000), by and large it took until the 1980s before teamwork came back to the forefront. But several forces converged in the 1980s to rekindle interest in, and application of, work teams. First, *total quality management* and its accompanying feature *quality circles* rose in popularity. Employees were looking for greater voice, and organizations were looking to leverage their inputs. Second, *global competitiveness* and *volatile environments* exposed the limits of large bureaucracies and the benefits of increased flexibility afforded by the use of project teams, modular production techniques, and other team-based design features. Sundstrom, De Meuse, and Futrell (1990) detailed how the use of teams proliferated during this period as organizations redesigned around advice and involvement, production and service, project and development, and action and negotiation arrangements. Third, tragic events in the mid-late 1980s in the Persian Gulf, including the failure to defend the USS *Stark* from enemy attack, followed by the downing of an Iranian commercial jetliner by the guided missile cruiser USS *Vincennes*, highlighted shortcomings of overreliance on automated decision aids and failures of team decision-making. In turn, resources and attention were devoted to better understanding the human (team)-technology interface to improve decision-making (see Salas, Cannon-Bowers, & Johnston, 1998). In short, from the 1980s through today, organizations have moved toward team-based arrangements and consider teams as a basic building block of modern organizational designs (Mathieu et al., 2008). Team and group research reflected this growth and began appearing more prominently in organizational research outlets (Sanna & Parks, 1997).

By the 1990s team research and application were flourishing. With flatter organizational structures came an increased appreciation for team empowerment (cf. Kirkman & Rosen, 1999; Mathieu, Gilson, & Ruddy, 2006), shared leadership (e.g., Pearce & Sims, 2002), and other forms of semiautonomous work group designs (Wellins, Byham, & Wilson, 1991). Research explored the role of shared mental models (e.g., Mathieu, Heffner, Goodwin, Salas, & Cannon-Bowers, 2000), particularly in high-reliability systems such as air-traffic control, nuclear power, plants, and military applications (Bowers, Salas, & Jentsch, 2006). Team composition and developmental processes gained renewed emphasis as many organizational strategies utilized temporary team designs and rapidly reconfigured members into different team arrangements in order to best align their human capital with changing competitive pressures (Morgan & Lassiter, 1992; Klimoski & Jones, 1994).

As we turned the corner into the 21st century team designs became still more complex and amorphous (Tannenbaum, Mathieu, Salas, & Cohen, 2012; Wageman, Gardner & Mortensen, 2012). Present-day teams are rapidly configured and dismantled, often with unclear boundaries and memberships. Individuals are often simultaneously members of multiple teams with different roles (Maynard, Mathieu, Rapp, & Gilson, 2012; O'Leary, Mortensen & Woolley, 2011). And with the establishment of empowerment, shared leadership, and semiautonomous work teams came new challenges associated with orchestrating their operations in larger forms such as multiteam systems that may span different organizations (Mathieu, Marks, & Zaccaro, 2001; Zaccaro, Marks, & DeChurch, 2011). On the research front, teams became one of the more popular topics of investigations, and numerous reviews of the literature were published (e.g., Kozlowski & Bell, 2003; Kozlowski & Ilgen, 2006; Mathieu et al., 2008; Salas, Stagl, & Burke, 2004). And yet again, technological advances qualitatively changed the nature of teamwork. With the advent of the Internet and high-speed connectivity, coupled with the destabilizing effects of the September 11, 2001, attacks on the United States, virtual forms of communication and coordination rose in popularity. Suddenly organizations could assemble global teams and create virtual environments for them to operate in. This capability brought to the forefront advantages and disadvantages of working through different mediums, as well as issues such as coordinating activities asynchronously, the use of knowledge repositories, and social psychological implications of interacting through technology (Kirkman & Mathieu, 2005; Martins, Gilson & Maynard, 2004). Global virtuality also, however, meant that far more diverse teams could be constituted than was logistically feasible in face-to-face designs. Accordingly, there were renewed interest and challenges associated with managing diversity – of a wide variety of sorts – in teams.

This brief review of the use and study of work teams in organizations well illustrates that contextual factors associated with different periods of time place a premium on different facets of teamwork. In other words, the historical context within which teams are operating drives the salience of different functions and activities, which in turn places emphases on different enabling conditions and team characteristics for success. Some common themes, however, deal with the nature of the interdependencies among members, the composition of the team as related to situational demands, and the implications of interfacing with technologies. Team-based arrangements are the organizational design of choice these days, but that is not because they are simply fashionable or the latest management fad. Organizational environments are extremely volatile, and competition is intense. Team-based designs enable organizations to quickly align, and realign, their human capital to meet these changing demands and are therefore adaptive and offer competitive value. Yet these "macro drivers" mean that teams need to be designed, comprised, enabled, and reinforced if they are to prove successful. And those needs change as a function of their developmental stages and episodic dynamics – that we consider next.

Time as a team developmental marker

Traditional longitudinal team models have noted the importance of development over the teams' life cycle (see Smith, 2001, for a review). Developmental theories suggest that teams go through a series of phases as members seek to understand their task environment and get to know one another. Team development is described as "the path a [team] takes over its life-span toward the accomplishment of its main tasks" (Gersick, 1988, p. 9), and many models of such processes exist (e.g., Ancona & Chong, 1996; Bennis & Shepard, 1956; Gersick, 1988; Kozlowski, Gully, Salas, & Cannon-Bowers, 1996; Morgan et al., 1993; Tuckman, 1965). Many of the developmental models of team development assume that groups progress in a linear fashion from one stage to another (Bennis & Shepard, 1956; Braaten, 1974/75; Caple, 1978; Heinen & Jacobson, 1976; Kormanski & Mozenter, 1987; Lacoursiere, 1980; Maples, 1988; Mills, 1964; Sarri & Galinsky, 1974; Tuckman, 1965; Tuckman & Jensen, 1977).

The most prominent *linear group development model* would be Tuckman's (1965; Tuckman & Jensen, 1977) stages of small group development. Tuckman's model includes four primary stages: forming, storming, norming, and performing. In the first stage of development group members become familiar with each other and the task and work to establish a sense of stability and purpose. This stage is consistently hypothesized in linear developmental models often utilizing Tuckman's *forming* label (Heinen & Jacobson, 1976; Maples, 1988; Tuckman, 1965; Tuckman & Jensen, 1977) in addition to 'encounter' (Mills, 1964), 'origin formative' (Sarri & Galinsky, 1974), 'pregroup' (Braaten, 1974/75), 'orientation' (Caple, 1978; Lacoursiere, 1980), and 'awareness' (Kormanski & Mozenter, 1987). While there are differences among this stage within the various linear models, they generally share a focus on testing boundaries, overcoming individual anxiety, and legitimizing leadership. The next stage generally refers to a time of conflict, unrest, and disagreement. Tuckman labeled this stage *storming*, noting that in this second phase teams define the mission, determine how to perform both independent and interdependent tasks, and define the leadership model. Members may quickly vet assumptions related to team functioning and determine a pattern allowing them to move to the next phases. However, Tuckman argued that some teams will be unable to resolve conflict and never move past the storming phase. In addition to the 'storming' label, which was also used by Maples (1988), researchers have categorized this phase as 'Testing Boundaries and Modeling Roles' (Mills, 1964), 'Intermediate 1' (Sarri & Galinsky, 1974), 'Initial Phase' (Braaten, 1974/75), 'Differentiation' (Heinen & Jacobson, 1976), 'Conflict' (Caple, 1978; Kormanski & Mozenter, 1987), and 'Dissatisfaction' (Lacoursiere, 1980). The common theme among these categorizations is that conflict arises in the process of members becoming acquainted with each other's strengths, weaknesses, and 'task' versus people orientations (Caple, 1978). Tuckman also argued that during this phase members are often fighting to maintain their identity.

Succeeding the period of conflict these types of development models argue that teams enter a phase of group identity and cohesion. Tuckman labeled this phase *norming*, indicating a time of mutual goal alignment and agreed-upon formation and processes. In addition to 'norming' (Maples, 1988; Tuckman, 1965; Tuckman & Jensen, 1977), this phase has been labeled 'negotiating an indigenous normative system' (Mills, 1964), 'revision' (Sarri & Galinsky, 1974), 'early phase' (Braaten, 1974/75), 'integration' (Heinen & Jacobson, 1976; Caple, 1978), 'resolution' (Lacoursiere, 1980), and cooperation (Kormanski & Mozenter, 1987). Tuckman (1965) described this phase as a period of cohesiveness and ingroup feeling, where the focus shifts to the assigned task. This phase has been argued to set up the next period (i.e., *performing*; Maples, 1988; Tuckman, 1965; Tuckman & Jensen, 1977), where groups actively produce or perform their task. This stage has been argued to be more flexible and dynamic (Braaten, 1974/75; Tuckman, 1965), as the team has developed effective responses to internal and external stresses (Sarri & Galinsky, 1974) and eagerly and mutually explores and resolves problems. In addition to performing (Tuckman, 1965; Tuckman & Jensen, 1977) this period has been described as 'production/productivity' (Kormanski & Mozenter, 1987; Lacoursiere, 1980; Mills, 1964), 'intermediate 2' (Sarri & Galinsky, 1974), 'full maturity' (Heinen & Jacobson, 1976), 'mature work phase' (Braaten, 1974/75), and achievement (Caple, 1978). Performing was the final stage in Tuckman's original 1965 classification; however, it was updated to include a closing phase in later conceptions (Tuckman & Jensen, 1977). The *adjourning* phase indicates a point where the team terminates or is disbanded as they have completed their work and are no longer needed by the organization (Tuckman & Jensen, 1977). This phase has also been described as 'separation' (Mills, 1964), 'maturation' (Sarri & Galinsky, 1974), 'termination' (Braaten, 1974/75; Lacoursiere, 1980), and 'order' (Caple, 1978).

In addition to linear stage developmental models researchers have advanced what might be categorized as the *contingency team development model*. This model argues that the observed patterns of development are largely the result of environmental factors that covary with temporal factors that affect the process. Gersick's (1988) *punctuated equilibrium* model has received the most attention both in academic literatures and popular press (Smith, 2001). Gersick's model largely co-opted a biological evolution perspective contrasting to Darwin's slow stream of small mutations explanation of evolution. The punctuated equilibrium (Eldredge & Gould, 1972) viewpoint argued that species exist in equilibrium (i.e., static form) over most of their histories and that new species abruptly arise through revolutionary (i.e., punctuation) change. Gersick argued that teams mirrored this same process as they alternated between times of inertia to times punctuated by massive change. Gersick argued that in the early phases of the team members define the situation and move forward based on limited or satisficing (Simon, 1976) information and generally do not have the storming phase. At roughly the group's midpoint teams are often forced to abandoned their original agendas and rechart the focus and course of the work. This change is often a discontinuous shift where members take advantage of their history and external pressure to transition into a new course of action. Following this shift, Gersick argued that teams enter a second period of inertia as changes from the shift begin to form.

Poole's (1983) *multiple-sequence model* suggested that in contrast to linear sequence models that team decision-making is a function of task structure, group composition, and conflict management strategies. Poole and Roth (1989) argued that teams are a series of intertwining threads of activity as opposed to blocks or periods. They believed that if teams dealt with functions such as task, composition, and conflict issues in an orderly fashion, then teams would evolve in fashions consistent with the type of linear models described earlier. However, if teams hit 'breakpoints' such as delays or disruptions the group may need to cycle back or completely reconsider its work process.

Taking aspects from Tuckman's (1965) and Gersick's (1988) model, Morgan et al. (1993) proposed a hybrid *Team Evolution and Maturation (TEAM) developmental model*. This model includes nine stages of development including preforming (i.e., development of task assignment and investigation of group), forming (orientation to task and testing of dependence), storming (i.e., emotional response to task demands and intragroup conflict), norming (i.e., open exchange of relevant interpretations and development of group cohesion), performing (i.e., emergence of solutions and development of role relatedness), reforming (adjustment of framework and refinement of roles), performing II (drive to completion and fulfillment of roles), conforming (i.e., completion and delivery of task and adjustment to environmental demands), and finally de-forming (i.e., review of accomplishments, withdrawal from task, exiting from group, and remembering group). While Morgan et al. (1993) have detailed development paths akin to Tuckman's work, they did not expect groups to either start or move through in a linear fashion. Instead it is anticipated that groups will respond to members' past experiences of the task, and environmental influences akin to Gersick's punctuated equilibrium model. Morgan et al. (1993) also believed that groups can recycle through previous phases in order to resolve conflict or correct misconceptions. In going through the various phases they suggested that there are two paths: one where the groups learn skills and possess the ability to complete the task, and one concerning the teamwork skills related to the interactions that occur among team members. Morgan and colleagues argued that the more the two paths overlapped (i.e., task-related and team-related skills merged) the stronger the team becomes.

In sum, developmental theories suggest that teams go through a series of phases as members seek to understand their task environment and get to know one another. Accordingly, events that occur early in a team's life span have important implications for their later functioning. For example, Mathieu and Rapp (2009) conducted a longitudinal analysis of team charters and formal planning activities on team performance trajectories. They concluded that "for those interested in maximizing team effectiveness . . . taking time out early in a team's life cycle to establish both task and people strategies can benefit team performance over time" (p. 100).

Developmental models also suggest that what constitutes effectiveness may radically change over time. Consider typical project teams assigned with, for example, the creation of a new product or service. During their initial stages, not only do members need to understand one another, their strengths and weaknesses, but also the team must scope out the project, generate options, consider the viability of alternative, and so forth. At this stage, effectiveness is gauged primarily in terms of the number of potential options that are identified and how well they are framed. The second stage involves the development of various prototypes from which the team can do proof of concept tests and narrow down their options. In short, the primary index of effectiveness at this stage, roughly halfway through the process, is to identify a primary design or course of action for moving forward.

Teams oftentimes discover dead ends during their third phase and must cycle back to select or generate other options to pursue. Inevitably, the teams complete a third phase with a prototype or specific proposal for what they think they should pursue going forward. The extent to which the teams' proposals are thoroughly researched and are feasible represents the primary indices of effectiveness at this point. In later stages, teams typically present their ideas to a review panel, receive feedback, and potentially move to implement their ideas. The ultimate criteria following this stage are whether the teams' proposals are creative and are implemented, and the extent to which they yield a positive cost/benefit ratio.

As detailed in the foregoing example, what constitutes team effectiveness changed over time, with the success of later stages dependent, in part, on the success of earlier stages. Importantly, given that the nature of effectiveness qualitatively changed over time, temporal-based comparisons become far more difficult, as compared to those of teams who perform the same tasks over time (e.g., production teams). While researchers may choose to employ fairly generic indices (e.g., observers' ratings of "overall effectiveness") in an effort to have comparable metrics over time, the disadvantage of that approach is that measures are less sensitive and less valid indices of effectiveness at any given phase. Alternatively, researchers may use earlier indices of effectiveness as predictors of later team states, processes, and effectiveness. Of course, this strategy presents serious logistical challenges if different teams are at different developmental stages during any calendar periods. In other words, adopting this phase-sensitive approach would mean that data collection efforts would need to be yoked to the developmental stage of each and every team. While this would help to align data collection with team developmental processes, it represents a daunting logistical challenge. For example, the lead author once adopted such an approach in a study of project teams, which necessitated nearly daily data collection efforts for almost a year to gather information for approximately 35 teams.

In sum, developmental theories of teams require researchers and practitioners to know what stage each of their teams have reached at any given point in time. In so doing, practitioners are better poised to introduce timely interventions to facilitate team development, and scholars are best positioned to gather meaningful data that will shed light on underlying team processes.

Episodic time and teams

Whereas team developmental models consider how they progress through various stages or phases of a maturation process, episodic theories refer to recurring cyclical processes that occur within teams over time as related to goal accomplishment. In other words, episodic approaches argue that teams must execute different processes at different times, depending on task demands that recur in a cyclical fashion (cf. Marks et al., 2001; McGrath, 1984). For example, McGrath's theory of time, interaction, and performance (TIP) suggests that teams simultaneously manage multiple bundles of activities over time. Such management represents the "complex matching of bundles of activities to particular periods of time" (McGrath, 1991, p. 163). Moreover, teams simultaneously juggle multiple tasks that may, or may not, be aligned temporally. This "creates an environment where members are engaged in complex sequences of interdependent tasks that comprise a larger project" (ibid., p. 149). Whereas McGrath referred to time as an environmental driver, Marks and her colleagues associated team activities to different periods of episodic processes. Their theory hinges on the notion of performance episodes, which serve as demarcation points for recurring cycles of task accomplishment (Marks et al., 2001). Similar notions were advanced by McGrath and Rotchford (1983), who discussed *recurrent periodicity*, and Ancona et al. (2001), who discussed *repeated activity mapping.* Episodes are distinguishable periods of time over which performance accrues and feedback is available (Mathieu & Button, 1992). They govern the rhythms of task performance for teams, and are distinguished by identifiable periods of action and transition periods between task accomplishments. Team tasks and technology impose certain episode durations (e.g., production runs, projects, quarterly goals), but members may also have some discretion on the duration of performance periods.

Marks et al. (2001) identified three primary *transition processes.* First, mission analysis involves the identification and evaluation of team tasks, challenges, environmental conditions, and resources available for performing the team's work. Second, goal specification refers to activities centered on the identification and prioritization of team goals. And third, strategy formulation and planning involve developing courses of actions and contingency plans, as well as making adjustments to plans in light of changes or expected changes in the team's environment.

Action processes reflect four types of activities that occur as the team works toward the accomplishment of its goals and objectives (Marks et al., 2001). First, monitoring progress toward goals involves members paying attention to, interpreting, and communicating information necessary for the team to gauge its progress toward its goals. Second, systems monitoring refers to activities such as tracking team resources (e.g., money) and factors in the team environment (e.g., inventories) to ensure that the team has what it needs to accomplish its goals and objectives. Third, team monitoring and backup behaviors involve members going out of their way to assist teammates in the performance of their tasks. Such assistance may involve indirect help, such as providing feedback or coaching, direct help with the task itself, or perhaps behaviors that directly compensate for teammates (taking on the task of a teammate who needs assistance). Team monitoring and backup behaviors have been studied in the context of research on synonymous concepts such as workload sharing (e.g., Campion, Medsker, & Higgs, 1993), and group-level organizational citizenship behavior (e.g., Hyatt & Ruddy, 1997). Finally, coordination refers to the process of synchronizing or aligning the activities of the team members with respect to their sequence and timing (Marks et al., 2001).

Whereas Marks and colleagues presented the transition and action processes as cyclically triggering one another over time, they submitted that managing members' *interpersonal processes* could be ongoing activities and be salient at any time. They identified three particular types of interpersonal processes. First, conflict management refers to the manner in which team members proactively and reactively deal with conflict. Effective conflict management includes showing mutual respect, willingness to compromise, and developing norms that promote cooperation and harmony. Second, motivating and confidence building refer to activities that develop and maintain members' motivation and confidence with regard to the team accomplishing its goals and objectives. Finally, affect management represents those activities that foster emotional balance, togetherness, and effective coping with stressful demands and frustration.

Marks et al. (2001) suggested that the successful execution of interpersonal processes might help a team to vent frustrations, stay focused during difficult times, and otherwise maintain a positive work atmosphere. Yet previous reviews have concluded that efforts to enhance team interpersonal relationships have yielded relatively little benefit in terms of team outcomes (e.g., Salas, Rozell, Mullen, & Driskell, 1999; Tannenbaum, Beard, & Salas, 1992). In contrast, Bradley, White, and Mennecke (2003, p. 361) argued that "the temporal dimensions of team and task are critical to the impact of interpersonal interventions on team performance." They noted that most previous studies included in the earlier reviews were conducted with teams that briefly performed contrived tasks and were then disbanded. Bradley et al.'s (2003) position was that interpersonal processes matter little if members know that their joint experiences will be relatively brief. In contrast, if members know that they will be working together for an extended period of time, interpersonal processes relate significantly to team performance. Their meta-analysis results demonstrated that team interpersonal processes did indeed have significant influences on important team outcomes to the extent that teams had longer histories of working together. Bradley et al. (2003, p. 367) concluded that "team members can endure poor interpersonal relationships for an hour or even a few days, but when team members must work closely together for an extended period of time, cooperative relationships are essential for cohesive team performance."

Marks et al. (2001) argued that "work teams strive toward collective goals that incorporate time as a component. . . . Time-based rhythms act to shape how teams manage their behavior" (pp. 358–359). The general idea is that longer-term efforts are broken down into more operational and meaningful subperiods. "Episodes' durations stem largely from the nature of the tasks that teams perform and the technology that they employ, and from the manner in which members choose to complete work. Episodes are most easily identified by goals and goal accomplishment periods" (Marks et al., 2001, p. 359). For example, year-long performance targets can be partitioned or "chunked" into quarterly, or even weekly, goals and monitored at a more fine-grained level. Production teams may chunk activities into periods that correspond to different product runs, shift changes, or other times that are meaningful to them. The point is simply that time is partitioned into recurring chunks that have meaning to members – usually in terms of being tied to goals and/or feedback delivery. This implies a natural nesting of phenomena where faster cycling team processes and performance outcomes unfold episodically within the context of longer time periods. It may also be the case that different team dimensions may have different episodic rhythms. For example, task-based episodic rhythms (i.e., transition and action phases) might cycle at one pace whereas interpersonal-based relations may cycle at a different pace. Moreover, the development and decline of team states may not be symmetrical. For example, we know that team trust is a slow-evolving emergent state that can be shattered in an instant by a single dysfunctional act (Wildman et al., 2012).

Research and meta-analyses of team process dimensions along the lines of Marks et al.'s (2001) framework have shown them to be highly correlated. LePine, Piccolo, Jackson, Mathieu, and Saul (2008) submitted that given the modal research design where team members are surveyed about all team processes simultaneously, which are then correlated with concurrent or lagged outcome measures (e.g., Mathieu et al., 2006), it is not surprising that team processes are highly correlated. No doubt various forms of response biases or "methods effects" are particularly likely to exist in such designs. If researchers simultaneously survey members about all team processes, then respondents must perform a mental synthesis of processes that have occurred over time as they formulate their answers. Even if researchers employ uninvolved observers of team processes (e.g., Mathieu et al., 2000), who are asked to evaluate transition processes while observing teams that are actively engaged in task performance, then observers' ratings may be artificially inflated as well. The point is that an adequate test of Marks et al.'s (2001) episodic process relationships requires time-based research designs whereby measures of *different team processes are aligned with*, and *measured when*, they are anticipated to occur and then correlated over time (e.g., DeChurch & Marks, 2006; Maynard et al., 2012). We anticipate that such designs should yield lower interprocess correlations and might begin to illustrate the utility of narrower teamwork process dimensions.

Episodic theories of team processes also suggest that the quality of transition processes sets the stage for later action processes. For example, Steiner (1972) defined comprehensive planning as "a process of deciding in advance what is to be done, how it is to be done, and who is going to do it" (p. 4). Hackman (1976) considered the effect of such activities when he proposed that good plans benefit a team by establishing appropriate boundaries, helping the team come to terms with their task, and developing norms that guide group behavior. Weingart (1992) suggested that preplanning (transition) activities should facilitate in-process planning efforts (i.e., transition processes), and the latter should relate more directly to team performance than the former, particularly in complex environments. Similarly, Janicik and Bartel (2003) found that formal plans related positively to subsequent team performance, both directly and as mediated by team coordination. Recall that transition processes also have a "backward glance" as members seek to learn from previous performance episodes. One such mechanism for doing so is team debriefs, where members (often with the help of a skilled facilitator) review their previous performances and search for lessons learned and areas of improvement. Tannenbaum and Cerasoli (2013) conducted a meta-analysis and concluded that team debriefs significantly improve subsequent team performance by as much as 20–25% as compared to controls. Eddy, Tannenbaum, and Mathieu (in press) demonstrated that teams can also successfully conduct effective self-guided debriefs with the aid of an automated debriefing tool.

Cyclical models such as Marks et al.'s (2001) suggest that different team outcomes will be salient at different times. Decision timeliness, the quality of strategies and plans, and so forth would constitute suitable criteria for teams in the transition stage. Alternatively, performance metrics, efficiencies, customer reactions, and the like would be more suitable criteria for teams performing in action phases. Traditionally, various effectiveness indices are aggregated over time, as described earlier. However, in so doing, important relationships and temporal variance may be obscured. For example, using students competing in a business simulation, Mathieu and Schulze (2006) found that unpacking transition-action periods led to far more significant results than when data were aggregated across episodes over time. In sum, cyclical theories of team activity raise issues surrounding the pace and frequency of performance episodes. Researchers need to discern the most appropriate temporal "chunks" or units of time to consider. Cyclical theories also highlight the fact that teams are doing different things at different times, and therefore the relevant indicators of effectiveness differ across time. Aligning their research designs and analyses with such cycles represents both a challenge for researchers and an opportunity for new insights.

Summary of theoretical frameworks

The three approaches to the study of temporal influences on teams that we outlined earlier (i.e., historical context, developmental phases, and episodic cycles) each and collectively emphasize the point that teams are doing different things at different times. This illustrates the fact that different processes (e.g., planning, execution, interpersonal dynamics) have different importance for task accomplishment at different times. Accordingly, it also suggests that enabling and supporting conditions (e.g., team composition, information and reward systems, leader-team interactions, etc.) are likely to have differential impact on team effectiveness at different times. Gaining a better understanding and appreciation of these temporal dynamics offers advantages for researchers and practitioners alike.

Notably, we have generally treated time in an absolute sense – as a contextual variable – that exists and influences team functioning. Yet we also recognize that there is value afforded by incorporating a more relativistic viewpoint – or one that focuses on time as experienced and interpreted by individuals and teams (see Ancona et al., 2001; Fried & Slowik, 2004). Individuals and teams respond to time as they see it, which naturally derives in large part from how it exists in the context. But individual and cultural differences, developed norms, salient cues and expectations, and a wide variety of other factors operate such that different people may experience and react differently to the same situational factors. These relationships are well articulated in other chapters of this book (e.g., Chapter 4, this volume). Therefore, blending contextual temporal themes with experiential time represents fertile ground for future research.

Additional methodological issues

Historical context, development phases, and episodic cycles represent substantive time-related team phenomena. As noted earlier, research methods and interventions need to be temporally aligned to optimize their effectiveness. Moreover, there are two other important methodological factors that should be considered in teams' research: 1) postdictive versus predictive research designs; and 2) aggregation lags and periods. At issue is how the outcomes measures relate in time to when various team activities occurred and whether the period of outcome observation is sufficient for making important distinctions.

Postdictive versus predictive research designs

It seems obvious to even say that predictive measures should be collected prior to one's criteria, but close examination of the literature reveals many instances where this was not the case. Many authors frame their study as a cross-sectional design if their predictor measures are collected at the same time as their criteria. However, even with that caveat, their design may actually be postdictive. For example, typically one collects information about team composition and mediators (e.g., emergent states or processes) from members while perhaps asking their supervisors to rate the team's effectiveness. No doubt the researcher wishes to justify depicting a causal order of team composition → team mediators → team outcomes. Given that compositional factors are typically based on member traits and characteristics, it is probably the case that the composition → mediator portion of such a model is easily defendable (see Mathieu & Taylor, 2006). This ordering would be less convincing, however, if the team composition was in terms of members' attitudes. However, the team mediators → outcome ordering is more problematic.

For sake of argument, assume that the team mediators were measured using members' survey responses at the end of the first quarterly performance period. Most likely, members' responses would reflect recent team activities unless survey items specifically referred to a designated time period (e.g., "Rate your team processes over the past three months"). What would be the salient period of performance for an external manager when it comes to rating the team's performance? Most likely it would be an extended period of performance dating back further than the past quarter. And, even if framed in terms of the "past three months," there would not likely be an alignment between the temporal focus of members' process responses and managers' effectiveness ratings. Assuming some ebb and flow between team processes and effectiveness over time, there is no way to ensure that the temporal focus of members is consistent with that of managers. At issue is that if team processes take some time to generate team effectiveness, then having members or their managers focus on the same period of time is more likely to yield process scores that are *consequent* to earlier team effectiveness than it is the reverse. Thus, the standard cross-sectional design is quite likely to yield postdictive data. The situation is exacerbated only if researchers were to associate team members' responses gathered in the first quarter with existing performance evaluations or organizational archives – which naturally would reflect earlier performance periods.

More generally, the problem outlined earlier is referred to as endogeneity effects in the strategic management literature (Hamilton & Nickerson, 2003). In brief, the endogeneity problem suggests that one's predictor variables may actually be the product, to varying degrees, of earlier states of one's outcome variable. Applied to this context, if previous team performance (i.e., t_0) generates future team states (e.g., team empowerment, t_1), and team performance is fairly consistent over time, one might easily observe an illusionary correlation between team empowerment and subsequent (i.e., t_2) team performance. This follows from the fact that the observed empowerment (t_1) $\lozenge$ performance (i.e., t_2) correlation really emanates from their common roots in earlier performance (i.e., t_0). Both Hamilton and Nickerson (2003) and Maxwell and Cole (2007) outline different ways in which the endogeneity threat to causal inferences may be addressed.

Aggregation lags and periods

The previous section made the point that criteria measures should represent outcomes that followed from earlier team activities. While the point may appear to be self-evident, it becomes tricky to implement in practice. At issue are two related factors: 1) when would outcomes become manifest; and 2) how long should criteria be accumulated (i.e., aggregated)? As for the first point, consider a study in which where some intervention is introduced (e.g., team task redesign) in the hopes of significantly improving team functioning and thereby team effectiveness. Assuming for the moment that the intervention worked and was powerful, how long would it take for members to adjust to the new design? How long would it take for those adjustments to produce changes in members' attitudes, states, or processes? And then how long would it take for their reactions and behaviors to result in changes in effectiveness indicators, whether those were productivity counts or customer reactions? Collectively, we submit, such presumably potent intervention changes may take several weeks or months to manifest changes in criteria measures. Therefore, an intervention introduced in the first quarter of the year may not begin to show its effects until the second quarter or even later. A tally of effectiveness indicators gathered immediately following the intervention may well miss such effects. In brief, there is very little in the literature that addresses the appropriate time lag to employ between team influences and their effects. And we further submit that such lags may well differ, depending on the nature of the intervention and the type of effectiveness indicator being considered. We urge researchers to consider such relationships, and to justify the lag periods that they employ.

The second point concerns how long a period of aggregation should be employed for the outcome measures. Note that this issue is pertinent no matter what method of measurement is used. Good survey measures direct the respondent to a particular time frame (e.g., "Rate the quality of the team's performance over the past three months"). Aggregation of archival indices and other types of measures also requires some specific time frame. Given that team criteria are often dynamic entities (Landis, 2001), the choice of aggregation period becomes particularly important. On one hand, the aggregation period should be sufficiently long so as to yield a psychometrically stable and representative composite. On the other hand, the aggregation period should not be so long as to become susceptible to other sources of contamination. Here again, the ideal period of time may well differ from one situation to another, and as a function of the criterion measure employed. In any event, it is important for researchers to articulate the rationale for the aggregation period(s) that they employ.

We should mention briefly one other temporal-related methodological concern – namely, seasonal and other historical trends. If performance values, customer preferences, other elements, and so forth are susceptible to factors that change systematically over time, one may fall prey to illusionary increasing or decreasing outcome patterns over time. Various forms of norming (e.g., efficiency rates) may help to control for such factors, such as considering performance relative to quotas, comparing quarterly performance against the same period in previous years, or making within-period comparisons across teams. In times of economic strife or resource shortages, expectancies, goals, quotas, or other forms of standards should be adjusted. In short, researchers may have to recalibrate outcome indicators to yield a "level playing field" for criteria measures over time.

The foregoing recommendations address how to best align traditional methods of measurement and studying teams with temporal considerations. As discussed, they may be exceedingly difficult to implement. However, an alternative may be to leverage various forms of digital traces and to index team variables on an ongoing basis. For example, with the advent of "virtual teams" and other technologically mediated or recorded forms of member interactions (e.g., knowledge communities of practice, knowledge repositories, customer resource management systems, etc.), process data may be available through nontraditional means. For example, a text analysis of a threaded discussion list may well reveal the types (and qualities) of processes that teams engage in over time. Alternatively, for teams who operate in the same time and space, members might be equipped with spatial badges that signal their whereabouts relative to other teammates. Some of these technologies include sensors that detect the intensity of discussions such that the effect associated with members' exchanges can also be indexed (Pentland, 2007).

Psycho-physiological measures are also advancing rapidly such that members might be monitored with anything from EEG sensors (if stationary), to heart, skin response, or breathing monitors associated with different cognitive or psychological states (e.g., Cleveland, Blascovich, Gangi, & Finez, 2011). Of course the use of such technologies may be limited to experimental environments or to relatively few applied settings (e.g., submarine crews, fire fighters, pilots), but they do offer intriguing possibilities for the future.

Applied implications

Developing a greater appreciation for time-related factors in teamwork also has numerous applied implications. Starting with the use of traditional surveys for diagnostic purposes, we noted that simultaneous assessment of all team processes may lead to more inflated correlations than would time-sensitive designs. Of course, field settings may simply not be amenable to multiple measurement occasions. Yet knowing that members report difficulties in interpreting their performance and developing performance strategies, versus that they know what they want to do but experience coordination breakdowns, versus the fact that failure to manage interpersonal relationships is undermining their performance, may be important as it relates to the potential utility of different interventions. Rather than merely rolling out a generic team-building type of intervention, organizational change agents armed with this type of information may be in a better position to focus their energies and development efforts. Moreover, a better appreciation of the temporal dynamics of team processes may well cue practitioners about when to monitor which types of team processes more closely in order to facilitate their development.

Consideration of teams' developmental patterns also offers guidance as to the timing of various interventions. For example, as suggested earlier, getting teams off to a good start pays multiple dividends over time. This suggests that, perhaps, greater attention should be devoted to team staffing than is typically the norm (Hollenbeck, DeRue, & Guzzo, 2004; Mathieu, Tannenbaum, Donsbach, & Alliger, in press). It is also the case that teams should be encouraged to "go slow in order to go fast" – by having them invest time in the development of well-articulated team charters and task plans (Mathieu & Rapp, 2009). Applied to developmental processes, practitioners can be attuned to ensure that teams go through the proper stages to establish a foundation for later actions. This does not preclude efforts to employ interventions aimed at, for example, enhancing "swift trust" among unfamiliar members in a newly constituted team. The point is to appreciate the developmental sequence that is associated with the targeted outcomes.

Teaching teams how to solicit and process feedback using techniques such as debriefs (Tannenbaum & Cerasoli, 2013) or timing when leaders provide guidance versus permit teams to address changes on their own (Morgeson, 2005) are not in the typical arsenal of change agents but offer great promise. And, naturally, team training offers a valuable means by which to enhance team effectiveness. But not all training and development efforts are the same (Shuffler,

DiazGranados, & Salas, 2011) – to which we would add that different forms of training are influential at different stages of development or cycling of team processes. Yet the science is still evolving regarding the timing of training interventions. For example, at what stage of a team's life cycle is it best to introduce team development? Done prematurely before members know one another or their task responsibilities, such efforts may seem trite and meaningless. Done too late in the team's life cycle, or perhaps after deep-seated interpersonal processes have already been established, and development activities may be perceived as a distraction or waste of members' time. At issue is not just *what* is done to enhance team functioning but also *when* it is done. When the timing is right, team training and building interventions can be powerful mechanisms for accelerating team development and effectiveness. But when the timing is wrong, those same interventions not only might be a waste of everyone's time but also might do more harm than good. Table 2.1 lists several questions for researchers and practitioners to consider as they seek to understand better the temporal dynamics associated with teamwork.

Table 2.1 Questions addressing temporal issues in team research

Historical contexts
> Are there any seasonal or recurring influences that should be considered?
> Are there historical factors (e.g., recession, staffing shortages) that should be adjusted for?
> Does team composition remain sufficiently stable to warrant temporal comparisons?

Formally incorporate developmental processes into research designs
> How long is the team life cycle?
> When are teams likely to move from one phase to another?
> What are the salient criteria for each stage of development?

Formally incorporate episodic processes into research designs
> How frequently do episodes cycle?
> What triggers or marks episodic transitions?
> Align the collection of predictor and criteria variables with episodic phases.

Methodological issues

Utilize predictive versus concurrent (or postdictive) designs
> Do the criteria occur after the predictive factors?
> When would changes in the criteria become evident?
> Have you modeled changes in trajectories?

Select appropriate aggregation periods
> Are they sufficiently long enough to provide stable criteria estimates?
> Are they not so long as to become overly susceptible to contamination?
> Have you sampled enough of them to permit adequate modeling of change?

Conclusions

The time for teams is now. Given the modern-day competitive environment, employee expectations, the dominant work-related technologies, and assorted other contextual drivers, team-based designs are the most suitable for aligning human capital with organizational needs. That said, they are not panaceas, and history shows us that their use may wax and wane as circumstances change. But for the time being and for the foreseeable future, teams will be a primary part of the organizational landscape. What teams are, however, and how they function are issues that are changing, and new forms of teamwork are evolving (Tannenbaum et al., 2012).

Whether teams are constituted quickly for a very brief purpose, or whether they are anticipated to continue long into the future, there are developmental processes that they typically mature through. Research has shown us that to the extent that they take time to establish a solid foundation, both for taskwork and for orchestrating teamwork, they tend to experience fewer breakdowns and are more effective. Timing various developmental efforts, from team building to team development, from skills training to cross-training, is a valuable point of leverage. These types of interventions need to be not only well aligned with their intended purposes and team needs but also introduced at the right times to maximize their impact. Many teams also function in recurring cycles where different activities are done at different times. Similar to how early experiences set the stage for later team development, the quality of transition processes facilitate or hinder the successful execution of action processes *within episodes* (i.e., the "forward glance"). And research has shown us that how well team members understand and learn from previous episodes (i.e., the "backwards glance") enhances their effectiveness and performance trajectories *across episodes.* And, again, to the extent that organizational interventions are timed and focused appropriately for different activities done at different periods of these performance episodes, their effectiveness can be maximized.

Finally on the research front, better understanding and incorporating temporal issues offer great promise for advancing our science. We are not the first to suggest that – nor do we expect to be the last. But doing so is difficult and costly. We offered insights concerning when measures should be collected, and for how long data should be accumulated. In other words, traditional methods such as observations, interviews, and surveys can be used more strategically to align with and reveal temporal dynamics. We believe that we can do better. However, we also advocate the incorporation of digital trace measures as a means of better understanding the *dynamics* of teamwork over time. Historically, trace measures have been used to index team performance (e.g., the quantity and quality of products produced or services provided). However, cutting-edge technologies can reveal more about cognitive, affective, and behavioral processes underlying teamwork than have previously been available or were practically feasible. Like any trace measures, they are alluring and should not be embraced blindly. We need to work hard to establish their construct validity and applicability to different types of teams in different circumstances. But if we do so, they offer great promise for enabling the monitoring and modeling of dynamic team processes.

In sum, the time is right for teams. It has been for a while, and is likely to be so in the foreseeable future. But it is also time for us to better appreciate and incorporate time into our theories, research investigations, and our practice. We need to invest our time and efforts in doing so, but we believe that the payoffs will be worth it. It is time that we get to work on it.

References

Ancona, D., & Chong, C. L. (1996). Entrainment: Pace, cycle, and rhythm in organizational behavior. *Research in Organizational Behavior, 18,* 251–284.

Ancona, D. G., & Caldwell, D. F. (1998). Rethinking team composition from the outside in. In M. A. Neale, E. A. Mannix, & D. H. Gruenfeld (Eds.), *Research on managing groups and teams* (Vol. 1, pp. 21–38). Greenwich, CT: JAI Press.

Ancona, D. G., Okhuysen, G. A., & Perlow, L. A. (2001). Taking time to integrate temporal research. *Academy of Management Review, 26*(4), 512–529.

Bennis, W. G., & Shepard, H. A. (1956). A theory of group development. *Human Relations, 9,* 415–437.

Bowers, C. A., Salas, E., & Jentsch, F. (2006). *High-tech teams: Making effective work teams with people, machines, and networks.* Washington, DC: American Psychological Association.

Braaten, L. J. (1974/75). Developmental phases of encounter groups and related intensive groups: A critical review of models and a new proposal. *Interpersonal Development, 5,* 112–129.

Bradley, J., White, B. J., & Mennecke, B. E. (2003). Teams and tasks – A temporal framework for the effects of interpersonal interventions on team performance. *Small Group Research, 34*(3), 353–387.

Bramel, D., & Friend, R. (1982). Is industrial psychology none of Marxism's business? *American Psychologist, 37*(7), 860–862.

Campion, M. A., Medsker, G. J., & Higgs, A. C. (1993). Relations between work group characteristics and effectiveness: Implications for designing effective work groups. *Personnel Psychology, 46,* 823–850.

Caple, R. B. (1978). The sequential stages of group development. *Small Group Behavior, 9,* 470–476.

Cleveland, C., Blascovich, J., Gangi, C., & Finez, L. (2011). When good teammates are bad: Physiological threat on recently formed teams. *Small Group Research, 42,* 3–31.

DeChurch, L. A., & Marks, M. A. (2006). Leadership in multiteam systems. *Journal of Applied Psychology, 91*(2), 311–329.

Eddy, E., Tannenbaum, S. I., & Mathieu, J. E. (in press). Helping teams to help themselves: Comparing two team-led debriefing methods. *Personnel Psychology.*

Eldredge, N., & Gould, S. (1972). Punctuated equilibria: An alternative to phyletic gradualism. In T. J. Schopf (Ed.), *Models in paleobiology* (pp. 82–115). San Francisco: Freeman, Cooper.

Fried, Y., & Slowik, L. H. (2004). Enriching goal-setting theory with time: An integrated approach. *Academy of Management Review, 29*(3), 404–422.

Gersick, C. J. G. (1988). Time and transition in work teams: Toward a new model of group development. *Academy of Management Journal, 31,* 9–41.

Gully, S. M. (2000). Work teams research: Recent findings and future trends. In M. M. Beyerlein (Ed.), *Work teams: Past, present and future* (pp. 25–44). Netherlands: Kluwer Academic.

Hackman, J. R. (1976). *The design of self-managing work groups* (No. TR-11). New Haven, CT: Yale University, School of Organization and Management.

Hamilton, B. H., & Nickerson, J. A. (2003). Correcting for endogeneity in strategic management research. *Strategic Organization, 1,* 51–78.

Heinen, J. S., & Jacobson, E. (1976, October). A model of task group development in complex organizations and a strategy of implementation. *Academy of Management Review,* 98–111.

Hollenbeck, J. R., DeRue, D. S., & Guzzo, R. (2004). Bridging the gap between I/O research and HR practice: Improving team composition, team training, and team task design. *Human Resource Management, 43*(4), 353–366.

Hyatt, D. E., & Ruddy, T. M. (1997). An examination of the relationship between work group characteristics and performance: Once more into the breach. *Personnel Psychology, 50,* 553–585.

Ilgen, D. R., Hollenbeck, J. R., Johnson, M., & Jundt, D. (2005). Teams in organizations: From I-P-O models to IMOI models. *Annual Review of Psychology, 56,* 517–543.

Janicik, G. A., & Bartel, C. A. (2003). Talking about time: Effects of temporal planning and time awareness norms on group coordination and performance. *Group Dynamics-Theory Research and Practice, 7*(2), 122–134.

Johns, G. (2006). The essential impact of context on organizational behavior. *Academy of Management Review, 31*(2), 386–408.

Kirkman, B. L., & Mathieu, J. E. (2005). The dimensions and antecedents of team virtuality. *Journal of Management, 31,* 700–718.

Kirkman, B. L., & Rosen, B. (1999). Beyond self-management: Antecedents and consequences of team empowerment. *Academy of Management Journal, 42*(1), 58–74.

Klimoski, R., & Jones, R. G. (1994). Staffing for effective group decision making: Key issues in matching people and teams. In R. A. Guzzo, E. Salas, et al. (Eds.), *Team effectiveness and decision making in organizations* (pp. 291–332). San Francisco, CA: Jossey-Bass.

Kormanski, C., & Mozenter, A. (1987). A new model of team building: A technology for today and tomorrow. In J. W. Pfeiffer (Ed.), *The 1987 Annual: Developing human resources* (pp. 255–268). San Diego, CA: Jossey-Bass.

Kozlowski, S. W. J., & Bell, B. S. (2003). Work groups and teams in organizations. In W. Borman, D. Ilgen, & R. Klimoski (Eds.), *Comprehensive handbook of psychology: Industrial and organizational psychology* (Vol. 12, pp. 333–375). New York: Wiley.

Kozlowski, S. W. J., Gully, S. M., Nason, E. R., & Smith, E. M. (1999). Developing adaptive teams: A theory of compilation and performance across levels and time. In D. R. Ilgen & E. D. Pulakos (Eds.), *The changing nature of work performance: Implications for staffing, personnel actions, and development* (pp. 240–292). San Francisco: Jossey-Bass.

Kozlowski, S. W. J., Gully, S. M., Salas, E., & Cannon-Bowers, J. A. (1996). Team leadership and development: Theory, principles, and guidelines for training leaders and teams. In M. M. Beyerlein, D. A. Johnson, & S. T. Beyerlein (Eds.), *Advances in interdisciplinary studies of work teams* (Vol. 3, pp. 253–291). Greenwich, CT: JAI Press.

Kozlowski, S. W. J., & Ilgen, D. R. (2006). Enhancing the effectiveness of work groups and teams. *Psychological Science, 7,* 77–124.

Lacoursiere, R. B. (1980). *The life cycle of groups.* New York: Human Sciences Press.

Landis, R. S. (2001). A note on the stability of team performance. *Journal of Applied Psychology, 86,* 446–450.

LePine, J. A., Piccolo, R. F., Jackson, C. L., Mathieu, J. E., & Saul, J. R. (2008). A meta-analysis of teamwork processes: Tests of a multidimensional model and relationships with team effectiveness criteria. *Personnel Psychology, 61*(2), 273–307.

Lewin, K. (1945). The Research Center for Group Dynamics at Massachusetts Institute of Technology. *Sociometry, 8*(2), 126–136.

Maples, M. F. (1988). Group development: Extending Tuckman's theory. *Journal for Specialists in Group Work, 13*, 17–23.

Marks, M. A., Mathieu, J. E., & Zaccaro, S. J. (2001). A temporally based framework and taxonomy of team processes. *Academy of Management Review, 26*(3), 356–376.

Martins, L. L., Gilson, L. L., & Maynard, M. T. (2004). Virtual teams: What do we know and where do we go from here? *Journal of Management, 30*, 805–835.

Mathieu, J., Maynard, M. T., Rapp, T., & Gilson, L. (2008). Team effectiveness 1997–2007: A review of recent advancements and a glimpse into the future. *Journal of Management, 34*(3), 410–476. doi:10.1177/0149206308316061

Mathieu, J. E., & Button, S. B. (1992). An examination of the relative impact of normative information and self-efficacy on personal goals and performance over time. *Journal of Applied Social Psychology, 22*, 1758–1775.

Mathieu, J. E., Gilson, L. L., & Ruddy, T. M. (2006). Empowerment and team effectiveness: An empirical test of an integrated model. *Journal of Applied Psychology, 91*(1), 97–108.

Mathieu, J. E., Heffner, T. S., Goodwin, G. F., Salas, E., & Cannon-Bowers, J. A. (2000). The influence of shared mental models on team process and performance. *Journal of Applied Psychology, 85*(2), 273–283.

Mathieu, J. E., Marks, M. A., & Zaccaro, S. J. (2001). Multi-team systems. In N. Anderson, D. Ones, H. K. Sinangil, & C. Viswesvaran (Eds.), *International handbook of work and organizational psychology* (pp. 289–313). London: Sage.

Mathieu, J. E., & Rapp, T. L. (2009). Laying the foundation for successful team performance trajectories: The roles of team charters and performance strategies. *Journal of Applied Psychology, 94*(1), 90–103. doi:10.1037/a0013257

Mathieu, J. E., & Schulze, W. (2006). The influence of team knowledge and formal plans on episodic team process-performance relationships. *Academy of Management Journal, 49*, 605–619.

Mathieu, J. E., Tannenbaum, S. I., Donsbach, J. S., & Alliger, G. E. (in press). Achieving optimal team composition for success. In E. Salas, S. I. Tannenbaum, D. Cohen, & G. Latham (Eds.), *Developing and enhancing high performing teams: Evidence-based best practices and guidelines*. San Francisco, CA: Wiley.

Mathieu, J. E., & Taylor, S. R. (2006). Clarifying conditions and decision points for mediational type inferences in organizational behavior. *Journal of Organizational Behavior, 27*, 1031–1056.

Maxwell, S. E., & Cole, D. A. (2007). Bias in cross-sectional analyses of longitudinal mediation. *Psychological Methods, 12*, 23–44.

Maynard, M. T., Mathieu, J. E., Rapp, T. L., & Gilson, L. L. (2012). Something(s) old and something(s) new: Modeling drivers of global virtual team effectiveness. *Journal of Organizational Behavior, 33*(3), 342–365. doi:10.1002/job.1772

McGrath, J. E. (1984). *Groups: Interaction and performance*. Englewood Cliffs, NJ: Prentice-Hall.

McGrath, J. E. (1991). Time, interaction, and performance (TIP): A theory of groups. *Small Group Research, 22*, 147–174.

McGrath, J. E., Arrow, H., & Berdahl, J. L. (2000). The study of groups: Past, present, and future. *Personality & Social Psychology Review, 4*(1), 95–105.

McGrath, J. E., & Rotchford, N. L. (1983). Time and behavior in organizations. *Research in Organizational Behavior, 5*, 57–101.

Mills, T. M. (1964). *Group transformation: An analysis of a learning group*. Englewood Cliffs, NJ: Prentice-Hall.

Mitchell, T. R., & James, L. R. (2001). Building better theory: Time and the specification of when things happen. *Academy of Management Review, 26*(4), 530–547.

Morgan, B. B., & Lassiter, D. L. (1992). Team composition and staffing. In R. W. Swezey & E. Salas (Eds.), *Teams: Their training and performance* (pp. 75–100). Norwood, NJ: Ablex.

Morgan, B. B., Salas, E., & Glickman, A. S. (1993). An analysis of team evolution and maturation. *Journal of General Psychology, 120*(3), 277–291.

Morgeson, F. P. (2005). The external leadership of self-managing teams: Intervening in the context of novel and disruptive events. *Journal of Applied Psychology, 90*(3), 497–508.

O'Leary, M., Mortensen, M., & Woolley, A. (2011). Multiple team membership: A theoretical model of its effects on productivity and learning for individuals and teams. *Academy of Management Review, 36*(3), 461–478.

Pearce, C. L., & Sims, H. P. (2002). Vertical versus shared leadership as predictors of the effectiveness of change management teams: An examination of aversive, directive, transactional, transformational, and empowering leader behaviors. *Group Dynamics-Theory Research and Practice, 6*(2), 172–197.

Pentland, A. (2007). Automatic mapping and modeling of human networks. *Physica A: Statistical Mechanics and Its Applications, 378*(1), 59–67.

Poole, M. S. (1983). Decision development in small groups, III: A multiple sequence model of group decision development 1. *Communications Monographs, 50*(4), 321–341.

Poole, M. S., & Roth, J. (1989). Decision development in small groups, IV. *Human Communications Research, 15*, 323–356.

Poole, M. S., Seibold, D. R., & McPhee, R. D. (1985). Group decision-making as a structurational process. *Quarterly Journal of Speech, 71*, 74–102.

Rice, A. K. (1953). Productivity and social organization in an Indian weaving shed: An examination of the socio-technical system of an experimental automatic loom shed. *Human Relations, 6*, 297–329.

Salas, E., Cannon-Bowers, J. A., & Johnston, J. H. (1998). Lessons learned from conducting the TADMUS program: Balancing science, practice, and more. In J. A. Cannon-Bowers & E. Salas (Eds.), *Making decisions under stress* (pp. 409–413). Washington, DC: American Psychological Association.

Salas, E., Rozell, D., Mullen, B., & Driskell, J. E. (1999). The effect of team building on performance – An integration. *Small Group Research, 30*(3), 309–329.

Salas, E., Stagl, K. C., & Burke, C. S. (2004). 25 years of team effectiveness in organizations: Research themes and emerging needs. *International Review of Industrial and Organizational Psychology, 19*, 47–91.

Sanna, L. J., & Parks, C. D. (1997). Group research trends in social and organizational psychology: Whatever happened to intragroup research? *Psychological Science, 8*(4), 261–267.

Sarri, R. C., & Galinsky, M. J. (1974). A conceptual framework for group development. In P. Glasser, R. Sarri, & R. Vinter (Eds.), *Individual change through small groups* (pp. 71–88). New York: Free Press.

Shuffler, M. L., DiazGranados, D., & Salas, E. (2011). There's a science for that. *Current Directions in Psychological Science, 20*(6), 365–372. doi:10.1177/0963721411422054

Simon, H. A. (1976). *Administrative behavior* (Vol. 3). New York: Free Press.

Smith, G. (2001). Group development: A review of the literature and a commentary of future research directions. *Group Facilitation: A Research and Applications Journal, 46*, 14–31.

Sonnenfeld, J. A. (1985). Shedding light on the Hawthorne studies. *Journal of Organizational Behavior, 6*(2), 111–130.

Steiner, I. D. (1972). *Group processes and productivity.* New York: Academic Press.

Sundstrom, E., De Meuse, K. P., & Futrell, D. (1990). Work teams: Applications and effectiveness. *American Psychologist, 45,* 120–133.

Sundstrom, E., McIntyre, M., Halfhill, T., & Richards, H. (2000). Work groups: From the Hawthorne studies to work teams of the 1990s and beyond. *Group Dynamics: Theory, Research, and Practice, 4*(1), 44.

Tannenbaum, S., Beard, R. L., & Salas, E. (1992). Team building and its influence on team effectiveness: An examination of conceptual and empirical developments. Issues, theory, and research in industrial/organizational psychology. In K. Kelley (Ed.), *Advances in psychology* (Vol. 82, pp. 117–153). New York: Elsevier Science.

Tannenbaum, S. I., & Cerasoli, C. (2013). Do team and individual debriefs enhance performance? A meta-analysis. *Human Factors, 55*(1), 231–245.

Tannenbaum, S. I., Mathieu, J. E., Salas, S., & Cohen, D. (2012). Teams are changing – Are research and practice evolving fast enough? *Industrial and Organizational Psychology: Perspectives on Science and Practice, 5*(1), 56–61.

Trist, E. L., & Bamforth, K. W. (1951). Some social and psychological consequences of the longwall method of coal getting. *Human Relations, 4,* 3–38.

Tuckman, B. W. (1965). Developmental sequence in small groups. *Psychological Bulletin, 63,* 384–389.

Tuckman, B. W., & Jensen, M. C. (1977). Stages of small-group development revisited. *Group and Organization Studies, 2*(4), 419–427.

Wageman, R., Gardner, H., & Mortensen, M. (2012). The changing ecology of teams: New directions for teams research. *Journal of Organizational Behavior, 33*(3), 301–315.

Waller, M. J. (1999). The timing of adaptive group responses to nonroutine events. *Academy of Management Journal, 42*(2), 127–137.

Weingart, L. R. (1992). Impact of group goals, task component complexity, effort, and planning on group performance. *Journal of Applied Psychology, 77,* 682–693.

Wellins, R. W., Byham, W. C., & Wilson, J. M. (1991). *Empowered teams.* San Francisco, CA: Jossey-Bass.

Wildman, J. L., Shuffler, M. L., Lazzara, E. H., Fiore, S. M., Burke, C. S., Salas, E., & Garven, S. (2012). Trust development in swift starting action teams: A multilevel framework. *Group & Organization Management, 37*(2), 137–170.

Zaccaro, S., Marks, M., & DeChurch, L. (2011). *Multiteam systems: An organizational form for dynamic and complex environments.* New York: Routledge Academic.

3 Time and leadership

David V. Day

*No little part of the torment of
existence lies in this, that time is
continually pressing upon us, never
letting us take a breath.*

*But always coming after us, a
taskmaster with a whip.*
      –A. C. Grayling (2011, p. 80)

Leadership takes time. It takes time to be perceived as a leader, to have one's actions (behaviors) as a leader influence others, and it certainly takes time to develop as a leader. Relatedly, the field is clear that leadership is a process – not a position – and process implies time. For all of these reasons, leadership and time should be inherently intertwined in theory and research. But just as time is continually pressing upon us, as noted by A. C. Grayling, it can also shroud causality and effects in a haze. The best way to cut through this epistemological murk in the scientific study of leadership is to pay careful attention to time.

Unfortunately, the treatment of time in the leadership literature has been cursory at best, and when it is addressed it is mainly at a theoretical rather than empirical level. As others have noted, the role of time in studying, understanding, and practicing leadership is critically important, yet it continues to be "an unexplored dimension in leadership studies" (Shamir, 2011, p. 307). This is troubling because what we think we know about leadership may not be as robust as we believe. Results from cross-sectional research may not generalize longitudinally, and if those results do generalize, we need to understand the time frame under which they operate. These are just a few of the many questions that are raised when we fail to consider time in leadership theory and research.

Process issues aside, questions might be raised as to why time is so important in leadership. One example is illustrative. For a period of time (pun intended), it was argued in the scholarly literature that CEOs and other top-level leaders had little or no influence on the economic outcomes of organizations (Calder, 1977; Pfeffer, 1977). This assertion was based primarily on executive succession data that appeared to support such claims (e.g., Lieberson & O'Connor, 1972; Salancik &

Pfeffer, 1977). Most of the interpretations were based on uncorrected outcome estimates with no time lags; however, when more appropriate outcomes were adopted (e.g., profit margin rather than raw sales or net income) and a three-year lag between succession and outcome measurement was incorporated, executive leadership was shown to explain as much as 45% of an organization's financial performance (Day & Lord, 1988).

This may seem like an obvious point, but it is necessary to address time lags in assessing the effects of anything (especially executive leadership) because "it takes time for causes to have effects" (Gollub & Reichardt, 1987, p. 80). Time matters, and it especially matters when the focus of study is leadership. This particular example is just one in which the failure to consider time potentially results in erroneous conclusions about leadership.

This chapter will pick up from recent commentators on the general theme of linking time and leadership (e.g., Bluedorn & Jaussi, 2008; Shamir, 2011). In particular, temporal issues will be explored across four domains of leadership research and theory: (a) Leader *behavior* regarding how much of a lag time between actions and effects is appropriate and related measurement implications; (b) leader *emergence* in terms of how followers' perceptions form and change over time; (c) leader-follower *relationships* (e.g., LMX) as to how quickly – or slowly – do such relationships develop and change over time; and (d) leader *development* in the form of how leaders acquire and otherwise develop leadership capacity and capabilities over time.

A central theme in the chapter will be on giving greater consideration to *temporal design* concerns – the sampling of times of measurement (Collins & Graham, 2002) – in leadership research, especially issues associated with determining how many times to measure and the appropriate intervals between measurement periods. The chapter will conclude with a brief discussion of the potential benefits associated with intensive longitudinal data, along with a nontechnical overview of the design and analyses of this type of data (e.g., Tan, Shiyko, Li, Li, & Dierker, 2012; Walls & Schafer, 2006).

The demands of time

If time is a taskmaster, always coming after us with a whip (metaphorically of course), it has a special fondness for leaders and leadership. The notion of having to do more with less and the perception that the pace of demands and expectations has accelerated seem ubiquitous. Or maybe relentless is the more appropriate term. This seems particularly the case with leadership. Investors and analysts expect to see quick returns on the appointment of a new CEO; the actions taken by leaders in other levels of an organization are hoped to immediately motivate, engage, and direct employees; and the pressing need to develop more and more effective leaders in an accelerated manner is an organizational imperative. These demands may seem unrealistic – especially to those subjected to them – yet researchers have aided and abetted those who are making these leadership demands by failing to incorporate temporal issues into relevant research.

This state of affairs may be partly due to a lingering misperception that time is not a theoretically interesting variable (Kelly & McGrath, 1988). Perhaps a more likely explanation is that time is a theoretically difficult variable to incorporate into research (Avital, 2000).

As noted by Mitchell and James (2001), the field of management and organizations has little if any theory about time, timing, or the specification of when things occur. This is especially troublesome given that time is a central concern in causality and in drawing causal inferences. As a result, those authors believe that the neglect of time in organizational theory and research "poses serious problems for the evolution and acceptance of our field" (p. 530).

As noted, this chapter addresses the need for more theoretical and (especially) research attention on the role of time in leadership. Where this chapter will go that is different from previous commentaries is to elaborate on four specific areas within the broad leadership domain that have particular relevance for integrating and understanding the influence of time: (a) leader behavior, (b) leader emergence and follower perceptions, (c) leader-follower relationships, and (d) leader development.

Leader behavior

One of the most popular research approaches to the scientific study of leadership is examining the effects of leader behavior (Bass, 2008). Either implicitly or explicitly it is assumed that leader behavior precedes followers' actions and other outcomes and influences them in a causal manner (e.g., DeRue, Nahrgang, Wellman, & Humphrey, 2011); however, the kinds of research designs needed to demonstrate such causal effects are the exception rather than the rule in leadership research. Although researchers have argued that over time followers will likely have more exposure to leaders' behavior and thus be more predictive of leader effectiveness this remains mainly speculative. Perhaps a bigger concern is that research from the social cognition and person perception literatures suggests that for the most part perceivers do not encode, store, and retrieve memories of specific behaviors.

As noted by the research evidence summarized by Gilbert (1998), the first stages of person perception involve categorization (what is she doing) and characterization (what personality trait is implied), both of which occur spontaneously and relatively effortlessly. What is stored in memory and recalled when needed is what the person is "like" (i.e., personality) rather than what he or she "did" (i.e., behavior), except in very unusual cases. Note that this is very much at odds with the behavioral measurement of leadership that is found in contemporary scales such as the Multifactor Leadership Questionnaire (MLQ) for transactional and transformational leadership (Bass & Avolio, 2000), Authentic Leadership Questionnaire (ALQ) (Walumba, Avolio, Gardner, Wernsing, & Peterson, 2008), and Servant Leadership Scale (SLS) (Liden, Wayne, Zhao, & Henderson, 2008), among others.

Despite their widespread use in leadership research, basic assumptions underpinning the use of questionnaire surveys to measure leader behavior are untenable.

Specifically, it is assumed that respondents (typically followers) encode, store, and recall observed leader behaviors while completing a leadership questionnaire such as the MLQ, ALQ, or SLS. But as discussed, the person perception literature maintains that observers quickly and spontaneously categorize and characterize (i.e., attach trait labels to) observed behaviors and then go back and correct those trait-based inferences in an effortful manner only if there are available cognitive resources and the motivation to correct initial impressions. Note also that the temporal focus (Shipp, Edwards, & Lambert, 2009) of leadership ratings is unclear. If followers are focused on the past, then person perception research shows that observed information is encoded in terms of semantic trait labels and not behavior. But another possibility is that leadership ratings have a future temporal focus in terms of what a follower expects a leader to do. This further confounds the meaning of behavioral measures of leadership.

Another implication of person perception processes with regard to leadership ratings is that behaviors consistent with an impression of a target ratee such as a leader will tend to be favorably rated even if the behavior never occurred (Sulsky & Day, 1992). This may explain why most leadership theories conceptualize leadership as a multidimensional construct yet empirical research reveals the various dimensions to be highly intercorrelated. There are also long-standing research findings showing that group members who receive bogus performance feedback distort (i.e., correct) group process ratings in the direction of that feedback (Downey, Chacko, & McElroy, 1979; Staw, 1975). Similar findings have been found with leadership ratings. Leaders who are portrayed (through bogus feedback) as being associated with successful group performance are rated more highly in their respective leadership behaviors than those who are thought to be leaders of unsuccessful groups, despite observing videotapes showing identical leadership behaviors (Lord, Binning, Rush, & Thomas, 1978; Mitchell, Larson, & Green, 1977). As I have noted elsewhere (Day, 2012a), "Researchers are fooling themselves if they believe that responses to questionnaires accurately reflect leader behavior and only leader behavior" (p. 705).

Although this discussion of the measurement of leader behavior appears to be tangential to the core issues of time and leadership, they are actually highly interrelated. In research that has largely been ignored in the leadership and applied personality literatures, Fleeson (2001) found a great deal of within-person variability in manifestations of individual personality. There was so much evidence of behavioral variability he concluded that "the typical individual regularly and routinely manifested *nearly all levels of all* [Big Five] *traits* in his or her everyday behavior" (p. 1011, italics added). Fleeson also concluded from his findings that the typical individual is "highly diverse, flexible, and responsive" in terms of everyday behavior (p. 1024). As an illustration, the average individual's distribution of states over two weeks is charted in Figure 3.1.

The implications of Fleeson's (2001) findings for leadership research, and specifically the relationship between time and leadership, are potentially profound. Consider what proportion of a leader's everyday behavior is observed or experienced by a follower. Whatever that percentage of behavior might be (and I would

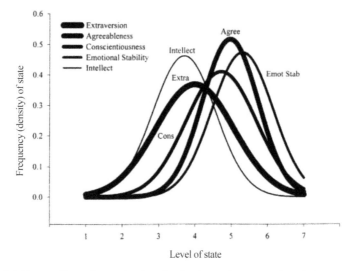

Figure 3.1 Personality traits as density distributions of states. Adapted from "Toward a structure- and process-integrated view of personality: Traits as density distributions of states," by W. Fleeson, 2001, *Journal of Personality and Social Psychology, 80*, p. 1016. Copyright 2001 by American Psychological Association. Reprinted with permission.

Note: The average individual's distributions of states over two weeks: Within-person variability is near the high end of expectations. How the typical individual acts over a two-week period: Normal distributions calculated with the means and standard deviations observed within the typical individual. The larger standard deviations (for Extraversion, 1.08; for Conscientiousness, 0.97) show that variability cannot be much larger on a seven-point scale while maintaining normality and that individuals must largely overlap with each other in their behavior. Conditional and contextual personality units are needed to describe this variation. Extra = Extraversion; Agree = Agreeableness; Cons = Conscientiousness; Emot Stab = Emotional Stability.

conjecture it is at best modest) it is clearly a sample, and probably a nonrepresentative sample, of leader behavior. This calls into question how accurate followers' impressions are of a leader, and the underlying leader behavior and personality (i.e., character) given the demonstrated diversity, flexibility, and responsiveness of such behavior on a daily basis.

In their meta-analytic integration of trait and behavioral theories of leadership, DeRue et al. (2011) posited that time would be an important moderator between leader personality and behavior and their effects on relevant outcomes. Specifically, over time followers are thought to have greater exposure to a leader's behavior, likely making it a more important explanation for the noted effects of leader traits on effectiveness (i.e., leader traits → leader behavior → leadership effectiveness). This seems sensible especially if we extrapolate from basic sampling theory that gathering more observations from a (representative) sample would better approximate the true (i.e., population) distribution of leader behavior. But a question that has not been addressed either theoretically or empirically is how much time with a leader is sufficient to form an accurate and representative impression given the noted within-person variability of everyday trait-based behavior. Surely impressions can change over time as well. Therefore, another question involves the amount of time associated with changing perceptions of someone as a leader (or not). These are not trivial questions when it comes to understanding and improving our measures of leadership. Although it is beyond the scope of this chapter to offer definitive answers to these questions, the general take-away point is that researchers need to treat leadership behavior and the related topic of leadership perceptions (which is taken up in more detail in the next section) as dynamic processes rather than as stable snapshots.

Related concerns involve the lag times associated with actions taken by a leader. The leadership literature is dominated by cross-sectional, questionnaire-based research designs, which cannot account for any precise understanding of when the actions of a leader have an effect on follower attitudes or behavior, let alone more macro outcomes associated with organizational performance. Causality and research design issues aside, another concern is in understanding what is meant by leader behavior and devising a theoretical perspective on when different types of leader behavior are likely to influence followers' attitudes or behaviors.

DeRue et al. (2011) proposed four general categories of leader behavior as part of their integrated model of leader traits, behaviors, and effectiveness, which were examined meta-analytically. Those types of leader behaviors are: (a) task-oriented (e.g., initiating structure, contingent reward), (b) relational-oriented (e.g., consideration, participative), (c) change-oriented (e.g., transformational, charismatic), and (d) passive (e.g., laissez-faire). Even at this broad level it is apparent that certain kinds of leader behaviors such as those that are change-oriented are likely to have considerably longer lag times associated with their potential effects than something relational-oriented such as showing consideration for a follower. This would seem especially true when the target of the behavior is affective- rather than performance-based. Furthermore, leadership theory and research make no suggestions as to how long it would take for a "do nothing" (i.e., laissez-faire) leader to be recognized as such or how long this lack of leadership would need to continue before it adversely affected relevant performance outcomes.

Another perspective on leader behavior has been offered under the guise of developing a more integrative ontology of leadership (Drath et al., 2008). From this perspective, leadership is about setting *direction*, creating *alignment*, and building *commitment* and anything that serves to bring about those processes – whether at the level of an individual or a broader collective – is thought to be a source of leadership. But imagine the different temporal imperatives associated with something like envisioning goals (direction) as compared with managing and achieving a workable unity (alignment), or motivating and renewing followers (commitment). Although unspecified by these (or other) authors, it can be easily imaged how different *timescales*, or intervals of time of different lengths (Zaheer, Albert, & Zaheer, 1999), might be needed to ascertain changes in setting a group's direction as compared with alignment of various individuals' mindsets and personal agendas in the group, or building and maintaining collective commitment across the length of engagement for a collective.

This section raises many more questions than it provides answers with regard to time and leader behavior. Nonetheless, it highlights some troubling assumptions researchers make about the measurement and effects of leader behavior. Related to points made by Mitchell and James (2001), continuing to ignore the temporal implications associated with the measurement and meaning of leader behavior runs the risk of undermining the further evolution and acceptance of leadership as a scholarly field of research. This is especially the case if a focus is on conducting additional studies of leader behavior, as some scholars have advocated (Judge, Piccolo, & Ilies, 2004).

Leader emergence and follower perceptions

An important area of theory and research is that of leader emergence. Predicting who emerges as a leader among a group of individuals and understanding the underlying perceptual processes are of long-standing interest to leadership researchers. Indeed, some have defined the essence of leadership as "the process of being perceived by others as a leader" (Lord & Maher, 1991, p. 11). Although this definition may seem overly simplistic, it recognizes an important point: it is easier to exercise influence over someone if one is first seen as a leader. And as many have argued (e.g., Katz & Kahn, 1978; Stogdill, 1950; Tead, 1935), the exercise of social influence is at the heart of leadership.

Leader emergence is conceptualized as a socioperceptual process guided by followers' perceptions that are grounded in their respective implicit leadership theories (ILT). In nontechnical terms, ILTs are preconceived notions or implicit expectations about what traits and behaviors are associated with leadership (Kenney, Schwartz-Kenney, & Blascovich, 1996). Rather than going into detail about the kinds of factors associated with ILTs and being perceived as a leader (see Epitropaki & Martin, 2004; Offermann, Kennedy, & Wirtz, 1994), I will instead briefly discuss the process of leader emergence and the temporal implications associated with leadership perceptions and the likelihood of these changing over time.

A stage model of leadership perceptions first proposed by Lord and Maher (1991) is based on human information processing and the person perception literatures. Leadership perceptions are initially guided by spontaneous, automatic, recognition-based processes using perceptual matching of what is observed of a target individual and the leadership prototype held by a perceiver as part of his or her ILT. This prototype match process creates a near-immediate recognition of someone as a leader. It is also thought that someone can be perceived as a leader through slower, more controlled, and attribution-based processing such as reasoning from outcomes. Rather than quickly matching perceived dispositional traits with a stored prototype of a leader, attribution-based processing involves reasoning backwards from some outcome (e.g., goal attainment, successful performance) to deduce that the cause of this outcome was effective leadership of a target individual. Attribution-based processes might also involve "word of mouth" associations based on what has been heard about a prospective leader. In these ways individuals can emerge as leaders either quickly through a type of "bottom up," recognition-based, prototype match process or more slowly through "top down," thoughtful, attributional reasoning. But a question that has not received much attention is how stable these perceptions are and how likely they are to change over time.

An implicit assumption in these models is that once someone is seen as a leader that perception will continue over time (i.e., is stable); however, there may be reasons to doubt this theoretically and practically. Human behavior can be inconsistent and someone who appears to be calm and rational one day can be seen as stubborn and argumentative the next day. Which of these is more "leader-like"? (Hint: probably the former.) This is consistent with Fleeson's (2001) personality research discussed in the previous section, demonstrating that individuals are quite flexible and responsive in their everyday behavior. When an interaction occurred with a leader could greatly determine the level of a given trait that was perceived. Given that potential followers do not see all of a leader's possible behaviors – and not necessarily even a representative sample of behavior – it is possible that perceptions fluctuate around some mean of manifested behaviors.

Empirical evidence at the group level regarding social network "churn" (Sasovova, Mehra, Borgatti, & Schippers, 2010), or changes in who is indicated as a friend in a particular context at different points in time, backs up this claim. Additional data from a 12-month leadership development program show considerable churn in terms of the number of leadership nominations gained and lost among participants (Day, 2013a). Across three time periods, results from a social network analysis of leadership perceptions (who is considered to be a leader in this program) indicated that 60–70% of leadership nominations were different across program participants between consecutive time periods. This compares with fewer than 50% change in friendship nominations across this same group of participants and time periods. Although these findings require replication before any firm conclusions can be drawn, they suggest that people's leadership perceptions may be much less stable than might be expected. But how stable or, conversely, how malleable are these perceptions? There is very little research on this potentially important topic.

Using one high-profile example of changes in leadership perceptions, we know that the job approval ratings of US presidents can vary remarkably over their tenures. The American Presidency Project (www.presidency.ucsb.edu/data/popularity.php) tracks the job approval ratings of every US president from Franklin Roosevelt (1941) through to the current president (Barack Obama at the time of this writing). A notable example of wide variability in leadership perceptions is that of George W. Bush, who attained a job approval rating of 89% shortly after the terrorist attacks of September 11, 2001, which dropped to a low of 25% immediately preceding the 2008 election. Although these are the widest swings in job approval ratings in this presidential sample, similar changes can be found with every president in the sample, with the possible exception of Franklin Roosevelt (high of 83% in January 1942, low of 65% in August 1941 and December 1943). Although presidential job approval ratings are not exactly the same as leadership perceptions, theory suggests that they are most likely related. One of the most robust aspects of ILTs is the connection in the minds of perceivers that successful performance is related to effective leadership (e.g., Lord et al., 1978). It is difficult to imagine someone strongly disapproving of a president's performance and also to see him or her as an effective leader. He or she might be considered to be a leader by virtue of position, but not in terms of behaviors or outcomes achieved.

As noted previously, the role of time in the study of leadership has been sorely overlooked. Although researchers have examined the influence of followers' ILTs on subsequent leader-member exchange relationships (Epitropaki & Martin, 2005), there is very little research that has examined changes in leadership perceptions over time. An exception to this general rule, Foti, Knee, and Backert (2008) examined the dynamic process of leadership perceptions from the perspectives of connectionist and catastrophe theories, respectively, across two independent studies. These studies used laboratory procedures and measured changes in leadership perceptions in terms of milliseconds in demonstrating how time and a dynamic nonlinear perspective can help clarify leadership perception processes. Besides this valuable experimental research, there is a very real need to understand the dynamics of leadership perceptions over time in nonlaboratory settings. The available evidence is beginning to accumulate suggesting that the fundamental processes of perceiving someone as a leader may be less stable and more dynamic than typically considered. Thus, more considered notions of time and leader emergence and leadership perceptions are needed.

Leader-follower relationships

The relationships that develop between a formal leader and followers have been an active area of theory and research for going on four decades (Dansereau, Graen, & Haga, 1975; Graen & Cashman, 1975). Typically conceptualized in terms of leader-member exchange (LMX) theory (Graen & Scandura, 1987; Graen & Uhl-Bien, 1995), high-quality relationships that develop between a leader and follower(s) have been shown to be associated with a host of positive work-related outcomes, including higher levels of job performance, satisfaction, commitment, and lower levels of role conflict and turnover intentions (Gerstner & Day, 1997), as well as higher levels of citizenship behavior (Ilies, Nahrgang, & Morgeson, 2007). Despite the hundreds of LMX studies that have been conducted, including examinations of various mediation models (Dulebohn, Bommer, Liden, Brouer, & Ferris, 2012), there are relatively few longitudinal studies of LMX and virtually no empirical treatment of time in the LMX research literature, with the exception of using tenure with supervisor as a control variable.

The general failure to incorporate time into studies of LMX is especially surprising – and disappointing – given theoretical perspectives on the so-called life-cycle process of leadership making and leadership relationship maturity (Graen & Uhl-Bien, 1995). The process has been conceptualized to initiate with a *stranger* stage in which a leader and a follower are newly introduced. The relationship tends to be relatively formal in nature and the leader-member exchanges mainly contractual. According to the model, after a period of time (unclear as to length) an offer is made by either party to improve the relationship for their mutual career benefit. This designates the start of the *acquaintance* stage in which the social exchanges move beyond being entirely contractual, and more information and other resources are shared at a personal and professional level. Over time, relationships may – or may not – develop to the next stage of *mature partnership*. At this level the exchanges are not just behavioral but also emotional in that "mutual respect, trust, and obligation grow throughout the [leadership] process" (p. 230).

Although this is a general process heuristic of the development of relationship maturity rather than a formal testable model, it is still surprising that so little LMX research has been conducted that incorporates time. There are a few notable exceptions to this that should be discussed. A foundational study in demonstrating that leaders negotiate different types of relationships (i.e., exchange quality) with followers was based on a nine-month longitudinal study involving four waves of interview data collection (Dansereau et al., 1975). The main finding from the research was that it is misleading to attempt to study an average leadership style of any leader:

> No longer need researchers examining leadership behavior be content to search only for the behavior of the leader toward his [*sic*] members in general on the average, but instead they might probe the exchange processes between the leader and each of his [*sic*] members. (ibid., p. 76)

This was a landmark study in paving the way for the development of LMX as a distinct field of leadership research, different especially from the behavioral approaches that studied a so-called average leadership style. However, questions remained regarding the potential factors that predict the development of exchange qualities between leaders and followers. Whereas many subsequent studies examined correlates of LMX using cross-sectional designs, Liden, Wayne, and Stilwell (1993) examined the development of LMX over the first six months of employment in a sample of newly hired employees. The expectations that leaders and followers held for each other in the first five days of interaction significantly predicted (i.e., correlated with) LMX qualities at two weeks and six weeks in the history of the dyad, as well as members' expectations of leaders' predicted LMX qualities at six months. This finding has been widely interpreted as suggesting that LMX is established very early in the history of a leader-member dyad (within the first five days) and is relatively stable over time. Although interesting, this study does not shed much light on how leader-follower relationships change over time, so arguing that relationships are stable cannot be supported by the Liden et al. correlational results. Demonstrating change or a lack of change in LMX over time requires different methodologies and analytics.

One such study examining LMX change appropriately using a longitudinal design and growth curve modeling (Nahrgang, Morgeson, & Ilies, 2009) showed that the trajectory of LMX relationships was positive and linear in terms of rated quality from initial contact through four weeks followed by a flattening of the trajectory through week eight. In other words, the trajectory of LMX development was distinctly curvilinear, showing positive changes until approximately halfway through data collection, followed by diminishing returns for the remainder of the study. The participants in the study consisted of groups of undergraduate students that were led by an MBA student as part of a university class experience. This raises potential generalizability concerns due to some artificiality associated with the classroom academic setting. Future research needs to examine the LMX development in leader-member dyads of supervisors and direct reports in other organizational settings and over longer time periods using different timescales.

A question of key interest is to what extent LMX relationships stabilize over time or whether there is ongoing volatility in terms of change. Part of this issue concerns the appropriate timescale of LMX relationship changes that might be best examined using more intensive longitudinal data methodologies (Tan et al., 2012). At issue is the important question of what the quality of one's relationship with a leader is right now. Is it the same every hour of the day or every day of the week? As noted, leaders are likely to manifest very different behaviors on a daily basis, and it is unclear how sensitive followers are to this behavioral variability. It may be that measuring LMX every couple of weeks is insufficient to detect more frequent changes in experienced relationship quality.

Other relevant research questions include how long it would take for employees to find ways to recover from the adverse effects of experiencing a low-quality exchange relationship with a leader. Such recovery seems necessary for employees to perform effectively in their jobs. Time may play an important role in the ability to create a functioning relational system despite low LMX or other types of dysfunctional leadership. It is possible that such recovery processes occur relatively quickly or in an ongoing manner. If the relationship one has with one's boss "is a lens through which the entire work experience is viewed" (Gerstner & Day, 1997, p. 840), then there is a need for further research on the potential dynamics of change in LMX across daily or weekly interactions with a leader, as well as the intriguing notions of recovery times from dysfunctional leadership processes. The importance of the timing and spacing of observations in longitudinal designs will be addressed in a final section of this chapter.

As segue into a discussion of the role of time in leader development, the Japanese career progress studies of Graen et al. should be mentioned (Graen, Dharwadkar, Grewal, & Wakabayashi, 2006; Wakabayashi & Graen, 1984; Wakabayashi, Graen, Graen, & Graen, 1988). In essence, this series of longitudinal research – some of which has been as long as 23 years (Graen et al., 2006) – demonstrated that the ability to develop high-quality relationships with a supervisor (leader) predicts subsequent exchange quality relationships with different supervisors. Furthermore, those employees (followers) who are effective in developing positive relationships progress faster throughout their careers relative to those who have difficulty negotiating positive leadership exchanges. This research is an interesting juxtaposition to Nahrgang et al. (2009), who examined LMX in academic classroom settings.

Over the course of a professional career most people will work with many different bosses (leaders). Thus, from a career perspective the relative impact of a single exchange quality relationship may be less important than the ability to consistently forge high-quality exchanges with different superiors. But from a single LMX perspective, the appropriate timescale in which to study development and change may need to be more intensive than has been previously adopted in order to understand and predict the underlying dynamics of any relationship, including that between a leader and follower(s). This highlights a potential need to think more carefully about the likely timescales involved and to design longitudinal LMX research accordingly, depending on whether something like a career or a relationship with a single leader is the intended focus of study.

Leader development

Of all the topics discussed thus far in this chapter, perhaps the one with the strongest implications regarding time is that of leader development. Before elaborating on the various temporal implications, it would be helpful to first define what is meant by leader development (for more detailed reviews of the relevant literature, see Day, 2011a, 2012b, 2013b). One prominent definition of leader development is "the expansion of a person's capacity to be effective in leadership roles and processes" (McCauley, Van Velsor, & Ruderman, 2010, p. 2). Note that from this definition the expansion of personal capacities could take on relatively short-term timescales (days or weeks) in training a particular skill, such as charismatic communication (Antonakis, Fenley, & Liechti, 2011), to more long-term perspectives (years or decades), such as becoming an expert leader through ongoing practice and internalizing a leader identity (Day, Harrison, & Halpin, 2009).

This provides one of the biggest challenges with regard to time and leader development: matching the target of development with an informed estimate of how long it would likely take to develop to an accepted standard. This is deceptively complex (and difficult) partly because of different traditions in the field. One tradition comes from Gestalt psychology and constructive-developmental theory (McCauley, Drath, Palus, O'Connor, & Baker, 2006), in which the focus is on the development of the whole leader. This might take an entire lifetime to master and reach the highest levels of developmental functioning as a leader.

The second tradition stems from the domains of skill acquisition, competency development, and expert performance (Day et al., 2009; Lord & Hall, 2005). In this tradition, there are various leadership-related skills and broader competencies to be learned and mastered, which are thought to help anyone perform more effectively as a leader. Where these two traditions tend to converge is in their respective estimates of the amount of time needed to develop as a leader – long or very long. The Gestalt tradition believes that development occurs across the entire life span and that it is never fully complete (Kegan, 1994). Research from the expertise and expert performance domains provides a somewhat more optimistic estimate: it takes a minimum of 10 years or 10,000 hours of dedicated practice to become an expert in a given domain (Ericsson, Krampe, & Tesch-Römer, 1993), which has been argued includes leadership (Day et al., 2009). Regardless of whether the perspective is developing the whole person (i.e., leader) or expert leadership skills and competencies, the projected timescale is at least a decade and probably longer.

Given these daunting estimates of the time needed to develop as a leader, it makes the prospect of conducting research on the process seem formidable. Nonetheless, it is clear that attempting to study the developmental processes of leaders requires a careful consideration of time. Development implies change and change requires time; thus, cross-sectional studies of leader development make little theoretical sense and add little value to our scientific understanding of the process or the factors that facilitate or impede it. Given the imperative for longitudinal research on leader development, which means explicit attention to the role of time methodologically and analytically, a few cautions and recommendations follow.

Scholars of longitudinal research (Collins, 2006; Singer & Willett, 2003) have proposed three requisite methodological features of any study of change: (a) multiple waves of data (at least three), (b) a "substantively meaningful" metric for time (Singer & Willett, p. 4), and (c) an outcome that changes systematically. Of particular interest in this discussion is having a sensible metric for tracking time. Some viable nonleadership examples might include psychological maturity scores at particular ages, achievement levels at different educational grades, or measures of well-being associated with various numbers of counseling therapy sessions. But what is disconcerting about these so-called sensible metrics is that "there is no single answer to the seemingly simple question about the most sensible metric for time" (Singer & Willett, 2003, p. 11). It comes down to mainly a subjective – but hopefully theoretically driven – decision about what is expected to be the most useful timescale for the outcome being studied. Unfortunately, it is typically the case that practical reasons for the choices made in the temporal design of longitudinal research are heeded rather than scientific, theoretical, or conceptual explanations. Perhaps more troubling is that "reasons for the choice of temporal design are rarely mentioned, and equally rare is any discussion of how this choice might have affected the statistical and substantive conclusions drawn from the study" (Collins & Graham, 2002, p. S85).

A primary concern in designing longitudinal research on any topic is to allow for the greatest likelihood of detecting and accurately modeling the hypothesized change form and its predictors. One issue is that any longitudinal study of leader development must extend sufficiently in time to allow for relevant changes to occur. Another issue is to design the timing of measurement in ways that avoid missing the underlying trend in the data or misrepresenting the true form of the change. For example, in Figure 3.2a (adapted from Ployhart & Vandenberg, 2010) the modeling of the data collected from measurement periods 1, 3, and 5 yield a slope indicating no change in the outcome of leadership effectiveness over time; however, the "true" form of change is not zero but actually curvilinear. There are demonstrated positive changes early on in the intervention (time periods 1 and 2)

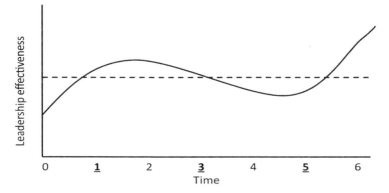

a. Wrong measurement occasions (**bolded**) miss the trend

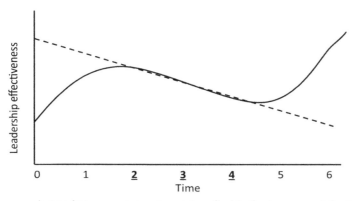

b. Too few measurement occasions (**bolded**) misrepresent the trend

Figure 3.2 Consequences of mismeasurement in longitudinal leader development research. Adapted from "Longitudinal research: The theory, design, and analysis of change," by R. E. Ployhart and R. J. Vandenberg, 2010, *Journal of Management, 36,* p. 106. Copyright 2010 by SAGE Publications. Reprinted with permission.

as well as positive and linear changes in times 5 and 6, but a slightly negative trend in times 3 and 4. Overall, leadership effectiveness improved over the course of measurement but not in a linear manner.

The choice of measurement periods in this example resulted in a Type II error – concluding no change occurred in leadership effectiveness when overall positive changes did occur when a longer timescale was considered. A different problem emerges if too few measurement occasions – or measurement occasions spaced too closely together – are used (see Figure 3.2b). Given the same underlying form of true change as in Figure 3.2a, this misrepresentation yields a linear, negative trend over time. Again, this misses the curvilinear nature of the change that shows overall positive growth and change when all time periods are included in the modeling. In this case, a form of a Type I error occurs in assuming change in leadership effectiveness is negative when it is really positive.

Relatedly, in longitudinal research the estimated size of an effect often depends on the timescale. Gollub and Reichardt (1987) provide an example of taking aspirin to reduce headache pain: the effect may be zero after two minutes, may be substantial after 30 minutes, near maximum effect after two or three hours, much reduced after five hours, and near zero again after 24 hours (p. 82). For this reason, understanding an effect size depends on knowing the time lag involved. And because different time lags have different effects, different timescales need to be studied to understand causal effects fully. This is an interesting example to consider within the realm of leader development, where it is commonly assumed that the effects of an intervention will continue to persist over time.

A study from the leader development literature demonstrates the potential risks of choosing an improper temporal design. Researchers examined the developmental trajectories of participants engaged in team-based action learning projects to promote leader development (Day & Sin, 2011). The leadership effectiveness of participants was rated on four occasions by an independent team advisor who was unique to each team. Growth modeling results indicated that the overall trajectory of leader development was negative with a slight upturn in the last wave of data collection (overall curvilinear trend). There are at least two relevant points to consider with this example. First, it is erroneous to think that the only possible trajectory of leader development is positive. The participants in this sample were all young, emerging leaders (first-year university students) who had little or no experience working in multicultural teams of peers without a formally appointed leader. This presented a significant developmental challenge, which appeared to stretch the leadership capabilities of participants – at least initially. Sometimes throughout the course of development overall effectiveness drops before it improves. Second, if the last wave of data collection had not occurred, then the overall conclusion would have been that the rated effectiveness of participants worsened over the course of the intervention. That is not a message that program sponsors would appreciate, especially in a different (e.g., corporate) context. But what is unknown is whether leadership effectiveness would continue in an upward trend beyond the 13 weeks of program data collection. Additional waves of data collection would be helpful; however, the intervention (course) had ended. This is a major shortcoming in leader development research: we do not know what happens after completion of a developmental intervention.

These examples and illustrations highlight that a critical decision in the design of longitudinal research is to have enough measurement periods to model the change appropriately and have the measurements close enough in time to detect changes when they occur. But there are always practical trade-offs between maximizing the number of measurement periods and the risks associated with potentially increasing participant attrition (due to research fatigue) and managing the increased expense. Two related points from this discussion are: (a) the timescale of longitudinal research can have important effects on results, and

(b) temporal design should be chosen in consideration of the characteristics of the phenomena being studied as well as important intervention features, if applicable (Collins & Graham, 2002).

Given the present focus on time and leader development, a pressing question to consider from a temporal design perspective is what is reasonable to expect with regard to change. What (if anything) would be expected to change for a participant involved in a seven-day leadership development program? What about a seven-month program? Clearly, the target of the developmental intervention is a critical concern. Another potential consideration is whether there are natural milestones such as key deliverables at various stages in the intervention that might constitute natural measurement periods. It is tempting to simply divide the total time of the study into equal intervals; however, without some better understanding of the nature of the developmental intervention – if there is an intervention – dividing measurement periods into equal intervals risks missing the true nature of change. Unfortunately, there are no quick and easy answers to these challenging questions. Researchers will need to match a deep understanding of what is transpiring within the intervention or over the course of data collection with insights into what is expected to change and the likely form of that change over time.

The discussion in this section on time and leader development has emphasized mainly concerns related to timescales and temporal design choices (Collins & Graham, 2002). Although this may seem overly method-focused, the point was made that leader development research is inherently longitudinal in nature given the focus on attempting to model and understand individual change (Day, 2011b). What researchers are struggling with in the field of leader development is not whether to model time in their research (that is a given) but how to do it most effectively. And as noted by eminent methodological scholars of longitudinal research (e.g., Collins, 2006; Collins & Graham, 2002; Ployhart & Vandenberg, 2010; Singer & Willet, 2003), there are no simple answers to these complex issues.

A note on intensive longitudinal data (ILD)

Something that can be said with some certainty in terms of temporal design concerns in longitudinal research is that everything else being equal, it is likely that any longitudinal study would benefit from including more observations that are more closely spaced. Of course, it is rare that everything is equal and the data collection efforts involved in longitudinal research are a major expense. Nonetheless, there are some distinct advantages in using temporal designs with condensed timescales. As noted by Collins and Graham (2002), short measurement intervals provide greater flexibility when the focus is on modeling dynamic processes. Specifically, it allows the researcher to model variability in change effects across various interval lengths. More compressed timescales can help detect when effects begin to emerge, when they reach a peak, and when the effect starts to dissipate (Gollub & Reichardt, 1987). Another advantage of more compressed timescales is that they can help detect when effects of different outcome variables peak at different times. This is especially relevant when leader development outcomes are studied, given the myriad possible effects of, for example, challenging experiences on personal development.

Advances in the field of longitudinal modeling illustrate how the thinking of researchers has evolved in terms of how change is conceptualized. For example, change had been thought of historically as the difference between two measurement points for some phenomenon of interest (Cronbach & Furby, 1970). Unfortunately, this ignores the possibility of different change forms. If there is a change between any two points in time, then the only possible course of change is linear. Gathering more intensive longitudinal data with compressed timescales may provide information that helps researchers better understand the underlying mechanisms of change, provide better prediction of behavior change, and uncover information leading to new theories of development (Tan et al., 2012).

Intensive longitudinal data (ILD) is generally considered to involve temporal designs with substantially larger number of observations for each participant compared to traditional longitudinal designs. Although there is no fixed number of observations needed for ILD, Tan et al. (2012) suggest that 10 or more observations is a reasonable number that should be able to be effectively modeled with their procedures if there are at least 100 research participants. Such dense timescales are driven by different types of research questions that focus on fine-grained temporal changes in human behavior or psychosocial processes with particular attention paid to issues of covariation and causation (p. 64). ILD are expected to contain detailed information about change that requires new, more flexible statistical approaches to effectively model such densely measured changes. Although it is beyond the scope of this chapter, Tan et al. present an extension of traditional multilevel modeling procedures, called a time-varying effect model, to analyze time-varying ILD relationships between covariates and outcomes. Because the recommended analytic approach is nonparametric and therefore does not impose strict assumptions regarding the nature (i.e., form) of change, it offers more flexibility in modeling change.

There is another distinct advantage with this recommended ILD approach. Rather than having to rely on prior knowledge about the shape of change, or on theory that is often unreliable or ill-defined when it comes to this issue, Tan et al. (2012) offer an inductive alternative. That is, one learns the shape of change directly from data. According to the authors, it potentially helps to speed up the iterative learning process inherent in understanding the nature of change in any context. What are needed to achieve this end are dense observations yielding data containing fine-grained information about the change and appropriate statistical models and estimation techniques. ILD fulfill the first requirement, and time-varying effect models fulfill the second. Although it is still early with regard to this approach, especially in terms of statistical power issues regarding requirements for sample size and number of repeated assessments, it offers a promising alternative to modeling and understanding the nature of change. Leadership researchers and especially those interested in leader development processes are urged to consider ILD-based temporal designs.

Conclusions

The point was made at the opening of this chapter that leadership takes time. Not only do the effects of leadership take time to be fully known, but also, if leadership is essentially about change and change requires time, time is fully implicated as a component of leadership research. Others have made similar points about the need to more carefully consider the effects of time on leadership (Bluedorn & Jaussi, 2008; Shamir, 2011). What this chapter offers above and beyond previous commentaries is a more focused treatment of four specific areas of leadership theory and research in which time is implicated. Those areas are leader behavior and the time needed to change the attitudes and behavior of followers, as well as issues of time that potentially undermine the accuracy of leadership ratings; leadership perceptions and who emerges as a leader (i.e., changes in eyes of others from nonleader to leader); leadership relationships and how long they take to develop and mature (i.e., change from one state to another); and leader development or the personal changes associated with becoming more effective as a leader. Knowledgeable readers will likely identify other leadership topics for consideration.

A relevant question to ask at this point is what is needed to help the leadership field to continue to evolve and be accepted among scientists and practitioners, rather than becoming obsolete and irrelevant as leadership was believed to be at one time. It is tempting to recommend a moratorium on all cross-sectional leadership research, as was proposed for the entire leadership discipline in the mid-1970s (Miner, 1975). But for better or worse, moratoriums are generally neither helpful nor effective in shaping research agendas in constructive ways (e.g., look what happened with leadership). In addition, these kinds of extreme measures tend to alienate the more junior members in a field and rightfully so. So, as tempting as it is to recommend a halt on cross-sectional leadership research, I think there are more measured actions that can be taken. At the top of that list is for researchers to take a more dynamic perspective on all aspects of leadership and not just leadership development. Another suggestion is to consider inductive research designs that incorporate intensive timescales and not just value theoretically driven, deductive research.

It has been argued that the scholarly management field has a "theory fetish" that impedes the publication of interesting results for which there is no extant theory (Hambrick, 2007, p. 1346). This is evident in the editorial guidelines in most of the major journals in management, organizational behavior, and applied psychology that say to one degree or another that a major gateway to publication is in clearly demonstrating a unique theoretical contribution (among other things). Hambrick argues that the contribution to theory requirement in our preeminent journals be replaced with this test: "Does the paper have a high likelihood of stimulating future research that will substantially alter managerial theory and/or practice?" (p. 1350). Widespread acceptance of this proposed criterion could open the way for intensive longitudinal data or ILD-type leadership research that does not have *a priori* theory as to the underlying change form, but uses data inductively to inform future studies of similar topics.

It is reasonable to question why this is needed. It has been over a decade since Mitchell and James (2001) published their piece in *Academy of Management Review* advocating building better theory that addresses "time and the specification of when things will happen" (p. 530). Given commentaries since this publication arguing essentially for this same thing, as well as the need for the present two-volume set of chapters on time and work, it is apparent that a different tack needs to be taken if there will ever be any empirical progress in understanding the effects of time in leadership or other related disciplines.

Encouraging ILD approaches is perhaps most relevant for longitudinal studies of leader development in which individual change over time is explicitly the focus of research. But in each of the other leadership areas addressed in this chapter (i.e., leader behavior, emergence and leadership perceptions, and leader-follower relationships) there is an inherent change component that would benefit from ILD approaches. If we could adopt intensive, inductive approaches *in addition to* theoretically driven, deductive tests it would potentially offer greater possibilities for better understanding the effects of time on leadership while helping to build better theory.

A more modest proposal would be to also encourage authors to be very clear in stating the time parameters under which their leadership research was conducted, as well as including a brief discussion of what are seen as the primary benefits and limitations of the timescales that were used. The former will help with future meta-analytic studies of various leadership phenomena that may yield insights into the role of time at a between-study level. The latter will help keep the issue salient in the minds of researchers and possibly generate additional ideas for future research. But, again, these are modest proposals for a scholarly area in which big changes are perhaps needed.

In closing, I want to emphasize and endorse statements made by others who have been involved in championing greater attention to time in our research. Kelly and McGrath (1988) argued there is a "vicious cycle of neglect" regarding the role of time in substantive, conceptual, methodological domains (p. 56). From this, Mitchell and James (2001) exhorted that "we can and should do better" (p. 545). I say amen to both sentiments and add that isn't it *time* we finally did something about it?

References

Antonakis, J., Fenley, M., & Liechti, S. (2011). Can charisma be taught? Tests of two interventions. *Academy of Management Learning & Education, 10,* 374–396.

Avital, M. (2000). Dealing with time in social inquiry: A tension between method and lived experience. *Organization Science, 11,* 665–673.

Bass, B. M. (2008). *The Bass handbook of leadership: Theory, research, and managerial applications* (4th ed.). New York: Free Press.

Bass, B. M., & Avolio, B. J. (2000). *MLQ: Multifactor leadership questionnaire* (2nd ed.). Redwood City, CA: Mind Garden.

Bluedorn, A. C., & Jaussi, K. S. (2008). Leaders, followers, and time. *Leadership Quarterly, 19,* 654–668.

Calder, B. J. (1977). An attribution theory of leadership. In B. M. Staw & G. R. Salancik (Eds.), *New directions in organizational behavior* (pp. 179–204). Chicago: St. Clair Press.

Collins, L. M. (2006). Analysis of longitudinal data. *Annual Review of Psychology, 57,* 505–528.

Collins, L. M., & Graham, J. W. (2002). The effect of the timing and spacing of observations in longitudinal studies of tobacco and other drug use: Temporal design considerations [Supplement]. *Drug and Alcohol Dependence, 68,* S85–S96.

Cronbach, L. J., & Furby, L. (1970). How should we measure "change" – Or should we? *Psychological Bulletin, 74,* 68–80.

Dansereau, F., Jr., Graen, G., & Haga, W. J. (1975). A vertical dyad linkage approach to leadership within formal organizations: A longitudinal investigation of the role making process. *Organizational Behavior and Human Performance, 13,* 46–78.

Day, D. V. (2011a). Leadership development. In A. Bryman, D. Collinson, K. Grint, B. Jackson, & M. Uhl-Bien (Eds.), *The SAGE handbook of leadership* (pp. 37–50). Los Angeles: SAGE.

Day, D. V. (2011b). Integrative perspectives on longitudinal investigations of leader development: From childhood through adulthood. *Leadership Quarterly, 22,* 561–571.

Day, D. V. (2012a). Leadership. In S. W. J. Kozlowski (Ed.), *The Oxford handbook of organizational psychology* (Vol. 1, pp. 696–729). New York: Oxford University Press.

Day, D. V. (2012b). The nature of leadership development. In D. V. Day & J. Antonakis (Eds.), *The nature of leadership* (2nd ed., pp. 108–140). Los Angeles: SAGE.

Day, D. V. (2013a, April). *Network churn and leadership development.* Paper presented at the 28th Annual Conference of the Society for Industrial and Organizational Psychology, Houston, Texas.

Day, D. V. (2013b). Training and developing leaders: Theory and research. In M. G. Rumsey (Ed.), *The Oxford handbook of leadership* (pp. 76–93). New York: Oxford University Press.

Day, D. V., Harrison, M. M., & Halpin, S. M. (2009). *An integrative approach to leader development: Connecting adult development, identity, and expertise.* New York: Routledge.

Day, D. V., & Lord, R. G. (1988). Executive leadership and organizational performance: Suggestions for a new theory and methodology. *Journal of Management, 14,* 453–464.

Day, D. V., & Sin, H.-P. (2011). Longitudinal tests of an integrative model of leader development: Charting and understanding developmental trajectories. *Leadership Quarterly, 22,* 545–560.

DeRue, D. S., Nahrgang, J. D., Wellman, N., & Humphrey, S. E. (2011). Trait and behavioral theories of leadership: An integration and meta-analytic test of their relative validity. *Personnel Psychology, 64,* 7–52.

Downey, H. K., Chacko, T., & McElroy, J. C. (1979). Attribution of the "causes" of performance: A constructive, quasi-longitudinal replication of the Staw study (1975). *Organizational Behavior and Human Performance, 24,* 287–299.

Drath, W. H., McCauley, C. D., Palus, C. J., Van Velsor, E., O'Connor, P.M.G., & McGuire, J. B. (2008). Direction, alignment, commitment: Toward a more integrative ontology of leadership. *Leadership Quarterly, 19,* 635–653.

Dulebohn, J. H., Bommer, W. H., Liden, R. C., Brouer, R. L., & Ferris, G. R. (2012). A meta-analysis of antecedents and consequences of leader-member exchange: Integrating the past with an eye toward the future. *Journal of Management, 38,* 1715–1759.

Epitropaki, O., & Martin, R. (2004). Implicit leadership theories in applied settings: Factor structure, generalizability, and stability over time. *Journal of Applied Psychology, 89,* 293–310.

Epitropaki, O., & Martin, R. (2005). From ideal to real: A longitudinal study of the role of implicit leadership theories on leader-member exchanges and employee outcomes. *Journal of Applied Psychology, 90,* 659–676.

Ericsson, K. A., Krampe, R. T., & Tesch-Römer, C. (1993). The role of deliberate practice in the acquisition of expert performance. *Psychological Review, 100,* 363–406.

Fleeson, W. (2001). Toward a structure- and process-integrated view of personality: Traits as density distributions of states. *Journal of Personality and Social Psychology, 80,* 1011–1027.

Foti, R. J., Knee, R. E., Jr., & Backert, R. S. G. (2008). Multi-level implications of framing leadership perceptions as a dynamic process. *Leadership Quarterly, 19,* 178–194.

Gerstner, C. R., & Day, D. V. (1997). Meta-analytic review of leader-member exchange theory: Correlates and construct issues. *Journal of Applied Psychology, 82,* 827–844.

Gilbert, D. T. (1998). Ordinary personology. In D. T. Gilbert, S. T. Fiske, & G. Lindzey (Eds.), *The handbook of social psychology* (4th ed., Vol. 2, pp. 89–150). Boston, MA: McGraw-Hill.

Gollub, H. F., & Reichardt, C. S. (1987). Taking account of time lags in causal models. *Child Development, 58,* 80–92.

Graen, G., Dharwadkar, R., Grewal, R., & Wakabayashi, M. (2006). Japanese career progress: An empirical examination. *Journal of International Business Studies, 37,* 148–161.

Graen, G. B., & Cashman, J. F. (1975). A role making model of leadership in formal organizations. In J. G. Hunt & L. L. Larson (Eds.), *Leadership frontiers* (pp. 143–165). Kent, OH: Kent State University Press.

Graen, G. B., & Scandura, T. A. (1987). Toward a psychology of dyadic organizing. *Research in Organizational Behavior, 9,* 175–208.

Graen, G. B., & Uhl-Bien, M. (1995). Relationship-based approach to leadership: Development of leader-member exchange (LMX) theory of leadership over 25 years: Applying a multi-level multi-domain perspective. *Leadership Quarterly, 6,* 219–247.

Grayling, A. C. (2011). *The good book: A secular bible.* London: Bloomsbury.

Hambrick, D.C. (2007). The field of management's devotion to theory: Too much of a good thing? *Academy of Management Journal, 50,* 1346–1352.

Ilies, R., Nahrgang, J. D., & Morgeson, F. P. (2007). Leader-member exchange and citizenship behaviors: A meta-analysis. *Journal of Applied Psychology, 92,* 269–277.

Judge, T. A., Piccolo, R. F., & Ilies, R. (2004). The forgotten ones? The validity of consideration and initiating structure in leadership research. *Journal of Applied Psychology, 89,* 36–51.

Katz, D., & Kahn, R. L. (1978). *The social psychology of organizations* (2nd ed.). New York: Wiley.

Kegan, R. (1994). *In over our heads: The mental demands of modern life.* Cambridge, MA: Harvard University Press.

Kelly, J. R., & McGrath, J. E. (1988). *On time and method.* Newbury Park, CA: SAGE.

Kenney, R. A., Schwartz-Kenney, B. M., & Blascovich, J. (1996). Implicit leadership theories: Defining leaders described as worthy of influence. *Personality and Social Psychology Bulletin, 22,* 1128–1143.

Liden, R. C., Wayne, S. J., & Stilwell, D. (1993). A longitudinal study on the early development of leader-member exchange. *Journal of Applied Psychology, 78,* 662–674.

Liden, R. C., Wayne, S. J., Zhao, H., & Henderson, D. (2008). Servant leadership: Development of a multidimensional measure and multi-level assessment. *Leadership Quarterly, 19,* 161–177.

Lieberson, S., & O'Connor, J. F. (1972). Leadership and organizational performance: A study of large corporations. *American Sociological Review, 37,* 117–130.

Lord, R. G., Binning, J. F., Rush, M. C., & Thomas, J. C. (1978). The effect of performance cues and leader behavior on questionnaire ratings of leadership behavior. *Organizational Behavior and Human Performance, 21,* 27–39.

Lord, R. G., & Hall, R. J. (2005). Identity, deep structure, and the development of leadership skill. *Leadership Quarterly, 16,* 591–615.

Lord, R. G., & Maher, K. J. (1991). *Leadership and information processing: Linking perceptions and performance.* Boston, MA: Unwin Hyman.

McCauley, C. D., Drath, W. H., Palus, C. J., O'Connor, P. M. G., & Baker, B. A. (2006). The use of constructive-developmental theory to advance the understanding of leadership. *Leadership Quarterly, 17,* 634–653.

McCauley, C. D., Van Velsor, E., & Ruderman, M. N. (2010). Introduction: Our view of leadership development. In E. Van Velsor, C. D. McCauley, & M. N. Ruderman (Eds.), *The Center for Creative Leadership handbook of leadership development* (3rd ed., pp. 1–26). San Francisco, CA: Jossey-Bass.

Miner, J. B. (1975). The uncertain future of the leadership concept: An overview. In J. G. Hunt & L. L. Larson (Eds.), *Leadership frontiers* (pp. 197–208). Kent, OH: Kent State University Press.

Mitchell, T. R., & James, L. R. (2001). Building better theory: Time and the specification of when things happen. *Academy of Management Review, 26,* 530–547.

Mitchell, T. R., Larson, J. R., Jr., & Green, S. G. (1977). Leader behavior, situational moderators, and group performance: An attributional analysis. *Organizational Behavior and Human Performance, 18,* 254–268.

Nahrgang, J. D., Morgeson, F. P., & Ilies, R. (2009). The development of leader-member exchanges: Exploring how personality and performance influence leader and member relationships over time. *Organizational Behavior and Human Decision Processes, 108,* 256–266.

Offermann, L. R., Kennedy, J. K., Jr., & Wirtz, P. W. (1994). Implicit leadership theories: Content, structure and generalizability. *Leadership Quarterly, 5,* 43–58.

Pfeffer, J. (1977). The ambiguity of leadership. *Academy of Management Review, 2,* 104–112.

Ployhart, R. E., & Vandenberg, R. J. (2010). Longitudinal research: The theory, design, and analysis of change. *Journal of Management, 36,* 94–120.

Salancik, G. R., & Pfeffer, J. (1977). Constraints on administrator discretion: The limited influence of mayors on city budgets. *Urban Affairs Quarterly, 12,* 475–498.

Sasovova, Z., Mehra, A., Borgatti, S. P., & Schippers, M. C. (2010). Network churn: The effects of self-monitoring personality on brokerage dynamics. *Administrative Science Quarterly, 55,* 639–670.

Shamir, B. (2011). Leadership takes time: Some implications of (not) taking time seriously in leadership research. *Leadership Quarterly, 22,* 307–315.

Shipp, A. J., Edwards, J. R., & Lambert, L. S. (2009). Conceptualization and measurement of temporal focus. The subjective experience of the past, present, and future. *Organizational Behavior and Human Decision Processes, 110,* 1–22.

Singer, J. D., & Willett, J. B. (2003). *Applied longitudinal data analysis: Modeling change and event occurrence.* New York: Oxford University Press.

Staw, B. M. (1975). Attribution of the "causes" of performance: A general alternative interpretation of non-sectional research on organizations. *Organizational Behavior and Human Performance, 13,* 414–432.

Stogdill, R. M. (1950). Leadership, membership and organization. *Psychological Bulletin, 47,* 1–14.

Sulsky, L. M., & Day, D. V. (1992). Frame-of-reference training and cognitive categorization: An empirical investigation of rater memory issues. *Journal of Applied Psychology, 77,* 501–510.

Tan, X., Shiyko, M. P., Li, R., Li, Y., & Dierker, L. (2012). A time-varying effect model for intensive longitudinal data. *Psychological Methods, 17,* 61–77.

Tead, O. (1935). *The art of leadership.* New York: McGraw-Hill.

Wakabayashi, M., & Graen, G. B. (1984). The Japanese career progress study: A 7-year follow-up. *Journal of Applied Psychology, 69,* 603–614.

Wakabayashi, M., Graen, G. B., Graen, M. R., & Graen, M. G. (1988). Japanese management progress: Mobility into middle management. *Journal of Applied Psychology, 73,* 217–227.

Walls, T. A., & Schafer, J. L. (Eds.). (2006). *Models for intensive longitudinal data.* New York: Oxford University Press.

Walumba, F. O., Avolio, B. J., Gardner, W. L., Wernsing, T. S., & Peterson, S. J. (2008). Authentic leadership: Development and validation of a theory-based measure. *Journal of Management, 34,* 89–126.

Zaheer, S., Albert, S., & Zaheer, A. (1999). Time scales and organizational theory. *Academy of Management Review, 24,* 735–741.

4 Cross-cultural perspectives on time

C. Ashley Fulmer, Brandon Crosby and Michele J. Gelfand

Introduction

The experience of time is universal. It is in the daily lives of people in developed and developing countries (Levine & Norenzayan, 1999) as well as in tribes deep in the Amazon and Papua New Guinea (Núñez, Cooperrider, Doan, & Wassman, 2012; Sinha, Sinha, Zinken, & Sampaio, 2011). Either explicitly or implicitly, conceptualizations and experiences of time exert impacts on individuals and groups in a wide range of domains, including cognition (Guo, Ji, Spina, & Zhang, 2012), motivation (Avnet & Sellier, 2011), communication and negotiation (Alon & Brett, 2007), work performance (Agranovich, Panter, Puente, & Touradji, 2011), team processes (Arman & Adair, 2012), and even health outcomes (Levine & Norenzayan, 1999) and economic progress (Hofstede & Minkov, 2010).

Just as time is an integral aspect of human experience, culture plays a crucial role in influencing the cognition, motivation, emotion, and behavior of individuals (Hofstede, 1980; Leung & Bond, 2004; Markus & Kitayama, 1991; Schwartz, 1994). As research increasingly demonstrates that many fundamental psychological processes exhibit cultural specificity (Markus & Kitayama, 1991), the conceptualizations and experiences of time should be no exception. In fact, as will be seen in this chapter, conceptualizations and experiences of time are highly culturally variable. However, cultural research has thus far devoted little attention to temporal diversity and its impact across cultures. Despite the immense progress that culture research has made (Aycan & Gelfand, 2012; Gelfand, Erez, & Aycan, 2007), its scope on temporal issues remains limited and fragmented, without a systematic integration of theoretical and empirical knowledge. The purpose of this chapter, therefore, is to provide an organized overview of the current state of the scholarly literature on the intersection of time and culture and a discussion of the future research on this topic.

In what follows, we first introduce key culture dimensions in temporal dimensions. Next we turn to the antecedents of cultural differences in these temporal dimensions, followed by a discussion of their consequences, which range from individual psychological and behavioral outcomes at the micro level to national economic progress at the macro level. We end with highlights of the measurement challenges in examining temporal differences cross-culturally and of future research directions in the intersection of culture and time.

Temporal differences as underlying culture dimensions

The wealth of studies on time and culture has identified a number of important temporal dimensions that vary across cultures, including 1) polychronicity and monochronicity, 2) past, present, and future orientation, 3) event time and clock time, 4) pace of life, and 5) time as cultural metaphor. We introduce each of them in turn before turning to the antecedents of these cross-cultural differences.

One of the most influential pieces of literature on the topic of culture and time is Edward T. Hall's 1959 book, *The Silent Language*. In his writings, Hall discussed the importance of the usage of people's time, and how this usage impacts their tendencies and behaviors (Brislin & Kim, 2003). Hall proposed that the rules surrounding social time and temporal understandings were deeply ingrained in each culture (Hall & Hall, 1990; Singelis, 1998). Learning these rules was considered analogous to learning a different culture's language, and is key to understanding and communicating with members of other cultures (Jandt, 2003; Rogers, Hart, & Miike, 2002). Though he was not the first to notice the different ways cultures view time, Hall is credited as being one of the first to provide multiple constructs that dictate how different groups of people value and spend their time (Brislin & Kim, 2003). In addition to developing his own constructs, Hall's early work inspired anthropologists, sociologists, and psychologists to examine other potential constructs that could explain the divergent ways in which cultures view time.

Polychronicity and monochronicity

Perhaps the most significant aspect of Hall's famous work on time was the introduction of the two concepts monochronic time (M-time) and polychronic time (P-time). Nonis, Teng, and Ford (2005) defined the two concepts when they wrote, "In general, M-time cultures view time as linear and separable, capable of being divided into units and therefore emphasize doing 'one thing at a time.' In contrast, P-time cultures view time as naturally re-occurring, and therefore emphasize doing 'many things at one time'" (p. 412). As stated, M-time cultures wait until one event is over before beginning the next one. This perception of time is similar to an assembly line where one task is completed before systematically moving to the next one. M-time cultures are typically found in developed nations where time is conceptualized as money. In these cultures, time not spent working on a specific task or working toward a specific goal is time wasted and is considered undesirable. Countries where M-time is prevalent include the United States, Germany, and Scandinavia (Kaufman, Lane, & Lindquist, 1991). On the other hand, P-time cultures focus more on a more naturally occurring flow of time, where time cannot be wasted because multiple goals can be completed at the same time (Manrai & Manrai, 1995). In general, polychronic individuals consider time to be more fluid and malleable, and as a result, are able to adapt or "go with the flow" (Nonis et al., 2005). In addition, P-time cultures typically focus more on human interactions such that time spent with others is considered a task because it helps build bonds that may be useful in the future (Kaufman et al., 1991). Given this aspect of P-time, it should not be too much of a surprise to find that collectivistic cultures are more likely to be polychronic (Billing et al., 2010; Leonard, 2008). It is also important to note that a polychronic person is not one who is simply good at multitasking, but also prefers to work on multiple tasks at once and interact with other people (Bluedorn & Denhardt, 1988; Persing, 1999). Countries that tend to be polychronic include Japan, Middle Eastern countries, and South Asian countries (Kaufman et al., 1991). Though the two concepts of time have their strengths and weaknesses, proponents of the different perspectives are sometimes at odds with each other. For example, polychronic individuals may view monochronic concepts as inefficient and narrow-minded (Kaufman-Scarborough, 2003).

Past, present, and future orientation

Not long after Hall's *The Silent Language* was published, Kluckhohn and Strodt-beck's (1961) seminal work, *Variations in Value Orientations*, was introduced. These researchers aimed to identify the key values of different societies that impact the behaviors of their people. Among the proposed concepts was how cultures value the past, present, and the future (Maznevski, Gomez, DiStefano, Noorder-haven, & Wu, 2002). Cultures with a past orientation tend to place more focus and value on tradition, elder members of society, and positive aspects of their history, communities, or organizations (Ji, Guo, Zhang, & Messervey, 2009; Spadone, 1992). Individuals from present-oriented cultures are more likely to live "in the moment," focus on the short-term consequences of their behaviors, value events that occurred relatively recently, and use recent events to predict future events (Brislin & Kim, 2003; Spadone, 1992). Lastly, individuals from future-oriented societies focus on the long-term consequences of their actions, and tend to focus more on tasks such as saving for the future and delaying gratification (Kluck-hohn & Strodtbeck, 1961). These temporal orientations developed by Kluckhohn and Strodtbeck have been used in several research programs, including the GLOBE project and Hofstede's work on the dimensions of cultural values (House, Javidan, Hanges, & Dorfman, 2002; Hofstede & Minkov, 2010). In addition, studies have been conducted in various countries around the world to investigate how different cultures value time. Research has shown that Asian countries tend to have more past-oriented societies (Block, Buggie, & Matsui, 1996; Guo et al., 2012; Núñez et al., 2012; Rojas-Méndez, Davies, Omer, Chetthamrongchai, & Madran, 2002; Spadone, 1992). On the other hand, the United States and other Western countries tend to be more present-oriented (Brislin & Kim, 2003; Sundberg, Poole, & Tyler, 1983).

Event time and clock time

Clock time, otherwise known as physical time, is the objective measure of time. Event time, on the other hand, is subjective and situational, and represents the time spent completing a task or attending an event (Plocher, Goonetilleke, Zhang, &

Liang, 2002). Many Western and industrialized countries tend to highly value clock time because it allows time to be added, borrowed, and divided (Rubin & Belgrave, 1999). Clock time also allows individuals to be precise with planning and rearranging time allocated for certain tasks and to have a measure of efficiency (Bluedorn & Denhardt, 1988; Levine & Norenzayan, 1999). Since the perspective on clock time focuses on precision, it is possible for individuals to be more rigid and have stricter expectations about following clock time than event time. In many Western organizations, clock time can take precedence over events, unless the events are urgent (Levine, 1997). For these reasons, clock time is typically utilized in organizations from countries with strong economies (Levine & Norenzayan, 1999). In contrast, event time features less rigid views on punctuality, and the passage of time is measured not by minute or hour, but instead by the time it takes for a task to be completed (Goldman & Rojot, 2003). Though event time is prevalent in less industrialized countries, globalization and the increase in international business have led to increased usage of clock time (Alon & Brett, 2007). In addition to clock and event time, there are other possible ways to view the passage of time. Dictated by religion, Saunders, Van Slyke, and Vogel (2004) discuss how Hinduism and Buddhism emphasize the meaninglessness of the passage of time as well as the cyclical nature of time. This diminishes the importance of punctuality and clock time. These authors also proposed the concept of harmonic time, which is characterized by highly valuing the time of oneself and others. This allows individuals to use time as a better way to increase harmony between people, society, and nature. Clearly, more research is needed to further investigate these temporal views.

Pace of life

The pace of life is a dimension that has been studied extensively in many academic disciplines (Macduff, 2006). Werner, Altman, and Oxley (1985) define pace of life as "the race, speed and relative rapidity or density of experiences, meanings, perceptions and activities" (p. 14). Research on the pace of life has been pioneered by Robert Levine, who has conducted several series of studies that investigated how the dimension differs across countries. His first major work on the topic investigated the pace of life in Japan, Taiwan, Indonesia, Italy, England, and the United States. By measuring postal efficiency, walking pace of individuals, and the accuracy of public clocks, Levine and Bartlett (1984) measured the pace of life across 12 different cities from each of the six countries. These researchers found significant positive correlations between economic development and the indicators of the pace of life for each country. This line of research was continued when Levine and Norenzayan (1999) examined the pace of life in 31 countries. Again, they used a variety of unique measures to evaluate the pace of life, including walking speed in downtown areas, postal clerk work speed, public clock accuracy, and work speed. These researchers found that Western European countries and Japan had the fastest pace of life, that the United States, Canada, and the Four Asian Tigers ranked middle, and that relatively non-industrialized countries were the slowest. However, since the three indicators measured the pace of life during business hours, Western Europeans were found to be better at slowing down after work than their American and Japanese counterparts (ibid.). These findings are not completely indicative of entire countries, however. Specifically, individuals from large urban areas across several different countries and cultural contexts tend to have faster paces of life than suburban or rural areas (Levine, 1997). Within the cities, Levine (1997) was able to find that the pace of life was predicted by the climate, economic welfare, and the dimension of individualism and collectivism. However, regardless of urban or rural areas, it has been consistently shown that wealthier and more developed areas possess less flexible definitions of punctuality (White, Valk, & Dialmy, 2011).

Time as cultural metaphor

In addition to the traditional dimensional approach, examining cultural metaphors can be another effective way to understand different temporal issues across cultures. Gannon, Locke, Gupta, Audia, and Kristof-Brown (2005) define a cultural metaphor as "an institution, phenomenon, or activity with which most citizens in each national culture identify cognitively or emotionally and through which it is possible to describe the culture and its frame of reference in depth" (p. 38). These metaphors can describe how different cultures perceive different aspects of society, as well as how different cultures conceptualize different abstract concepts, such as time. From this vein of study, researchers have considered space to be a metaphor for time (Hubbard & Teuscher, 2010). In this metaphor, time is considered to be an empty void that humans travel through from one event to the next (Fuhrman et al., 2011; Miles, Tan, Noble, Lumsden, & Macrae, 2011). Americans typically view time horizontally in a backward to forward manner and also view time as moving from left to right (Cooperrider & Núñez, 2009). On the other hand, Chinese view time as vertically moving from bottom to top (Fuhrman et al., 2011). Another popular metaphor is the concept of time being money (Brodowsky, Anderson, Schuster, Meilich, & Venkatesan, 2008). Tied with monochronic, industrialized societies, individuals from these cultures perceive time as something that can be spent, invested, and wasted (Leclerc, Schmitt & Dube, 1995). Individuals who believe something or someone is wasting their time will react negatively in most situations (Macduff, 2006; White et al., 2011). These cultural metaphors have provided a valuable lens that reveals a unique perspective of a culture on time, and it would be beneficial to try to understand what other cultural metaphors could describe time.

Antecedents of cross-cultural differences in temporal dimensions

Given the marked differences in these temporal dimensions, research has examined the antecedents that may explain why people perceive and approach time differently across cultures. These studies have uncovered a wide array of factors, some of which are inherent within a culture – such as values, religion, social structure, and language – while others are related to the environment – such as natural climate and social and economic conditions.

A number of studies have examined the relationships between cultural values and cross-cultural differences in temporal orientations. Among the various cultural values, collectivism/individualism, regulatory focus, and belief in one's control in life have been examined. Specifically, collectivism and individualism have been shown to influence cross-cultural differences in an orientation toward the future, present, and past. Shirai and Beresneviciene (2005) have found that individualistic cultures are more future-oriented while collectivistic cultures are more present-oriented, because collectivists tend to focus on concrete events and particularistic rules in the "here and now" as compared to individualists, who focus on abstract events and universal rules that apply across situations. Individualism and collectivism also have an effect on how much individuals attend to context and background, which is related to differences in temporal orientation. Chinese have been found to pay closer attention to contextual information than North Americans, predominantly individualists (Choi, Nisbett, & Norenzayan, 1999). Ji et al. (2009) suggest that Chinese may view the past as a background for the present, leading to more proximal perception and better memory of the past as compared to North Americans.

Cross-cultural differences in regulatory focus have also been examined, particularly in relation to different reliance on clock time and event time. Avnet and Sellier (2011) suggest that a promotion focus emphasizes maximizing gains, which is consistent with the use of clock time that can provide an objective deadline for a task. In contrast, a prevention focus emphasizes minimizing errors, which is consistent with the use of event time that ends a task only when no more mistakes can be detected. Cultures also differ in their emphasis on and belief in control in life. The focus on the future in North American cultures may be due to the people's belief that their future can be controlled; in contrast, East Asian cultures are less future-oriented as the people typically endorse the mentality of adjustment and perceive the future to be less in their control (Guo et al., 2012).

In addition to cultural values, myths and religion make up another factor that might explain cross-cultural differences in temporal orientation. The different views of Christians and Muslims, for example, can lead them to perceive time dissimilarly. Muslims view time as existing both on earth and in heaven, and while secular time (time on earth) is limited, heavenly time is believed to be unlimited. The additional consideration of the heavenly time may in part explain why Muslims, from the Christian perspective, do not exhibit a high time urgency or feel the need to rush (Alon & Brett, 2007). Likewise, researchers have found that the myths of a culture can also affect how its people conceptualize time. For example, the Yupnos of Papua New Guinea believe their ancestors traveled from an island offshore to settle in a valley among hills, which may be why they view the past as downhill and the future as uphill (Núñez et al., 2012). Closely linked to religion in many cultures, social structure has also been identified as an influence of the cross-cultural differences in temporal orientation. As social structure, such as festivals and gatherings, dictates how activities are organized in the past, present, and future, individuals' roles and participation in social activities influence how they view time (Eisenstadt, 1949).

Language is yet another major internal factor that influences a culture's temporal orientation. Metaphors unique to a culture may explain why its people conceptualize time differently from people in other cultures. For example, the Aymara culture of South America has an adage, "knowing is seeing," which may be attributed to why they see the past as in the front, where they can see, whereas the future is in the back, where they cannot see. In contrast, most cultures view the past in the back and the future in the front, consistent with the typical bodily movement of going forward. Related to metaphors, people across cultures also conceptualize time differently depending on how they describe time. English and Indonesian speakers tend to talk about duration in linear distances. In contrast, Greek and Spanish speakers tend to talk about duration in quantity. Consequently, individuals have been found to be more adept at estimating duration that is in a manner consistent with their native languages, such as Greeks estimating duration in terms of quantity (Casasanto et al., 2004).

Other aspects of languages also have implications for cultural differences in time perception. In particular, differences in writing systems have been extensively studied as an explanation for cross-cultural differences in temporal orientation. For example, the writing direction of English from left to right has been compared to the writing directions of Mandarin Chinese from top to bottom and from right to left. The difference in writing direction has been found to influence how the two languages' speakers think of time and organize temporal events spatially. Consistent with the direction in which they read their text, Mandarin Chinese speakers have been found to conceptualize time vertically from top to bottom, with earlier events placed toward the top and later events placed toward the bottom. As Chinese can also be read horizontally from right to left, they have also been found to conceptualize time accordingly, placing earlier events on the right and later events on the left. In contrast, English speakers have been found to conceptualize time horizontally from left to right, with earlier events on the left and later events on the right (Boroditsky, 2001; Boroditsky, Fuhrman, & McCormick, 2011; Tse & Altarriba, 2008). As the writing direction of Hebrew is from right to left, the same difference in temporal mapping has been found between Hebrew and English speakers (Fuhrman & Boroditsky, 2010). The same pattern has also been found between Hebrew and Spanish speakers (Ouellet, Santiago, Israeli, & Gabay, 2010), as Spaniards write from left to right, the same as English-speakers, and map temporal events from left to right (Santiago, Lupáñez, Pérez, & Funes, 2007). The effect on temporal orientation has even been observed among people using the same writing system but different writing direction, such as between Mainland Chinese and Taiwanese Chinese (Bergen & Lau, 2012) and between younger and older Chinese from Hong Kong and Macau (de Sousa, 2012). Interestingly, for bilinguals, the effect of languages on their temporal orientation depends on the priming (i.e., the language of testing either in writing or listening; Fuhrman et al., 2011; Miles et al., 2011) and the age when the second language is learned (Boroditsky, 2001).

In addition to the writing system, tense in languages has also been examined in relation to their speakers' temporal orientation. The Indonesian language does not have tense markers, which may explain why research has found that Indonesians perform worse in memory of temporal sequences than English speakers, as tense facilitates the organization of temporal events in order (Boroditsky, Ham, & Ramscar, 2002). These researchers also found that the performance of Indonesian-English bilingual speakers was between that of Indonesian speakers and English speakers. Other research has suggested that a lack of measurement of time may be one of the reasons why some cultures, such as the Amondawa in the Amazon, rely on event time (Sinha et al., 2011). Similarly, differences in the size of a unit of temporal measurement have been attributed to cultural differences in the definition of punctuality. When the temporal measurement unit is larger and therefore less precise, the definition of punctuality is more flexible and it allows for broader interpretations of punctuality (Levine, West, & Reis, 1980; White et al., 2011). However, while a large unit of temporal measurement has been linked to inaccuracies in public clocks, Levine et al. (1980) note that the direction of causality is unclear. While it is possible that imprecision of public clocks promotes a larger unit of temporal measurement to allow for more flexibility, it is also possible that a larger unit of temporal measurement makes imprecision of public clocks more acceptable.

Beyond these factors within a culture, the environment that its people face can also influence temporal orientations of a culture. When organizing temporal events spatially, Pormpuraawans in Australia and Nheengatu in Brazil both follow the east to west direction, the same as the path of sun from the perspective of Earth (Boroditsky & Gaby, 2010; Floyd, 2008). Temperature in climate has also been linked to cross-cultural difference in temporal orientation. For example, Levine and Norenzayan (1999) have found that the pace of life is generally faster in colder climates than in warmer climates, as warmer climates pose lower demands on productivity for clothing and housing needs and, at the same time, are more taxing of physical energy.[1]

Social and economic conditions can also exert an impact on people's temporal orientations. Agarwal and Tripathi (1984) have found that individuals who have suffered a high level of prolonged deprivation tend to be more future-oriented than those who have suffered a lower level. Some researchers suggest that an orientation toward the future may be a coping mechanism of the difficulties in the present. For example, Kolesovs (2005) observes a positive correlation between dissatisfaction with the present situation and future orientation. Finally, national leadership has also been used to explain the temporal orientation of a culture. Poole and Cooney (1987) attributed the future orientation among Singaporeans to the values espoused by the country's leaders.

Consequences of cross-cultural differences in temporal dimensions

Having discussed the antecedents of temporal differences across cultures, we now turn to the consequences of these differences. Given the essential role of time in our daily lives, it is not surprising that cross-cultural differences in temporal orientation have been found to have an important impact ranging from the micro level to the macro level. At the micro level, these differences influence individuals' psychological, behavioral, and health outcomes, as well as negotiation, teamwork, and job performance. At the macro level, they influence human resource management, strategic planning, marketing, and the economic development of countries.

Cross-cultural differences in temporal orientations have been linked to individual psychological outcomes, including how people value the past, present, and future and their belief in how changes occur. These differences can have an effect on the extent to which they decide to choose to "enjoy the moment" versus "save for the future." Specifically, a present orientation is associated with a higher level of impulsivity than past and future orientations (Jones, 1994). The relationship between a present orientation and impulsivity may be due in part to the negative effect of time pressure on decision quality (Zakay & Wooler, 1984). Cross-cultural differences in temporal orientation also influence how people anticipate changes. The attention to the information proximal to the present among North Americans has been related to a tendency to expect things to remain unchanged or to follow an established pattern of changes, whereas the attention to the information distal to the present among Chinese has been related to a tendency to expect things to change nonlinearly and unpredictably over time (Ji et al., 2009).

In addition to psychological outcomes, cross-cultural differences in temporal orientation have also been found to influence individuals' behaviors, including their communication and relationship building. People in Islamic cultures that are characterized by high past orientation and low future orientation, for example, can communicate in a manner distinct from people in other cultures. Alon and Brett (2007) have found that communication in the Arabic-speaking world frequently cites history and traditions and that discussion of the future is often accompanied by the phrase *in sha'a Allah* (if God wills) to account for potential changes and uncertainty. Likewise, these differences exert an impact on the development of a social relationship, particularly intercultural relationships. In particular, in such cultures that are high on past orientation and low on future orientation, the process of trust building tends to take much longer and, at the same time, patience is highly valued (Alon & Brett, 2007).

As trust building plays a critical role in negotiation (Lee, Yang, & Graham, 2006), temporal orientation differences likewise affect cross-cultural negotiation. For example, Alon and Brett (2007) discuss how the tendency to operate in event time in Islamic cultures may afford their negotiators opportunities to use stalling and delaying as a tactic to influence Western negotiators, who operate in clock time and are more prone to feel pressure from time urgency. In addition to the different perspectives on timeliness, Macduff (2006) suggests that cross-cultural negotiators should consider issues related to the amount of time allocated for varying activities (e.g., business talk vs. small talk) and temporal reference (e.g., when the past is taken into account and when future remedy occurs). All of these issues have been observed in the negotiations between Palestinians and Israelis, where Zakay and Fleisig (2010) have concluded that it has been challenging to reach an agreement in part because Palestinians prefer a slow negotiation process whereas

Israelis prefer a quick resolution. Further, both parties have a past orientation such that the emphases they place on past conflicts make resolutions difficult. Zakay and Fleisig (2011) thus suggest that the negotiations between Palestinians and Israelis may be facilitated if both parties can adopt an orientation toward the future.

Extending from the dyadic level to the team level, research has examined the effect of temporal orientation on teams. When people from cultures with different temporal orientations work in a team, special care needs to be taken to ensure smooth team functioning. Temporal diversity can influence a myriad of team processes, including mission analysis, goal monitoring, and coordination (Arman & Adair, 2012). For example, when conducting a team mission analysis, members may focus on divergent aspects of a mission: past-oriented members tend to value traditions, present-oriented members tend to value efficiency and fast results, and future-oriented members tend to value long-term macro consequences. Likewise, members can also differ in the extent to which they check on the team's progress: team members who are concerned about time may engage in more goal monitoring than team members who are less concerned about time. The potential problems of temporal diversity among team members may be particularly salient in global virtual teams that have little face-to-face interaction, and members must find other ways to communicate how to schedule deadlines, divide time across tasks, and synchronize work activities (Saunders et al., 2004). These authors suggest that creating awareness of temporal differences, developing team norms, and using technology and automated tools to manage time can help alleviate problems stemming from temporal diversity. While Zerubavel (1981) proposes that planning and scheduling are especially critical in teams high in temporal diversity to ensure smooth functioning and coordination, Arman and Adair (2012) suggest that even the effect of planning may vary depending on the temporal orientation of team members – it tends to be more effective for polychronic team members than for monochronic members.

Differences in temporal orientations have also been found to influence how people conduct their work and their performance. People from cultures that operate in clock time, such as Americans, have been found to perform better on time-limited activities than people from cultures that operate in event time, such as Russians (Agranovich et al., 2011). Employees from clock-time cultures may place more importance on punctuality and planning than employees from event-time cultures (Ali & Azim, 1996). Performance has also been found to be higher when tasks are scheduled in a manner that matches the regulatory focus (Avnet & Sellier, 2011): organizing tasks on clock time facilitates performance of individuals' high promotion focus because they strive for efficiency, whereas organizing tasks on event time facilitates performance of individuals high on prevention focus because they strive for effectiveness.

In addition to the distinction between clock time and event time, people differ across cultures in how they allocate activities at work. Brislin and Kim (2003) have found that employees in collectivistic cultures tend to spend 50% of their work time on tasks and 50% on social activities, whereas employees in individualistic cultures tend to spend 80% of their work time on tasks and 20% on social activities. While individualists may view the work time distribution of collectivists to be inefficient, in collectivistic cultures, tasks are often completed during social activities through interpersonal relationships. Research has also found effects of polychronicity and monochronicity on job performance. Goal setting and planning tend to be more conducive to performance for polychronic individuals than monochronic individuals (Nonis et al., 2005).

Finally, at the micro level, cross-cultural differences in temporal orientations have been linked to health implications. For example, people in cultures with faster pacing tend to have higher rates of smoking and of death from coronary heart disease, but to enjoy greater subjective well-being than people in cultures with slower pacing (Levine & Bartlett, 1984; Levine & Norenzayan, 1999). Levine and Norenzayan (1999) suggest that the link to coronary heart disease is due to a stronger sense of time urgency while the link to subjective well-being is related to greater economic productivity. The health implication of present orientation has also been examined. Within the United States, people high in present orientation may be less effective in managing hypertension, believing more in home remedies and less in prescribed medication, as well as seeing themselves as less susceptible to the consequences of hypertension.

Beyond the micro-level outcomes, research has examined consequences at the macro level and has linked cross-cultural differences in temporal orientations to human resource management, strategic planning, marketing, and the economic development of countries. Firms across cultures have been found to focus on different aspects of employee selection and performance appraisal depending on the cultures' temporal orientation. For example, because the Chinese culture is high in past orientation, Chinese firms tend to place more emphasis on employees' past accomplishments when making HR decisions; in contrast, the American culture is high in future orientation, which leads American firms to place more emphasis on employees' future potential (Guo et al., 2012). In addition, HRM in clock-time cultures may evaluate employees based on whether deadlines are met, while HRM in event-time cultures may evaluate employees based on the types of tasks performed (Saunders et al., 2004).

Temporal orientations also have implications on the strategic planning of a firm. In particular, Bluedorn and Denhardt (1988) suggest that firms in cultures that focus on time horizon proximal to the present may have suboptimal results for their planning, as these firms tend to plan for the short term even though firm-level goals typically require a longer time horizon. Likewise, temporal orientation will also influence a firm's pattern of activities and the timeliness of its responses to demands from the environment (Tuttle, 1997). Voss and Blackmon (1998) observed that the simultaneous emphases on the past and present in the Japanese culture make quality management an attractive strategic focus for many Japanese firms, as quality management can be achieved through daily reflection of current situations and the emphasis on continuous improvement. Differences in temporal orientation may also influence the innovation and creativity output of a firm and an economy. Polychronicity has been proposed to facilitate creativity because of the range of ideas and activities individuals engage in during a given moment, as compared to monochronicity (Persing, 1999).

Cross-cultural differences in temporal orientation also have important implications in marketing. For cultures high in past orientation, such as in Asia and Latin America, products should be marketed in ways that connect them with past events (Brodowsky et al., 2008) or emphasize its history (Spears, Lin, & Mowen, 2000). Consumers in these cultures may be more willing to stay with products that they have used previously than to switch to products that are more innovative (Guo et al., 2012) or to try new products in general (Legohérel, Daucé, Hsu, & Ranchhold, 2009). By comparison, in cultures high in present and future orientations, products should be marketed to illustrate how they can improve life, while downplaying the influences of past events (Spears et al., 2000). In addition to temporal orientation, marketing strategies should also match how people in a culture use their time, on dimensions such as prioritizing work or leisure, as well as engaging in activities individually or collectively and monochronically or polychronically (Manrai & Manrai, 1995). For example, Kaufman et al. (1991) propose that in polychronic cultures businesses should offer ways to learn about and use a product or a service while engaging in other day-to-day activities, such as during a commute or while running errands.

Finally, cross-cultural differences in temporal orientations have also been linked to the economic progress of different countries. Hofstede, Hofstede, and Minkov (1991) categorized cultures high in values such as thrift and perseverance as long-term–oriented and culture high in social convention and stability as short-term–oriented. Based on the relationship between long-term orientation and the rapid economic growth in Asia between 1965 and 1984 (Chinese Cultural Connection, 1987), Hofstede and Minkov (2010) predicted that long-term orientation of Eastern European cultures would also propel their countries to recover quickly from economic crisis. In contrast, the short-term orientation of the Muslim African and Latin American cultures, due to their emphasis on tradition and security, may slow the economic growth of these countries.

Measurement challenges of cross-cultural differences in temporal dimensions

As can be seen in our discussion, the intersection between time and culture has received increasing research attention and, together, the body of research has yielded important insights into how and why people across cultures perceive and approach time differently and the effects of the differences. Nevertheless, the research still suffers from other issues frequently encountered in cross-cultural investigations. Among those are different issues surrounding the development and measurement of different instruments. Given the large number of theories and hypotheses surrounding the different ways cultures perceive time, it is important to create accurate and reliable measures for the established cross-cultural temporal dimensions. By examining how different articles in the past have encountered these challenges, researchers can become better equipped to deal with them.

An early example of a measurement issue surrounding work on temporal understanding is Schriber and Gutek's (1987) study on time and organizational culture. The researchers created the Time Dimension Scale, which contained 13 subscales surrounding different time-based organizational concepts. However, only three of the subscales (Schedules and Deadlines, Punctuality, and Future Orientation) had Cronbach's α greater than .70. As will be seen in this section, reliability-related issues have been present in the development of many instruments that measure temporal constructs, perhaps due to insufficient development of the original measures and/or translation and equivalence issues. When faced with these limitations, researchers have found various ways to justify or improve their scales.

Similarly, Kaufman et al. (1991) found difficulty developing a reliable scale for polychronicity. The researchers' Polychronic Attitude Index (PAI) was found to have a Cronbach's α of .68. However, they argued that this relatively low value was acceptable since their index was developed early in the research on polychronicity. Years after this study, Lindquist et al. (2001) created another version of their initial PAI, the Modified Polychronic Attitude Index 3 (MPAI3). Research conducted by Plocher et al. (2002) found that the MPAI3 had improved slightly as compared to its predecessor, with a Cronbach's α of .72. However, Plocher et al. (2002) found that Bluedorn et al.'s (1999) Inventory of Polychronicity Value (IPV) was more reliable as the Cronbach's α for the IPV was 0.87.

Issues with reliability may become more complex as researchers investigate data from different countries. For example, Ko and Gentry (1991) designed a study on past and future time orientation in Korea and the United States. After developing two instruments to measure the two forms of time orientation, the researchers found that the Cronbach's α for both scales were below the recommended level (past: Korea = .59, U.S. = .51; future: Korea = .38, U.S. = .55). The researchers discussed that Koreans were inconsistent about their ideas of future orientation, whereas Americans were more inconsistent about their ideas of past orientation (ibid.). Rojas-Méndez et al. (2002) encountered similar issues with reliability. These researchers developed and utilized their Time-Attitude Scale to measure a culture's attitude about time. The scale contained five attitudes about time: past, present, future, planning (time as succession), and time pressure (time as duration). Unfortunately, the measure did not have a satisfactory Cronbach's α in most countries (Chile = .63, UK = .55, Thailand = .71, and Saudi Arabia = .63). However, like Kaufman et al. (1991), they suggested that these were acceptable for exploratory analysis because research on temporal perspectives within different countries needed to be further examined (Rojas-Méndez et al., 2002).

These issues are still common within more recent cross-cultural work on time. For example, Leonard (2008), along with the aid of cross-cultural collaborators, was also unable to develop a reliable measure for polychronicity. Across the entire international sample, the average Cronbach's α for the scale was .55, with the lowest being .47 in the United States and the highest being .60 in Venezuela (ibid.). In another study, while Legohérel et al.'s (2009) Temporal Styles Scale was found to be valid, the instrument encountered problems within the Chinese version. These investigators found that the Chinese data did not fit their confirmatory analysis model, and that their construct did not apply to both English and Chinese question-naire groups. This is a common issue in other cross-cultural research, and requires researchers to consider how their methodology will be implemented among different societies (Gelfand, Raver, & Ehrhart, 2002). Finally, Shipp, Edwards, and Lambert (2009) developed the Temporal Focus Scale, which focuses on the amount of attention an individual places on the past, present, and future, and contains a subscale for each focus. Across multiple studies, the authors found that the items consistently and significantly loaded onto their respective factors, with values ranging from .65 to .84. Each subscale also demonstrated good Cron-bach's α (past = .89; current = .74; future = .86). As the study is based on data from the United States, future research should examine its validity and reliability cross-culturally.

The issues researchers have encountered when studying time and culture extend beyond problems with developing reliable measures. Nevertheless, difficulty in creating valid, reliable measures for established constructs of interest such as polychronicity and future orientation illustrate issues within the field to accurately assess and understand the temporal dimensions across cultures. Future research should not neglect to create and improve developed instruments so that the phe-nomena can be better understood. Also, these issues may imply that different ways to examine these phenomena may be in order. Behavioral measures for some con-structs may not have some of the issues present in surveys and questionnaires, and more consistent findings and interpretations may be discovered.

Frontiers of research on culture and time

Building on our analysis of the research on time and culture, we now turn to a discussion of the research areas that are ripe for further investigation. In particu-lar, we have identified four questions that are in particular need of future research attention, including 1) how are the temporal dimensions interrelated, 2) what is the impact of globalization on time orientations across cultures, 3) are conceptualiza-tions of time similar or different across cultures, and 4) what are the neural bases of cross-cultural differences in temporal orientations?

Our chapter shows that much progress has been made in the research on temporal orientations across cultures. Beyond documenting similarities and dis-similarities, the research has examined the causes and impacts of these cultural differences. Nevertheless, research has thus far examined each temporal dimen-sion independently, even when multiple dimensions are considered (e.g., Ancona, Okhuysen, & Perlow, 2001; Bluedorn & Denhardt, 1988; Macduff, 2006). It is important to acknowledge that these temporal dimensions are interrelated and can co-occur as a result. Future research is thus needed on the theoretical and empiri-cal integration of the divergent temporal dimensions to provide a systematic and comprehensive picture of these cultural dimensions. For example, the emphasis on efficiency and multitasking in polychronicity is consistent with the use of clock time (Arman & Adair, 2012), wherein multiple activities tend to take place in a given time to obtain fast results. In contrast, the emphasis on process is consistent with the use of event time, wherein events are scheduled one at a time to ensure sufficient time for completion and quality of the results. In a similar vein, present time orientation and a fast pace of life may be related to polychronicity and clock time due to their common focus on quick turnarounds and fast results. Likewise, cultural metaphors of time reflect the temporal orientations of a culture. For example, the use of clock time has been linked to the conceptualization of time as a valuable economic resource (Alon & Brett, 2007; Bluedorn & Denhardt, 1988). Accordingly, future research needs to include multiple dimensions of time simultaneously and examine the underlying latent factors that account for their interrelationships to better integrate research on culture and time. From a methodological point of view, it is critical to create inventories that include different measures of time so that we can understand how a more parsimonious set of dimensions captures multiple temporal orientations. To further understand effects of temporal dimensions, either independently or jointly, on outcomes, future research should also consider how to *prime* different dimensions of time to examine causality.

As communication and transportation technologies continue to advance, the distances among cultures are decreasing at a rapid rate. There is an urgent need for researchers to document and study changes in temporal orientations across cultures due to globalization. Brislin and Kim (2003) predict that cultures in East Asia, Latin America, and the Mediterranean region will over time adopt the use of clock time and schedule events polychronically, consistent with the practices in the United States. As another example, the popular English phrase "time is money" has become increasingly common in many cultures. Usunier (1991) has observed that the phrase prompts Chinese, Brazilians, and Moroccans, who traditionally follow event time, to conceptualize an "ideal economic time" that is similar to the typically Western clock time, while their behaviors may not be consistent with the new conceptualization of time and continue to follow event time in reality. As another example, as the level of competitiveness increases in the global environment, cultures may change how they schedule events and "budget" their time. In the 1980s and early 1990s, cultures in North America were described as monochronic (Hall, 1983; Kaufman et al., 1991). However, due to the common practice of multitasking in organizations, these cultures now tend to be described as polychronic (e.g., Arman & Adair, 2012; Brislin & Kim, 2003). More research is needed to examine conflicts and integration between the traditional and introduced temporal dimensions within cultures and their impacts on micro- and macro-level outcomes. Research can also examine cross-generational differences in temporal dimensions within and across cultures. For example, it is possible that as globalization continues to advance, we may expect that the cross-cultural differences narrow with each succession of generation.[2] At the same time, globalization can also yield psychological reactance and a rejection of Western culture (Gelfand, Lyons, & Lun, 2012; Huntington, 1993). Thus, it is possible that Western notions of clock time and related orientations will be rejected in order to maintain one's cultural distinctiveness.

As can be seen in the previous section, the research on cross-cultural differences in temporal dimensions has its inherent challenges, foremost among them being measurement. Given the difficulties in establishing cultural equivalency of temporal orientations, it is important to take into account the ways the constructs are conceptualized differently across cultures. For example, the very idea of "the future" can vary from one culture to another. Ko and Gentry (1991) suggest that past-oriented cultures tend to view the future as stable, whereas future-oriented cultures tend to view the future as dynamic. They have also found that future orientation is associated with divergent factors across cultures: while Koreans high in future orientation endorse Confucian values, Americans high in future orientation do not, and yet Americans high in past orientation endorse Confucian values. Likewise, Poole and Cooney (1987) have found that while both Singaporeans and Australians are future-oriented, they focus on divergent aspects of the future. Singaporeans focus more on future education and careers, while Australians focus more on future lifestyle, environment, and psychological well-being. These studies point to the possibility that the categorization of individuals and their cultures as past, present, or future orientation, as monochronic or polychronic, and as operating in clock time or event time may be overly simplistic. Research should take into account the context in which people adhere to a temporal orientation. Given that many cultural construals are affected by situational factors (Gelfand et al., 2007), it is critical to see how they vary depending on organizational, situational, and individual difference characteristics. For example, individuals in a culture that has been observed to operate in clock time may nevertheless operate in event time for certain activities and under some circumstances. This is consistent with the increasing emphasis on cultural dynamics in the cultural literature (Gelfand & Realo, 1999; Hong, Morris, Chiu, & Benet-Martinez, 2000; Morris & Gelfand, 2004), where the effects of culture may change depending on the situational context and/or individual attributes. For example, the relationship between dissatisfaction with the present situation and future orientation (Kolesovs, 2005) raises the possibility that a culture's temporal orientation may change over time based on its people's current experiences. As another example, bicultural and multicultural individuals' experiences with time would be a very interesting future direction to examine how they manage temporal conflicts that stem from divergent world views.

Finally, research using methodology in neuroscience also holds promise to further our understanding of the relationship between time and culture. For example, using neuroimaging, neuropsychology, and monkey physiology, Hubbard and Teuscher (2010) have found that the common conceptualization of time as space across cultures is based on a common region associated with both time and space within the parietal lobe. They thus suggest that the prevalence of conceptualizing time as space may be due to brain-based structures. Clearly, more research is needed to understand the relationship between neural bases and cross-cultural differences in temporal orientations. Such research has potential to help illuminate the extent to which cross-cultural temporal differences are due to nature (e.g., the preexisting neural wiring) or to nurture (e.g., the physical, cultural, social, and economic environments). Above all, methodological diversity can improve our understanding of this promising topic.

Conclusion

As with the majority of human experiences, conceptualizations of time and approaches toward time show great diversity across cultures. The importance of understanding cultural differences in time cannot be overstated in today's world. As intercultural interactions increasingly become the norm rather than the exception, the ability of individuals, groups, and organizations to manage time effectively in cross-cultural settings is critical to the success of these interactions. As this chapter shows, temporal differences are important cultural dimensions that influence how individuals across cultures think, behave, and work (e.g., Alon & Brett, 2007; Brislin & Kim, 2003; Ji et al., 2009). These differences also influence how organizations manage employees, plan activities, and market products (e.g., Brodowsky et al., 2008; Saunders et al., 2004; Tuttle, 1997). Given these important consequences, it is clear that there is an urgent need to incorporate temporal dimensions into the mainstream of cultural research to allow further development and enrichment of the theoretical and empirical bases of the topic. Likewise, temporal research will benefit from a broad empirical scope beyond the Western context and an explicit consideration of differences across cultures to assess the extent to which findings or propositions are cultural-universal or cultural-specific. In this age of global interdependence, knowledge about cultural diversity in temporal perspectives and practices holds valuable practical implications that are part of the "cultural toolkit" to facilitate international relations at the individual, organizational, and national levels.

Acknowledgment

This chapter is based upon research funded by the US Army Research Laboratory and the US Army Research Office under W911NF-08–1-0144, and the National University of Singapore Start-Up Grant. We give special thanks to Kristie Chua and Gavin Goh for their assistance on the preparation of this chapter.

Notes

1. There is also a possibility that a curvilinear relationship exists between pace of life and climate temperature in that pace is slower in both extremely cold and warm climates. We thank the editors for this comment.
2. We thank the editors for this comment.

References

Agarwal, A., & Tripathi, K. K. (1984). Influence of prolonged deprivation, age and culture on the development of future orientation. *European Journal of Social Psychology, 14*(4), 451–453.

Agranovich, A. V., Panter, A. T., Puente, A. E., & Touradji, P. (2011). The culture of time in neuropsychological assessment: Exploring the effects of culture-specific time attitudes on timed test performance in Russian and American samples. *Journal of the International Neuropsychological Society, 17*(4), 692–701.

Ali, A. J., & Azim, A. (1996). A cross-national perspective on managerial problems in a non-western country. *Journal of Social Psychology, 136*(2), 165–172.

Alon, I., & Brett, J. M. (2007). Perceptions of time and their impact on negotiations in the Arabic-speaking Islamic world. *Negotiation Journal, 23*(1), 55–73.

Ancona, D. G., Okhuysen, G. A., & Perlow, L. A. (2001). Taking time to integrate temporal research. *Academy of Management Review, 26*(4), 512–529.

Arman, G., & Adair, C. K. (2012). Cross-cultural differences in perception of time: Implications for multinational teams. *European Journal of Work and Organizational Psychology, 21*(5), 657–680.

Avnet, T., & Sellier, A. (2011). Clock time vs. event time: Temporal culture or self-regulation? *Journal of Experimental Social Psychology, 47*(3), 665–667.

Aycan, Z., & Gelfand, M. J. (2012). Cross-cultural organizational psychology. In S. Kozlowski (Ed.), *The Oxford handbook of organizational psychology* (pp. 1103–1160). New York: Oxford University Press.

Bergen, B. K., & Lau, T. T. C. (2012). Writing direction affects how people map space onto time. *Frontiers in Psychology, 3,* 109.

Billing, T. K., Bhagat, R. S., Lammel, A., Leonard, K. M., Ford, D. L., Jr., Brew, F., . . . Kuo, B. (2010). Temporal orientation and its relationships with organizationally valued outcomes: Results from a 14-country investigation. In A. Gari & K. Mylanos (Eds.), *Quod erat demonstrandum: From Herodotus' ethnographic journeys to cross-cultural research* (pp. 211–220). Athens, Greece: Pedio Books.

Block, R. A., Buggie, S. E., & Matsui, F. (1996). Beliefs about time: Cross-cultural comparisons. *Journal of Psychology, 130*(1), 5–22.

Bluedorn, A. C., & Denhardt, R. B. (1988). Time and organizations. *Journal of Management, 14*(2), 299–320.

Bluedorn, A. C., Kalliath, T. J., Strube, M. J., & Martin, G. D. (1999). Polychronicity and the Inventory of Polychronic Values (IPV): The development of an instrument to measure a fundamental dimension of organizational culture. *Journal of Managerial Psychology, 14*(3/4), 205–231.

Boroditsky, L. (2001). Does language shape thought? Mandarin and English speakers' conceptions of time. *Cognitive Psychology, 43*(1), 1–22.

Boroditsky, L., Fuhrman, O., & McCormick, K. (2011). Do English and Mandarin speakers think about time differently? *Cognition, 118*(1), 123–129.

Boroditsky, L., & Gaby, A. (2010). Remembrances of times East: Absolute spatial representations of time in an Australian Aboriginal community. *Psychological Science, 21*(11), 1635–1639.

Boroditsky, L., Ham, W., & Ramscar, M. (2002). What is universal in event perception? Comparing English & Indonesian speakers. In W. D. Gray & C. D. Schunn (Eds.), *Proceedings of the 24th Annual Meeting of the Cognitive Science Society* (pp. 136–141). Mahwah, NJ: Erlbaum.

Brislin, R. W., & Kim, E. S. (2003). Cultural diversity and people's understanding and uses of time. *Applied Psychology: An International Review, 52*(3), 363–382.

Brodowsky, G. H., Anderson, B. B., Schuster, C. P., Meilich, O., & Venkatesan, M. V. (2008). If time is money is it a common currency? Time in Anglo, Asian, and Latin cultures. *Journal of Global Marketing, 21*(4), 245–257.

Casasanto, D., Boroditsky, L., Phillips, W., Greene, J., Goswami, S., Bocanegra-Thiel, S., . . . & Gil, D. (2004). How deep are effects of language on thought? Time estimation in speakers of English, Indonesian, Greek, and Spanish. In K. Forbus, D. Gentner, & T. Regier (Eds.), *Proceedings of the 26th Annual Meeting of the Cognitive Science Society* (pp. 575–580). Hillsdale, NJ: Lawrence Erlbaum.

Chinese Cultural Connection. (1987). Chinese values and the search for culture-free dimensions of culture. *Journal of Cross-Cultural Psychology, 18,* 143–164.

Choi, I., Nisbett, R. E., & Norenzayan, A. (1999). Causal attribution across cultures: Variation and universality. *Psychological Bulletin, 125*(1), 47–63.

Cooperrider, K., & Núñez, R. (2009). Across time, across the body: Transversal temporal gestures. *Gesture, 9*(2), 181–206.

de Sousa, H. (2012). Generational differences in the orientation of time in Cantonese speakers as a function of changes in the direction of Chinese writing. *Frontiers in Psychology, 3,* 1–8.

Eisenstadt, S. N. (1949). The perception of time and space in a situation of culture-contact. *Journal of the Anthropological Institute of Great Britain and Ireland, 79,* 63–68.

Floyd, S. (2008, May). *Solar iconicity, conventionalized gesture and multimodal meaning in Nheengatú.* Paper presented at the Arizona Linguistics and Anthropology Symposium, Tucson, Arizona.

Fuhrman, O., & Boroditsky, L. (2010). Cross-cultural differences in mental representations of time: Evidence from an implicit nonlinguistic task. *Cognitive Science, 34*(8), 1430–1451.

Fuhrman, O., McCormick, K., Chen, E., Jiang, H., Shu, D., Mao, S., & Boroditsky, L. (2011). How linguistic and cultural forces shape conceptions of time: English and Mandarin time in 3D. *Cognitive Science, 35*(7), 1305–1328.

Gannon, M. J., Locke, E. A., Gupta, A., Audia, P., & Kristof-Brown, A. L. (2005). Cultural metaphors as frames of reference for nations: A six-country study. *International Studies of Management and Organization, 35*(4), 37–47.

Gelfand, M. J., Erez, M., & Aycan, Z. (2007). Cross-cultural organizational behavior. *Annual Review of Psychology, 58,* 479–514.

Gelfand, M. J., Lyons, S., & Lun, J. (2012). Toward a psychological science of globalization. *Journal of Social Issues, 67,* 841–853.

Gelfand, M. J., Raver, J. L., & Ehrhart, K. (2002). Methodological issues in cross-cultural organizational research. In S. Rogelberg (Ed.), *Handbook of industrial and organizational psychology research methods* (pp. 216–241). New York: Blackwell.

Gelfand, M. J., & Realo, A. (1999). Individualism-collectivism and accountability in intergroup negotiations. *Journal of Applied Psychology, 84*(5), 721–736.

Goldman, A. L., & Rojot, J. (2003). *Negotiation: Theory and practice.* Netherlands: Kluwer Law International.

Guo, T., Ji, L. J., Spina, R., & Zhang, Z. (2012). Culture, temporal focus, and values of the past and the future. *Personality and Social Psychology Bulletin, 38*(8), 1030–1040.

Hall, E. T. (1959). *The silent language.* New York: Doubleday,

Hall, E. T. (1983). *The dance of life.* New York: Doubleday.

Hall, E. T., & Hall, M. R. (1990). *Understanding cultural differences.* Yarmouth, ME: Intercultural Press.

Hofstede, G. (1980). *Culture's consequences: International differences in work-related values.* Thousand Oaks, CA: SAGE.

Hofstede, G., Hofstede, G. J., & Minkov, M. (1991). *Cultures and organizations.* London: McGraw-Hill.

Hofstede, G., & Minkov, M. (2010). Long-versus short-term orientation: New perspectives. *Asia Pacific Business Review, 16*(4), 493–504.

Hong, Y. Y., Morris, M. W., Chiu, C. Y., & Benet-Martinez, V. (2000). Multicultural minds. *American Psychologist, 55*(7), 709–720.

House, R., Javidan, M., Hanges, P., & Dorfman, P. (2002). Understanding cultures and implicit leadership theories across the globe: An introduction to project GLOBE. *Journal of World Business, 37*(1), 3–10.

Hubbard, E., & Teuscher, U. (2010). *Neural constraints on temporal-spatial metaphors.* Unpublished manuscript. Retrieved from http://ssrn.com/abstract=1632025

Huntington, S. P. (1993). The clash of civilizations? *Foreign Affairs, 72,* 22–49.

Jandt, F. E. (2003). *Intercultural communication: An introduction.* Thousand Oaks, CA: SAGE.

Ji, L. J., Guo, T., Zhang, Z., & Messervey, D. (2009). Looking into the past: Cultural differences in perception and representation of past information. *Journal of Personality and Social Psychology, 96*(4), 761–769.

Jones, J. M. (1994). An exploration of temporality in human behavior. In C. R. Schank & E. Langer (Eds.), *Beliefs, reasoning and decision making: Psycho-logic in honor of Bob Abelson* (pp. 389–411). Mahwah, NJ: Lawrence Erlbaum.

Kaufman, C. F., Lane, P. M., & Lindquist, J. D. (1991). Exploring more than 24 hours a day: A preliminary investigation of polychronic time use. *Journal of Consumer Research, 18*(3), 392–401.

Kaufman-Scarborough, C. (2003). Two perspectives on the tyranny of time: Polychronicity and monochronicity as depicted in *Cast Away. Journal of American Culture, 26*(1), 87–95.

Kluckhohn, F. R., & Strodtbeck, F. L. (1961). *Variations in value orientations.* Evanston, IL: Peterson.

Ko, G., & Gentry, J. W. (1991). The development of time orientation measures for use in cross-cultural research. *Advances in Consumer Research, 18*(1), 135–142.

Kolesovs, A. (2005). Time perspective of Latvian and Russian (ethnic minority) high school students in Riga and Latgale. *Baltic Journal of Psychology, 6*(1), 5–20.

Leclerc, F., Schmitt, B. H., & Dube, L. (1995). Waiting time and decision making: Is time like money? *Journal of Consumer Research, 22*(1), 110–119.

Lee, K. H., Yang, G., & Graham, J. L. (2006). Tension and trust in international business negotiations: American executives negotiating with Chinese executives. *Journal of International Business Studies, 37*(5), 623–641.

Legohérel, P., Daucé, B., Hsu, C. H., & Ranchhold, A. (2009). Culture, time orientation, and exploratory buying behavior. *Journal of International Consumer Marketing, 21*(2), 93–107.

Leonard, K. M. (2008). A cross-cultural investigation of temporal orientation in work organizations: A differentiation matching approach. *International Journal of Intercultural Relations, 32*(6), 479–492.

Leung, K., & Bond, M. H. (2004). Social axioms: A model for social beliefs in multicultural perspective. *Advances in Experimental Social Psychology, 36,* 119–197.

Levine, R. (1997). *A geography of time: The temporal misadventures of a social psychologist.* New York: Basic.

Levine, R. V., & Bartlett, K. (1984). Pace of life, punctuality, and coronary heart disease in six countries. *Journal of Cross-Cultural Psychology, 15*(2), 233–255.

Levine, R. V., & Norenzayan, A. (1999). The pace of life in 31 countries. *Journal of Cross-Cultural Psychology, 30*(2), 178–205.

Levine, R. V., West, L. J., & Reis, H. T. (1980). Perceptions of time and punctuality in the United States and Brazil. *Journal of Personality and Social Psychology, 38*(4), 541–550.

Lindquist, J. D., Knieling, J., & Kaufman-Scarborough, C. (2001). Polychronicity and consumer behavior outcomes among Japanese and US students: A study of response to culture in a US university setting. In H. Spotts, L. Meadow, & S. Smith (Eds.), *Proceedings of the Tenth Biennial World Marketing Congress.* Cardiff, UK: Academy of Marketing Science.

Macduff, I. (2006). Your pace or mine? Culture, time, and negotiation. *Negotiation Journal, 22*(1), 31–45.

Manrai, A. L., & Manrai, A. K. (1995). Effects of cultural-context, gender, and acculturation on perceptions of work versus social/leisure time usage. *Journal of Business Research, 32*(2), 115–128.

Markus, H. R., & Kitayama, S. (1991). Culture and the self: Implications for cognition, emotion, and motivation. *Psychological Review, 98*(2), 224.

Maznevski, M. L., Gomez, C. B., DiStefano, J. J., Noorderhaven, N. G., & Wu, P. C. (2002). Cultural dimensions at the individual level of analysis: The cultural orientations framework. *International Journal of Cross Cultural Management, 2*(3), 275–295.

Miles, L. K., Tan, L., Noble, G. D., Lumsden, D., & Macrae, C. N. (2011). Can a mind have two time lines? Exploring space-time mapping in Mandarin and English speakers. *Psychonomic Bulletin & Review, 18*(3), 598–604.

Morris, M. W., & Gelfand, M. J. (2004). Cultural differences and cognitive dynamics: Expanding the cognitive perspective on negotiation. In M. J. Gelfand & J. M. Brett (Eds.), *The handbook of negotiation and culture* (pp. 45–70). Stanford, CA: Stanford University Press.

Nonis, S. A., Teng, J. K., & Ford, C. W. (2005). A cross-cultural investigation of time management practices and job outcomes. *International Journal of Intercultural Relations, 29*(4), 409–428.

Núñez, R., Cooperrider, K., Doan, D., & Wassmann, J. (2012). Contours of time: Topographic construals of past, present, and future in the Yupno valley of Papua New Guinea. *Cognition, 124*(1), 25–35.

Ouellet, M., Santiago, J., Israeli, Z., & Gabay, S. (2010). Is the future the right time? *Experimental Psychology, 57*(4), 308–314.

Persing, D. L. (1999). Managing in polychronic times: Exploring individual creativity and performance in intellectually intensive venues. *Journal of Managerial Psychology, 14*(5), 358–373.

Plocher, T., Goonetilleke, R. S., Zhang, Y., & Liang, S. F. M. (2002). Time orientation across cultures. In J. Coronado, D. L. Day, & B. Hall (Eds.), *Proceedings of the 4th Annual International Workshop on Internationalisation of Products and Systems* (pp. 23–31). Rochester, NY: Product & Systems Internationalisation, Inc.

Poole, M. E., & Cooney, G. H. (1987). Orientations to the future: A comparison of adolescents in Australia and Singapore. *Journal of Youth and Adolescence, 16*(2), 129–151.

Rogers, E. M., Hart, W. B., & Miike, Y. (2002). Edward T. Hall and the history of intercultural communication: The United States and Japan. *Keio Communication Review, 24*, 3–26.

Rojas-Méndez, J. I., Davies, G., Omer, O., Chetthamrongchai, P., & Madran, C. (2002). A time attitude scale for cross cultural research. *Journal of Global Marketing, 15*(3–4), 117–147.

Rubin, D. F., & Belgrave, F. Z. (1999). Differences between African American and European American college students in relative and mathematical time orientations: A preliminary study. *Journal of Black Psychology, 25*(1), 105–113.

Santiago, J., Lupáñez, J., Pérez, E., & Funes, M. J. (2007). Time (also) flies from left to right. *Psychonomic Bulletin & Review, 14*(3), 512–516.

Saunders, C., Van Slyke, C., & Vogel, D. R. (2004). My time or yours? Managing time visions in global virtual teams. *Academy of Management Executive, 18*(1), 19–37.

Schriber, J. B., & Gutek, B. A. (1987). Some time dimensions of work: Measurement of an underlying aspect of organization culture. *Journal of Applied Psychology, 72*(4), 642.

Schwartz, S. H. (1994). *Beyond individualism/collectivism: New cultural dimensions of values.* Thousand Oaks, CA: SAGE.

Shipp, A. J., Edwards, J. R., & Lambert, L. S. (2009). Conceptualization and measurement of temporal focus: The subjective experience of the past, present, and future. *Organizational Behavior and Human Decision Processes, 110*(1), 1–22.

Shirai, T., & Beresneviciene, D. (2005). Future orientation in culture and socio-economic changes: Lithuanian adolescents in comparison with Belgian and Japanese. *Baltic Journal of Psychology, 6*(1), 21–31.

Singelis, T. M. (1998). *Teaching about culture, ethnicity, and diversity: Exercises and planned activities.* Thousand Oaks, CA: SAGE.

Sinha, C., Sinha, V. D. S., Zinken, J., & Sampaio, W. (2011). When time is not space: The social and linguistic construction of time intervals and temporal event relations in an Amazonian culture. *Language and Cognition, 3*(1), 137–169.

Spadone, R. A. (1992). Internal-external control and temporal orientation among Southeast Asians and white Americans. *American Journal of Occupational Therapy, 46*(8), 713–719.

Spears, N., Lin, X., & Mowen, J. C. (2000). Time orientation in the United States, China, and Mexico. *Journal of International Consumer Marketing, 13*(1), 57–75.

Sundberg, N. D., Poole, M. E., & Tyler, L. E. (1983). Adolescents' expectations of future events – A cross-cultural study of Australians, Americans, and Indians. *International Journal of Psychology, 18*(1–4), 415–427.

Tse, C. S., & Altarriba, J. (2008). Evidence against linguistic relativity in Chinese and English: A case study of spatial and temporal metaphors. *Journal of Cognition and Culture, 8*(3–4), 3–4.

Tuttle, D. B. (1997). A classification system for understanding individual differences in temporal orientation among processual researchers and organizational informants. *Scandinavian Journal of Management, 13*(4), 349–366.

Usunier, J. C. G. (1991). Business time perceptions and national cultures: A comparative survey. *MIR: Management International Review, 31*(3), 197–217.

Voss, C., & Blackmon, K. (1998). Differences in manufacturing strategy decisions between Japanese and Western manufacturing plants: The role of strategic time orientation. *Journal of Operations Management, 16*(2), 147–158.

Werner, C. M., Altman, I., & Oxley, D. (1985). Temporal aspects of homes: A transactional perspective. *Home Environments, 8,* 1–32.

White, L. T., Valk, R., & Dialmy, A. (2011). What is the meaning of "on time"? The sociocultural nature of punctuality. *Journal of Cross-Cultural Psychology, 42*(3), 482–493.

Zakay, D., & Fleisig, D. (2010). The time factor as a barrier to resolution of the Israeli-Palestinian conflict. In Y. Bar-Siman-Tov (Ed), *Barriers to peace in the Israeli-Palestinian conflict* (pp. 264–299). Jerusalem, Israel: Jerusalem Institute for Israel Studies.

Zakay, D., & Fleisig, D. (2011). Psychological time, time perspective, culture and conflict resolution. In S. Han & E. Pöppel (Eds.), *Culture and neural frames of communication* (pp. 123–137). Berlin, Germany: Springer-Verlag.

Zakay, D., & Wooler, S. (1984). Time pressure, training and decision effectiveness. *Ergonomics, 27*(3), 273–284.

Zerubavel, E. (1981). *Hidden rhythms*. Chicago: University of Chicago Press.

5 Human resource management is out of time

Robert E. Ployhart and Donald Hale, Jr.

The scholarly field of human resource (HR) management is out of time. We do not mean that the profession has run its course, but rather that the field has generally neglected the study of temporal dynamics within HR theories and phenomena. For example, when implementing a new selection or training program, we rarely know (a) when the benefits will manifest, (b) how long they will last, or (c) the functional form of change postintervention. Similarly, even though theory and empirical research suggest that employee collective resources, such as human capital and social capital, are likely to fluctuate and change over time, there is almost no scholarly attention devoted to understanding these dynamics. The modeling of time within HR is slightly more developed at the individual level, but even here the literature provides little guidance into how individual knowledge, skills, abilities, and other characteristics (KSAOs) (a) develop over time, (b) relate to performance or other criteria over time, or (c) influence the functional form of these relationships over time. Thus, in nearly every corner of HR scholarship, the literature is silent with respect to the time, timing, duration, and dynamics of HR practices, and the resources that are created from those practices (Gerhart, 2005; Wright & Haggerty, 2005). This lack of knowledge is both frustrating and embarrassing because it inhibits HR's progression as a science, and limits HR's impact in practice.

This chapter provides an overview of this state of affairs, emphasizing how "taking time seriously" would improve the rigor of HR theories, research, and practice. In the section that follows, we first review the HR field, at both micro and macro levels, to argue that there is little theory or research that incorporates time. We then provide a framework, based largely on Roe (2008), to identify the key principles of time, duration, timing, and temporal dynamics. This framework is then used to generate specific recommendations for incorporating time into the theory, design, and analysis of HR practices and resources. The main focus of this chapter will be on HR practices (e.g., selection; training), the individual and unit-level collective employee resources that are influenced by HR practice, and performance outcomes.

The timeless nature of human resource research

There is a wealth of HR research that is timeless, in the sense that there are "classic" insights that last through time. However, our use of the term "timeless" reflects a more discouraging tone, one that implies most HR research neglects consideration of time or temporal issues in even a superficial manner. This neglect is present in both the strategic (macro) and individual (micro) literatures.

Macro HR research

The macro HR literature makes important distinctions between HR practices, policies, and systems. HR practices are "specific organizational actions designed to achieve some specific outcomes" (Lepak, Liao, Chung, & Harden, 2006, p. 221). HR policies are "the firm or business unit's stated intentions about the kinds of HR programs, processes, and techniques that should be carried out in the organization" (Wright & Boswell, 2002, pp. 263–264). HR systems are the highest level of abstraction and represent a collection of HR policies and practices. Employees do not experience HR practices in isolation; they experience the combination of practices – the system – that drives employee perceptions and resulting behaviors (Bowen & Ostroff, 2004; Delery, 1998; Lepak et al., 2006). HR systems are focused around specific organizational goals, such as occupational safety HR systems (Zacharatos, Barling, & Iverson, 2005), customer service HR systems (Liao & Chuang, 2004), and knowledge-intensive HR systems (Jackson, Chuang, Harden, & Jiang, 2006). HR practices are nested within HR policies, which are in turn nested within HR systems (e.g., Becker & Gerhart, 1996; Lepak et al., 2006; Schuler, 1992). However, HR practices have a more proximal relationship to employee cognition, affect, and behavior (Bowen & Ostroff, 2004; Lepak et al., 2006; Wright & Boswell, 2002). Researchers have recognized that HR systems, policies, or practices impact firm-performance via mediating processes (Becker, Huselid, Pickus & Spratt, 1997). These mediating processes are employee behavior, cognition, and affect. Ostroff and Bowen (2000) and Lepak et al. (2006) proposed multilevel models in which HR systems have a direct impact on employee human capital, motivation, and opportunity, which, when aggregated, have a direct impact on unit performance.

Time and the temporal dynamics of the relationships between HR (systems, policies, practices), mediating processes (i.e., employee characteristic), and unit performance have received little explicit attention (Wright & Haggerty, 2005). There are some exceptions that have explicitly incorporated time. For example, Wright, Dyer, and Takla (1999) examined the amount of time it takes to develop and deploy human resources management (HRM) systems. HR managers were asked how long it would take to implement a major overhaul of the current HRM system. The results suggest that it takes 9–10 months to develop and 10–12 months to deliver a new HRM system. Similarly, Birdi et al. (2008) looked at the longitudinal relationship between HR systems and firm performance in UK manufacturing firms over the span of up to 22 years. They found that HR systems impacted longitudinal performance while other management practices did not. There are also some theoretical models that make more explicit consideration of time (e.g., Wright, Dunford, & Snell, 2001; Wright & Snell, 1998).

However, reviews of the HRM literature find most research gives little to no consideration of time. For example, Wall and Wood (2005) examined 25 articles related to the role of HRM. Only 2 of the 25 they examined had true longitudinal study designs (i.e., Capelli & Neumark, 2001; Ichniowski, Shaw, & Prennushi, 1997). In addition, Wright, Gardner, Moynihan, and Allen (2005) found that only 10 out of 70 designs (in 66 studies) reviewed actually measured HRM practices prior to the performance measurement period. Astonishingly, 50 out of the 70 designs employed a model in which HR practices were measured *after* the performance period.

Micro HR research

The micro HR research considered in this chapter emphasizes the study of HR practices on individual behavior, cognition, and affect. Note that we do not review individual-level research in great detail because it is already covered in other chapters in this book (e.g., Parker, Andrei, & Li, Volume 1; Roe, Volume 1). The most common theme in micro HR research is that a given HR practice produces (usually positive) effects on employee behavior, cognition, and/or affect. For example, training programs are implemented to enhance individual employee knowledge, selection programs are implemented to acquire higher-quality skills and abilities, and performance management programs are implemented to maintain or enhance motivation and performance behavior. The emphasis in this research is usually to evaluate the potential improvement in employee behavior, cognition, or affect, relative to a baseline (doing nothing) or using an alternative HR practice. The focus is on change relative to some standard, *not change over time.*

Most micro HR research has neglected to consider temporal issues. There are small pockets of temporal research that occur within specific content areas. For example, there is some longitudinal research on recruiting (Barber, 1998; Breaugh, 2013), dynamic performance (Sonnentag & Frese, 2012), and training (Baldwin & Ford, 1988). However, we will see that even this research is fairly limited once we take a more comprehensive consideration of time in HR. There is also little theoretical attention given to temporal issues. For example, there is no theory that we know of that specifies how long a training program, selection system, or performance management practice should enhance employee behavior. "Box and arrow" models of HR practices or processes are helpful for organizing constructs and their interrelationships, but they do not convey much information about time or timing, except only to propose which construct is expected to occur first (Wright & Haggerty, 2005). In turn, the majority of micro HR research is cross-sectional (Mitchell & James, 2001). When the research involves repeated measurements, there are usually only a few time periods, and they are used only to reduce concerns about method bias (Ployhart & Vandenberg, 2010). The micro HR research gives even less attention to issues about causal direction than does the macro literature. The micro literature almost always starts with the HR practice, so causal direction is not part of the theory or design.

Consequences of a human resource literature devoid of time

A knowledge of when things happen, why and how they happen, and for how long signifies the existence of an advanced scientific literature. The HR field has a long way to go before it is capable of discussing such issues in an informed manner. To the extent the HR field ignores these temporal issues, it marginalizes itself in both theory and practice. In terms of theory, an inability to explain why HR effects occur, when, or for how long only adds support to critics who claim HR is practice-based and lacks theoretical rigor. In terms of practice, an inability to explain why HR effects occur, when, or for how long only adds support to critics who claim HR research does not offer meaningful, actionable practical implications. The domain of HR scholarship straddles theory and practice, yet it is criticized as offering few insights into either area (Wright & McMahan, 1992). Ignoring temporal issues in HR only fuels the flames of criticism.

We are not the first to express such concerns. Wright and Haggerty (2005, p. 166) noted, "Current theory exploring the relationship between HRM and economic success has not deeply considered temporal issues. In most cases, time is either assumed as a constant, or considered in a relatively shallow way." Others have questioned the nature of HR-performance relationships, questioning the logic of causal direction and how employees tie into these relationships (Becker & Huselid, 2006; Gerhart, 2005; Wright et al., 2005).

What are the consequences of an HR field devoid of time? First, if there is not a clear understanding of the causal order between HR systems/policies/practices and performance, then it becomes difficult to know how changes in one affect changes in the other. For example, in Wright et al.'s (2005) review it could be argued that a majority of the strategic human resource management (SHRM) literature is actually measuring the impact of firm performance on HR systems, instead of the impact of HR systems on firm performance. Indeed, HR practices are uncorrelated with future performance when previous or current performance is controlled for. Ignoring time creates a scenario where the most basic question of causal order is open for debate (Wall & Wood, 2005).

Second, failing to understand the temporal dynamics underlying HR and employee or firm outcomes means we essentially don't know why HR systems or practices affect employee behavior, cognition, or affect. Current multilevel models link HR to individual and firm performance through aggregate employee behavior, cognition, and affect (e.g., Lepak et al., 2006). Human capital and social capital are the most common aggregate employee constructs (Adler & Kwon, 2002; Crook, Todd, Combs, Woehr, & Ketchen, 2011), but both take time to develop. If HR systems are related to firm performance via their impact on human and social capital, then there is a necessary role of time in the model because these resources need time to emerge.

Third, we don't know much about how fast or how long change will occur following the implementation of an HR practice or change in HR system or policy. If we don't know how long it will take for change to occur, then we don't know when we should measure change or evaluate the system or practice's effectiveness. According to most existing HR research, the benefits of HR interventions extend indefinitely. For example, two sacred HR findings are that more intelligent and more conscientious employees perform better. A *literal* reading of the HR literature would suggest this is expected to always be true over time. Our point is that HR theories and hypotheses rarely specify an "ending" point.

Fourth, HR theories and research have little to say about the functional form of HR effects over time. Are effects linear, do they decay, are there diminishing returns, or do they follow a nonlinear function? In some areas, such as dynamic performance, it appears there are curvilinear effects, such that performance follows a learning curve (Sonnentag & Frese, 2012). However, even this research is based on relatively small spans of time. Without knowing the shapes of these trends, the HR field has little to say about when additional HR investments are necessary. In some cases one may need to increase the intensity of the HR practice; in other cases one may need to change to a different practice entirely.

We conclude with one final concern. HR investments are expensive. To not know when, for how long, or why HR effects will occur is to put the HR field in an unfavorable position against other functions such as finance, accounting, or marketing, which usually have much more sophisticated models that incorporate temporal issues (e.g., depreciation in accounting). Boudreau (2010), Boudreau and Ramstad (2003, 2007), Cascio and Aguinis (2008), and Cascio and Boudreau (2011) have discussed these issues at some length. Their arguments are relevant to this chapter because they imply that we need to know how HR effects occur over time, so that it is possible to estimate the true return on HR investments.

A temporal framework for human resources

It is easy to criticize the HR field as one that neglects temporal issues. It is another thing entirely to propose specific actions for changing this state of affairs. It is our belief that the field will not significantly change unless there is an organizing framework that positions HR topics, theories, and operationalizations within a temporal lens. Just as theories or frameworks serve to direct future research by guiding the choice of constructs, relationships, and processes, a temporal framework for HR can help to guide future research by setting direction. Toward this end, we adapt general frameworks from other scholars (Lepak et al., 2006; Ployhart, 2006) that are particularly well suited for understanding temporal issues in HR. Figure 5.1 provides an overview of this framework.

We take as given that a temporal framework for HR must incorporate the following features. First, HR systems, policies, and practices have a reasonably precise starting and ending. HR systems and policies are broad plans for achieving the organization's vision and mission, while HR practices are the specific actions undertaken to achieve those plans. Path 1 in Figure 5.1 shows the influence of policies on practices. HR practices are essentially contextual interventions designed to produce change in employee behavior, cognition, or affect. Sooner or later, most (perhaps all) HR systems, policies, or practices have a starting point and an ending point. For example, a paper-based selection process gets replaced with an online process, and a new training program is then introduced for hiring managers to learn how to operate the online selection system. Unlike many organizational phenomena, there is often a specific date and time when HR policies and practices become "operational" and eventually "terminated." By terminated, we simply mean one practice ends and is replaced with another. Thus, a framework for HR

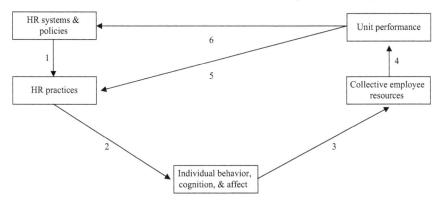

Figure 5.1 Model of HR systems, policies, and practices.

must recognize the beginning and possibly ending points of a given HR system, policy, or practice.

Second, HR practices influence employee behavior, cognition, and affect (Path 2 in Figure 5.1). As noted earlier, traditional strategic HR research, for example, focused on relationships between practices and unit-level outcomes (e.g., Huselid, 1995). This research evolved to focus more squarely on the intervening factors that explain why HR practices contribute to unit performance (Becker & Huselid, 2006). Looking inside this "black box," as it is frequently called, led to the development of multilevel HR models. HR practices are ways of communicating the organization's goals and climate (Bowen & Ostroff, 2004). They are unit-level phenomena because they are introduced and exist at a higher organizational level. For example, a firm policy forbidding the use of tests with adverse impact should be implemented across all departments and subunits. Yet, at the same time, HR practices produce effects that cross levels because they influence the behavior, cognition, and affect of *individuals* (Lepak et al., 2006). Therefore, HR systems and policies (indirectly), and practices (directly), are a cross-level effect on individual behavior, cognition, and affect.

Third, if administered and communicated consistently, HR practices contribute to the emergence of collective employee resources (e.g., human capital, social capital, collective performance behavior) from individual-level employee characteristics. This is shown in Path 3 in Figure 5.1. Emergence occurs when higher-level phenomena (e.g., aggregate employee skills or attitudes) originate from lower levels (e.g., individual skills or attitudes) through employee interaction and coordination (Kozlowski & Klein, 2000). To the extent HR policies and practices are communicated and implemented consistently, they contribute to the emergence of unit-level, collective resources such as human capital and climate perceptions because they shape the perceptions and nature of interactions among employees (Ployhart & Moliterno, 2011; Schneider, Ehrhart, & Macey, 1990).

Fourth, collective (unit-level) employee resources are the intervening explanatory variables that link HR policies and practices to unit-level performance. It is the unit-level resources that influence unit performance (Lepak et al., 2006; Ployhart, 2006), not HR policies and practices directly. This can be seen in Path 4 in Figure 5.1. The influence of HR practices on unit performance is indirect (through employee characteristics) and multilevel (from unit-level to employees [Path 2], and from employees to collective resources [Path 3]).

Finally, HR systems, policies, and practices, collective resources, and unit performance are dynamically and reciprocally related over time. Paths 5 and 6 in Figure 5.1 suggest the relationship goes from performance to systems, policies, and practices. As noted earlier, prior studies have sought to determine whether HR practices or unit performance comes first, but in reality, we believe this to be an unanswerable question. HR practices and unit performance are interrelated over time. Which variable comes first is likely to be more determined by the slice of time one uses for a given study. We demonstrate how such reciprocal relationships might occur shortly.

The HR framework shown in Figure 5.1 appears static, in that "time" is not illustrated in the model, nor are there indications of temporal processes. However, like many HR theories, time is implicit in the model. For every path in Figure 5.1, there is a corresponding time lag. For example, there will be a period of time that occurs between the implementation of an HR practice and changes to employee behaviors, cognitions, and attitudes. Likewise, resource emergence takes time, and more time will be required if one is trying to change the nature of the resource. Yet even by recognizing these lags, it is difficult to conceptualize time in the model shown in Figure 5.1.

What is needed is a means to transform the framework shown in Figure 5.1 into a *temporal* framework. The temporal framework offered by Roe (2008) offers a particularly useful starting point for developing a temporal HR framework. This framework contains four key elements: onset, offset, duration, and dynamics. The *onset* is the time at which an intervention or event occurs; the *offset* is the time at which an intervention or event ends. The time occurring between these two end points is the *duration*. Onset, offset, and duration are rather static entities; they define the scope (end points) and scale (duration) of a phenomenon. However, what happens between the onset and offset must be addressed, and this is the more difficult challenge because it involves understanding changes in the behavioral, cognitive, and affective processes. All of the action takes place in the dynamics that occur between onset and offset. *Dynamics* capture the types of change taking place, the variability over time in behavior, cognition, and affect, and the fluctuations that may occur in these constructs or relationships. Because the term dynamics is already in usage for other phenomena, we instead use the term *functional form* to emphasize the shape or trajectory of change in a construct over time between the onset and offset time points.

Mitchell and James (2001) offer more substance and variations to understanding temporal dynamics between two variables. They provide multiple configurations illustrating how two constructs may be related over time. As such, they provide a nice elaboration of several potential temporal dynamics that may exist through the duration period in Roe's (2008) framework. They also raise a number of issues

that are important for understanding temporal dynamics, including the lag or timing between constructs or events.

Drawing from these frameworks, it becomes possible to place the paths in
the HR framework shown in Figure 5.1 into a more dynamic, temporal structure
(note that all key terms are italicized to make them easier to identify). Figure 5.2
translates the relationship between an HR practice, individual employee behavior,
cognition, or affect (Path 2 in Figure 5.1), and resource emergence (Path 3 in Figure 5.2) into a general temporal framework. As the HR practice is implemented
at a specific time (*practice onset*), there is a corresponding lag after which individual employee behavior, cognition, or affect will begin to change. This *practice
onset lag* may be nearly immediate, or it may take days or months, if not longer
(expectations or anticipations for such lags may also affect employee reactions).
Assuming the practice is applied consistently, then over time individual behavior,
cognition, and affect begin to become more similar, and hence these individual
characteristics begin to coalesce into a unit-level collective resource (i.e., *resource
emergence*). The *rate of emergence* is essentially how fast the resource transforms
from individual attributes to a collective resource. Finally, for illustration we
assume there is some point at which the resource reaches a peak (*resource asymptote*), and then begins to decline. As the resource begins to erode, it is ultimately
decided that the HR practice is not achieving its goals and must be terminated
(*practice offset*), perhaps to be replaced with a different practice. Of course, the
functional form shown in the figure is merely an example, and it is not limited to
resources but could also apply to other phenomena such as unit performance. Not
all phenomena will change, grow, or decline as shown in the figure.

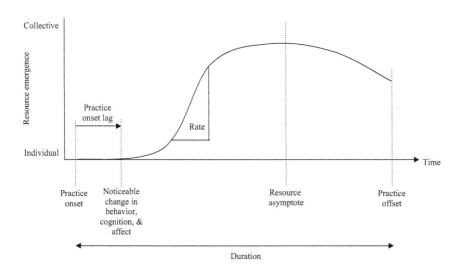

Figure 5.2 The Y-axis represents the degree of resource emergence. As resource emergence increases, it means that individual behavior, cognition, and affect
become more of a collective phenomenon.

Consider Figure 5.2 with an example. Assume that the HR practice is a training program designed to improve salespeople's knowledge of a new software system that helps with customer prospecting. As the training program is administered (*practice onset*), it takes six months to change the knowledge of individual salespeople (*practice onset lag*). As the number of salespeople trained increases, and as they begin to use the software collaboratively, this knowledge begins to comprise a firm-level collective resource (*resource emergence* and *rate of emergence*). However, after some extended period of time, salespeople begin to quit using the software, and new hires fail to complete the training, so the knowledge about it begins to deteriorate (it has passed *asymptote*). At some point, the knowledge declines to the point where HR managers believe the training is no longer valuable, and hence abandon the program (*practice offset*).

Let us now consider a more dynamic example. Figure 5.3 presents a temporal process entirely at the unit level, with just one HR practice (e.g., training), one collective resource (e.g., human capital), and unit-performance (e.g., profitability), interrelated over time. We assume that the HR practice has been implemented at a specific time, that this practice enhanced the quality of the collective resource that in turn enhanced unit performance. We then assume that unit performance begins to decline over time, and there is a point where it is recognized that the HR practice needs to be terminated (perhaps to be replaced with a different practice). In Figure 5.3, the collective resource is denoted by "X" and unit performance is denoted by "Y."

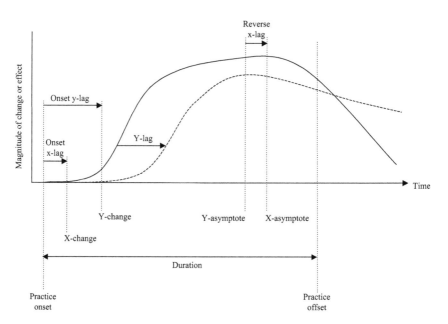

Figure 5.3 Dynamic relationship between HR practice, collective resource emergence, and unit performance. Solid line is quality of human capital resource (X); dashed line is unit performance (Y).

When the HR practice is implemented, there is a *practice onset* as before. However, now there are two lags: one for the lag between the implementation of the practice and the emergence of the collective resource (*onset x-lag*), and one between the implementation of the practice and change in unit performance (*onset y-lag*). Notice that the *onset x-lag* corresponds to Paths 2 and 3 in Figure 5.1, while the *onset y-lag* corresponds to Paths 2–4 in Figure 5.1. There is also a lag that exists between changes in the collective resource and changes in unit performance (*y-lag*). For illustration, we assume that unit performance reaches a peak (*y-asymptote*) and then begins to decline (perhaps due to an external event, such as a recession or change in the competitive environment). This, in turn, requires a reduction in HR investment, which begins to erode the quality of the collective resource (i.e., a decline past the *x-asymptote*). The *reverse x-lag* represents the amount of time that occurs between a decline in performance and a decline in the resource. As profits decline, investments in HR are cut to the point where the collective resource begins a free fall. Consequently, the firm decides to terminate the HR practice (*practice offset*).

Figures 5.2 and 5.3 are merely illustrative of the types of dynamic processes that we all know occur within HR systems. However, they are novel in the sense that they specify how HR systems, policies, and practices may evolve over time – in essence, they operationalize the temporal relationships implied in Figure 5.1. In doing so, the temporal HR framework lays bare the many assumptions that exist within HR scholarship. If one uses the temporal framework developed in this chapter to review existing HR scholarship, it is apparent that the literature says almost nothing about any of the key temporal elements: *practice onset lags*, *y-lags*, *x-lags*, points of *asymptote*, or even rates of change. We cannot offer managers much guidance as to when the benefits of an HR practice may begin, how long they may last, or when they might decline. We don't know when it will be necessary to reinvest in a HR practice, reconfigure it, or end it. Simply put, we implement HR practices with an almost blind faith that they will produce positive returns for some extended period of time – according to the HR literature, these returns last indefinitely. Yet we all know this cannot be true. Therefore, the following section describes a research agenda for understanding time in HR.

Time for a change: a temporal research agenda for human resources

This chapter concludes by proposing an agenda to bring time more prominently into HR scholarship. To date, the HR field has been fixated with establishing a causal direction for HR practices and performance, a "which comes first" question. While important, we suggest that long-term understanding of HR systems, policies, and practices requires a different point of view, one that emphasizes long-term dynamic relationships among systems, policies, practices, resources, and performance. In the following sections we consider several of the main HR practice areas, and consider how they might change if adopting the temporal framework described in the prior section (we do not cover all HR practices

Table 5.1 Key research directions for a temporally based human resource literature

1. For any given HR practice, what is the specific: (a) practice onset lag, (b) duration, (c) functional form, or (d) asymptote?
2. To what extent are the functional forms of HR effects linear or nonlinear?
3. Are there limits or diminishing returns to HR interventions or investments? Where is the point of asymptote?
4. What contextual, social, or individual factors influence these temporal attributes?
5. How does the HR practice influence the speed or timing of the emergence of collective employee resources?
6. What is the lag between implementing an HR system or practice and changes to, or the emergence of, collective employee resources?
7. What is the lag between changes in collective employee resources and firm performance?

because some are already addressed by other chapters in this volume). Readers should recognize that the ideas forwarded in these sections are based more on the temporal framework described earlier than they are on existing theory or research. For each HR practice area, we focus on only a few research questions that we believe are most important – at this point in time, of course. Table 5.1 summarizes these questions.

Recruiting

The main purposes of recruiting are to attract a sufficient number of qualified candidates to the organization, and increase the odds that they will accept potential offers from the firm. Prior recruiting research has considered time in a fairly general way. For example, Barber (1998) discusses three stages of recruiting (generating applicants, maintaining applicants, influencing job choice), and the applicant processes and recruiting practices that may occur at each stage should differ. Another area where there has been some systematic research is with respect to applicant perceptions of time lags in learning of hiring decisions. Simply put, the more time that lapses between applying for a job and learning of an offer, the more negative the applicant's perceptions of the organization and hiring process (Ryan & Ployhart, 2000). However, lacking in either individual- or unit-level recruiting research is a serious integration of time.

We find the broader neglect of time in recruiting research curious because in practice, metrics such as "time-to-hire" are used to evaluate the effectiveness of recruiting practices. Time-to-hire metrics are the amount of time that passes between when an applicant applies for a job and when he or she is hired. Further, those who work as recruiters or recruiting vendors emphasize speed in recruiting and sourcing as a source of competitive advantage. Finally, social and professional media, such as LinkedIn and Facebook, are used to enhance the speed and customization of recruiting processes. Time is very much a prominent concern in real-world recruiting.

Time is central to recruiting because recruiting is a process that occurs dynamically between applicants and organizations. The manner in which applicants attend to information, weigh information, and make judgments and choices will differ depending on the stage of the recruiting process (Barber, 1998; Harold & Ployhart, 2008; Osborn, 1990). At early stages, applicants are seeking to narrow a large list of potential employers to those that fit their needs and preferences. After choosing which firms to apply to, applicants then must decide which to pursue formally through applying and completing the necessary selection systems. To the extent these systems are lengthy or seen as unfair or non-job-related, they may withdraw (Gilliland, 1993; Ryan & Ployhart, 2000). If the applicant continues through the selection process, then he or she must decide which offer to accept, and negotiate the terms of the offer. Thus, at each stage the applicant is attending to different types of information and using different judgment and decision-making strategies. In turn, organizations can and should customize their recruiting practices to better influence the applicant at each stage. Organizations should emphasize fit, brand, and culture information at early stages to enhance the odds that applicants will find them a desirable employer. At later stages, organizations should emphasize job-specific information, working conditions, and co-worker attributes as a means to distinguish the firm from competitors. For example, a longitudinal recruiting study found that applicant fit perceptions change over time, such that fit and compensation attributes become more important as applicants proceeded through the process (Harold & Ployhart, 2008).

A research agenda to incorporate time and recruiting would emphasize the relationships between time, quality of hire, and recruiting strategy and practices. First, how long do applicant perceptions last before they decay? Using the temporal framework noted earlier, how long is the practice onset lag? Research has increasingly emphasized the importance of fairness perceptions, employer image, and brand for attracting and maintaining applicants (Ryan & Ployhart, 2000). But what is the duration of these perceptions; at which point might they asymptote, and for how long will they persist? Hausknecht, Sturman, and Roberson (2011) provide an initial investigation of perceptions over time. Those in advertising know that consumer attention spans are short, and that organizations must constantly evolve and change their advertising to maintain customer attention. In a similar manner, how long do applicants maintain their perceptions of organizational brand? Given likely decay, at what point should an organization reinvest or retool their branding?

Second, many recruiters emphasize the importance of speed in recruiting. Time-to-hire metrics are key, and this is one of the reasons they are increasingly adopting social media. Yet time-to-hire is essentially a practice onset lag measure, and, as the temporal HR framework suggests, a relatively static one. There is essentially no scholarly research on this topic, and we know nothing (scientifically) about whether recruiting over social media truly does increase speed of hire or quality of hire. Likewise, is there a speed versus quality trade-off that exists in recruiting? How much time are applicants willing to invest in a hiring process? Do higher-quality applicants demand faster recruiting processes? Is there a point where a selection process may be seen as so fast that the quality of the process is questioned? And do all of these temporal effects differ by context, such as industry or culture?

Third, does the customization of organizational information at different stages truly influence or change applicant perceptions, and does it truly change applicant behavior and job choice? Meta-analyses suggest time factors into recruiting as well (Chapman, Uggerslev, Carroll, Piasentin, & Jones, 2005), but what is missing is truly longitudinal research that tracks applicants from beginning to end, and customizes the hiring strategy and policy for different stages. For example, if the effectiveness of different organizational and fit information truly changes across different stages, then one might propose a dynamic process. One could examine the onset, duration, and offset of culture, fit, or job information presented at each stage of the recruiting process, to determine whether the duration for perceptions is the same at each stage.

Selection

There are now 100 years of research on personnel selection, but only a small handful of studies that address temporal issues. This is interesting given that personnel selection is about the future: the ability of a firm to identify the KSAOs today that are needed for performance in the future (Binning & Barrett, 1989). Selection is inherently future-oriented. And while there is a reasonably large literature on the stability and durability of KSAOs (Ackerman, 1987), not a great deal of that research has filtered over to the personnel selection field. The main exception is research on dynamic criteria. Because selection is future-oriented, one has to have some evidence that performance criteria and KSAOs are reasonably stable. If they are not, then predictive relationships will vary over time and hence one's ability to select "the best employees" will be short-lived. After nearly two decades of debate about dynamic criteria, the consensus today is that while criteria may vary over time, the variability is not so great that the value of selection is diminished (Sonnentag & Frese, 2012). In a sense, the field seems to have moved on to other questions, but we believe there is still much to learn about time in personnel selection.

First, it is still unknown how long predictive relationships will last for different KSAOs, tasks, or dimensions of job performance (e.g., task, citizenship). We need to know how long predictive relationships should last, and their functional form over time. In selection practice, it is typical not to conduct a validation study unless an employee has been on the job for at least six months, but there is to our knowledge no scientific basis for this suggestion. It is clear that at least some predictive relationships can last years (Judge, Higgins, Thoresen, & Barrick, 1999; Schmidt & Hunter, 2004).

Second, given the rapid nature of workplace change, are the KSAOs needed for stable performance the same that are needed for adaptive performance? Murphy (1989; see also Ackerman, 1987) proposed that performance follows maintenance and transition periods. Maintenance performance is relatively stable and thus most influenced by personality, while transition performance requires new learning and is most influenced by cognitive ability. For example, some research suggests that when tasks change dramatically, those with greater cognitive ability may actually perform worse (Lang & Bliese, 2009; but see Beier & Oswald, 2012). One reason is because experts have developed automatic routines to free up cognitive resources; once the task changes these routines are no longer effective. Thus, as job performance changes due to environmental or task-related changes, predictive relationships can also change. The question becomes, how long does it take to recover from a change? How long are maintenance and transition periods for different types of jobs? With rapid workplace changes, is there any distinction between maintenance and transition?

Finally, to what extent do more valid selection practices contribute to human capital resources? Personnel selection practices should be a strong determinant of the formation and emergence of human capital resources. Selection practices determine the types of KSAOs admitted to the firm, and it is these KSAOs that are the origins of human capital resources (Ployhart, 2006; Ployhart & Moliterno, 2011; Schneider, 1987). Beyond consideration of criterion-related validity at the individual level, one may question how long it takes for a selection practice to create a human capital resource. What is the practice onset lag for resource creation? Do different types of selection practices also differ in their practice onset lags? Are some KSAOs able to be developed into human capital resources more quickly (i.e., steeper slopes)? For example, training programs may accelerate the emergence of malleable KSAOs such as knowledge or skills more quickly than generic KSAOs such as cognitive ability or personality.

Training and development

Relative to other HR practice areas, training and development have given more significant attention to temporal issues. One tends to see more frequent use of longitudinal designs and longitudinal experimental designs, and there is a greater concern about issues such as decay and nonlinear change over time (Aguinis & Kraiger, 2009; Noe & Peacock, 2002). For example, when discussing transfer of training, Baldwin and Ford (1988) note there are two main dimensions: maintenance and generalization. Maintenance is the duration of how long the newly learned material is applied and used on the job. Generalization is the degree to which the newly learned material is applied and used in other work contexts. Similarly, employee development is inherently about the future, and usually takes a longer time frame than does training (which tends to be more immediate and task-focused).

However, there are many areas where training and development can incorporate temporal issues more deeply. Adopting the temporal HR framework mentioned earlier, we believe there are three major areas. First, research needs to attend to the basic issues of training onset lags, duration, asymptote, and functional form of different training programs for specific KSAOs. For example, given two training programs, which one has the shortest onset lag? Which has the least amount of decay? What are the functional forms of the KSAOs affected by different training programs? Some of this work has been conducted in the laboratory, where it is easier to collect repeated measures from subjects (Kozlowski et al., 2001). However, more of this research needs to be conducted in field settings to capture potential nonlinearities and X- or Y-lags.

Second, employee development research often takes a long-term orientation, but its treatment of time is theoretically underdeveloped. For example, there are many theories of adult learning that can be used to better understand how time affects such developmental phenomena as stretch assignments, job rotations, and promotions. Kanfer and Ackerman (2004) offer a number of interesting functional forms to describe the nature of adult development. These functional forms should be tested, although we recognize that to do so requires decades of data that is probably only now becoming available. Other interesting questions ask whether the development needs of employees differ across their careers.

Finally, research needs to take a more strategic view of training and development. The vast majority of research has focused on individual outcomes. More recent research has begun to emphasize training within groups and teams (Ilgen, Hollenbeck, Johnson, & Jundt, 2005). What is missing is consideration of whether training or development practices actually influence collective employee resources – both their nature and emergence. For example, it is employee training that should most strongly affect the creation of firm-specific human capital (Hatch & Dyer, 2004). There is research that shows how the use of training may influence unit-level outcomes (Ployhart, Van Iddekinge & MacKenzie, 2011; Van Iddekinge et al., 2009), but not how training influences human capital resources. Further, this research can then begin to study the lags and duration of training programs on collective resource emergence. For example, do the effects of a new training program on human capital resources begin to decay? Is it sensible to propose an asymptote to training practices? Studying relationships dynamically, such as those illustrated in Figure 5.3, would provide considerable insight.

Compensation

Compensation serves to motivate, attract, and retain human resources (Lawler, 1981; Rynes, Gerhart, & Parks, 2005). For example, as compared to a fixed pay scheme, pay for performance is expected to select and motivate higher-performing employees (Cadsby & Tapon, 2007). Compensation research implicitly holds a temporal component. For example, agency (Jensen & Meckling, 1976) and tournament (Lazear & Rosen, 1981) theories take a longer-term view of rewards in organizations, and emphasize how employees may act over time in response to such rewards. Likewise, research has examined how the timing and nature of financial rewards may influence future behavior (e.g., Peterson & Luthans, 2006). However, as with the other HR practice areas, most of this research has not considered temporal issues very completely. The study of temporal issues in compensation research offers several interesting avenues for future research.

First, for any given compensation system, how long will it take for the system to influence employee behavior, cognition, and affect, how long will the effects last, and why? Research needs to examine how temporal components change across the stages of one's career. It also needs to examine how employees perceive pay growth, relative to actual changes in their pay or the pay of their co-workers. Not knowing the duration of any such effects, or when or how they might decay, introduces a great deal of risk into the HR plan.

Second, how does compensation affect dynamic behaviors and outcomes such as job search or turnover over time? Research is starting to examine collective (unit-level) turnover from a more dynamic temporal lens (Hausknecht & Holwerda, 2013; Nyberg & Ployhart, 2013), but this theoretical work raises a number of questions. For example, we need to know how different compensation programs affect the rate of turnover over time. Does making greater distinctions between employees in their pay contribute to greater or lesser amounts of turnover over time? Does compensation influence job search at different stages of recruiting?

Finally, research needs to examine the extent to which compensation programs affect the speed by which collective employee resources emerge. For example, resource emergence may occur more quickly with merit-based than seniority-based systems. How might compensation, collective turnover, collective employee resources, and unit performance co-evolve over time? The dynamic nature of these interrelationships, and the various lags that may exist between them, is an entirely new area for research.

Strategic HR

We noted earlier how strategic HR research has been largely fixated on establishing causal precedence between practices and unit performance. We believe this is still an important question to address. However, we consider this question in light of the HR temporal framework presented earlier, and, in doing so, suggest some complementary paths for future research.

First, it is going to be difficult to definitively answer whether practices or performance comes first because they are dynamically and reciprocally related. Untangling causal direction in dynamic relationships can be difficult (DeShon, 2012). The question should perhaps not be "which comes first?" but rather "how do they co-evolve?" For example, there might be different environmental conditions (e.g., prerecession vs. recession periods) that contribute to HR practices leading or lagging behind unit performance, and vice versa. Similarly, how do shocks or changes in one system (e.g., collective employee resources) influence changes in the other system (e.g., performance)? Causal direction implies a static view; understanding a dynamic relationship requires different theory and methods.

Second, future research should focus more on lags between the implementation of a practice and changes in collective employee resources and unit performance. Such a framework is illustrated in Figure 5.3, and would create a fairly dramatic shift in the nature of strategic HR research. For example, does a certain HR system or practice shorten the resource lag, performance lag, or increase the speed (rate) of resource emergence, relative to a different HR system? Or, looking from the other direction, how long does it take for firm profits to translate into changes in HR? Knowing when the effects of HR policies or practices will influence collective resources or performance would make the strategic HR literature not only richer theoretically but also more compelling practically.

Finally, research should seek to understand the duration and functional form of HR practice effects on resources and performance. We need to know the duration of high-performance HR system effects on collective resources and unit performance. One might propose that practices that are more synergistic contribute to longer-duration benefits because they are mutually reinforcing. In contrast, misalignment among HR practices may contribute to decay or a lower asymptote. As a resource evolves over time, might different practices have a differential impact on its functional form (e.g., Sirmon, Hitt, & Ireland, 2007)? For example, training may affect human capital resource emergence more quickly than recruitment.

Conclusions

The field of HR is out of time. Although the field has a lot to say about how to increase the individual and collective behavior, cognition, affect, and motivation of employees, it has almost nothing to say about (a) how long it will take for the effects to occur, (b) how long they will last, or (c) how they will vary over time. We believe that more formally incorporating temporal issues into the study of HR topics will only serve to make it more interesting from a theoretical perspective, and more actionable from a practical perspective. Both of these are positive outcomes, and we hope the temporal HR framework proposed in this chapter offers a means to help stimulate change.

References

Ackerman, P. L. (1987). Individual differences in skill learning: An integration of psychometric and information processing perspectives. *Psychological Bulletin, 102,* 3–27.
Adler, P. S., & Kwon, S. W. (2002). Social capital: prospects for a new concept. *Academy of Management Review, 27,* 17–40.
Aguinis, H., & Kraiger, K. (2009). Benefits of training and development for individuals and teams, organizations, and society. *Annual Review of Psychology, 60,* 451–474.
Baldwin, T. T., & Ford, J. K. (1988). Transfer of training: A review and directions for future research. *Personnel Psychology, 41,* 63–105.
Barber, A. E. (1998). *Recruiting employees: Individual and organizational perspectives.* Thousand Oaks, CA: SAGE.
Becker, B., & Gerhart, B. (1996). The impact of human resource management on organizational performance: Progress and prospects. *Academy of Management Journal, 39,* 779–801.
Becker, B. E., & Huselid, M. A. (2006). Strategic human resources management: Where do we go from here? *Journal of Management, 32,* 898–925.

Becker, B. E., Huselid, M., Pickus, P., & Spratt, M. (1997). HR as a source of shareholder value: Research and recommendations. *Human Resources Management, 36,* 39–47.

Beier, M. E., & Oswald, F. L. (2012). Is cognitive ability a liability? A critique and future research agenda on skilled performance. *Journal of Experimental Psychology: Applied, 18,* 331–345.

Binning, J. F., & Barrett, G. V. (1989). Validity of personnel decisions: A conceptual analysis of the inferential and evidential bases. *Journal of Applied Psychology, 74,* 478–494.

Birdi, K., Clegg, C., Patterson, M., Robinson, A., Stride, C. B., Wall, T. D., & Wood, S. J. (2008). The impact of human resource and operational management practices on company productivity: A longitudinal study. *Personnel Psychology, 61,* 467–501.

Boudreau, J. W. (2010). *Retooling HR: Using proven business tools to make better decisions about talent.* Boston, MA: Harvard Business School Press.

Boudreau, J. W., & Ramstad, P. M. (2003). Strategic industrial and organizational psychology and the role of utility analysis models. In W. Borman, D. Ilgen, & R. Klimoski (Eds.), *Handbook of psychology* (Vol. 12, pp. 193–221). New York: Wiley.

Boudreau, J. W., & Ramstad, P. M. (2007). *Beyond HR: The new science of human capital.* Boston, MA: Harvard Business Press.

Bowen, D., & Ostroff, C. (2004). Understanding HRM-firm performance linkages: The role of the strength of the HRM system. *Academy of Management Review, 29,* 203–221.

Breaugh, J. A. (2013). Employee recruitment. *Annual Review of Psychology,* 64, 389–416.

Cadsby, C. B., & Tapon, F. (2007). Sorting and incentive effects of pay for performance: An experimental investigation. *Academy of Management Journal, 50,* 387–405.

Capelli, P., & Neumark, D. (2001). Do "high performance" work practices improve establishment-level outcomes? *Industrial and Labor Relations Review, 54,* 737–775.

Cascio, W. F., & Aguinis, H. (2008). Research in industrial and organizational psychology from 1963 to 2007: Changes, choices, and trends. *Journal of Applied Psychology, 93,* 1062–1081.

Cascio, W. F., & Boudreau, J. W. (2011). *Investing in People* (2nd ed.). Upper Saddle River, NJ: Pearson Education.

Chapman, D. S., Uggerslev, K. L., Carroll, S. A., Piasentin, K. A., & Jones, D. A. (2005). Applicant attraction to organizations and job choice: A meta-analytic review of the correlates of recruiting outcomes. *Journal of Applied Psychology, 90,* 928–944.

Crook, T. R., Todd, S. Y., Combs, J. G., Woehr, D. J., & Ketchen Jr., D. J. (2011). Does human capital matter? A meta-analysis of the relationship between human capital and firm performance. *Journal of Applied Psychology, 96,* 443–456.

Delery, J. E. (1998). Issues of fit in strategic human resource management: Implications for research. *Human Resource Management Review, 8,* 289–310.

DeShon, R. P. (2012). Multivariate dynamics in organizational science. In S.W.J. Kozlowski (Ed.), *The Oxford handbook of organizational psychology* (pp. 117–142). New York: Oxford University Press.

Gerhart, B. (2005). Human resources and business performance: Findings, unanswered questions, and an alternative approach. *Management Revue,* 16, 174–185.

Gilliland, S. W. (1993). The perceived fairness of selection systems: An organizational justice perspective. *Academy of Management Review, 18,* 694–734.

Harold, C. M., & Ployhart, R. E. (2008). What do applicants want? Examining changes in attribute judgments over time. *Journal of Occupational and Organizational Psychology, 81,* 191–218.

Hatch, N. W., & Dyer, J. H. (2004). Human capital and learning as a source of sustainable competitive advantage. *Strategic Management Journal, 25,* 1155–1178.

Hausknecht, J. P., & Holwerda, J. A. (2013). When does employee turnover matter? Dynamic member configurations, productive capacity, and collective performance. *Organization Science, 24,* 210–225.

Hausknecht, J. P., Sturman, M. C., & Roberson, Q. M. (2011). Justice as a dynamic construct: Effects of individual trajectories on distal work outcomes. *Journal of Applied Psychology, 96,* 872–880.

Huselid, M. A. (1995). The impact of human resource management practices on turnover, productivity, corporate financial performance. *Academy of Management Journal, 38,* 635–672.

Ichniowski, C., Shaw, K., & Prennushi, G. (1997). The effects of human resource management practices on productivity: A study of steel finishing lines. *American Economic Review, 87,* 291–313.

Ilgen, D. R., Hollenbeck, J. R., Johnson, M., & Jundt, D. (2005). Teams in organizations: From input-process-output models to IMOI models. *Annual Review of Psychology, 56,* 517–543.

Jackson, S. E., Chuang, C. H., Harden, E. E., & Jiang, Y. (2006). Toward developing human resource management systems for knowledge-intensive teamwork. In J. Martocchio (Ed.), *Research in personnel and human resources management* (Vol. 25, pp. 27–70). Boston: Elsevier JAI.

Jensen, M., & Meckling, W. (1976). Theory of the firm: Managerial behavior, agency costs, and ownership structure. *Journal of Financial Economics, 3,* 305–360.

Judge, T. A., Higgins, C. A., Thoresen, C. J., & Barrick, M. R. (1999). The big five personality traits, general mental ability, and career success across the life span. *Personnel Psychology, 52,* 621–652.

Kanfer, R., & Ackerman, P. L. (2004). Aging, adult development, and work motivation. *Academy of Management Review, 29,* 440–458.

Kozlowski, S. W., Gully, S. M., Brown, K. G., Salas, E., Smith, E. M., & Nason, E. R. (2001). Effects of training goals and goal orientation traits on multidimensional training outcomes and performance adaptability. *Organizational Behavior and Human Decision Processes, 85,* 1–31.

Kozlowski, S. W., & Klein, K. J. (2000). A multilevel approach to theory and research in organizations: Contextual, temporal, and emergent processes. In K. J. Kline & S. W. Kozlowski (Eds.), *Multilevel theory, research, and methods in organizations* (pp. 3–90). San Francisco: Jossey-Bass.

Lang, J. W., & Bliese, P. D. (2009). General mental ability and two types of adaptation to unforeseen change: Applying discontinuous growth models to the task-change paradigm. *Journal of Applied Psychology, 94,* 411–428.

Lawler, E. E. (1981). *Pay and organization development.* Reading, MA: Addison-Wesley.

Lazear, E. P., and Rosen, S. (1981). Rank-order tournaments as optimum labor contracts. *Journal of Political Economy, 89,* 841–864.

Lepak, D. P., Liao, H., Chung, Y., & Harden, E. E. (2006). A conceptual review of human resource management systems in strategic human resource management research. *Research in Personnel and Human Resources Management, 25,* 217–271.

Liao, H., & Chuang, A. (2004). A multilevel investigation of factors influencing employee service performance and customer outcomes. *Academy of Management Journal, 47,* 41–58.

Mitchell, T. R., & James, L. R. (2001). Building better theory: Time and the specification of when things happen. *Academy of Management Review, 26,* 530–547.

Murphy, K. R. (1989). Is the relationship between cognitive ability and job performance stable over time? *Human Performance, 2,* 183–200.

Noe, R. A., & Peacock, M. (2002). *Employee training and development.* Boston, MA: McGraw-Hill/Irwin.

Nyberg, A. J., & Ployhart, R. E. (2013). Context-emergent turnover (CET) theory: A theory of collective turnover. *Academy of Management Review, 38,* 109–131.

Osborn, D. P. (1990). A reexamination of the organizational choice process. *Journal of Vocational Behavior, 36,* 45–60.

Ostroff, C., & Bowen, D. E. (2000). Moving HR to a higher level: HR practices and organizational effectiveness. In K. J. Klein & S. W. J. Kozlowski (Eds.), *Multilevel theory, research, and methods in organizations: Foundations, extensions, and new directions* (pp. 211–266). San Francisco, CA: Jossey-Bass.

Peterson, S. J., & Luthans, F. (2006). The impact of financial and nonfinancial incentives on business-unit outcomes over time. *Journal of Applied Psychology, 91,* 156–165.

Ployhart, R. E. (2006). Staffing in the 21st century: New challenges and strategic opportunities. *Journal of Management, 32,* 868–897.

Ployhart, R. E., & Moliterno, T. P. (2011). Emergence of the human capital resource: A multilevel model. *Academy of Management Review, 36,* 127–150.

Ployhart, R. E., & Vandenberg, R. J. (2010). Longitudinal research: The theory, design, and analysis of change. *Journal of Management, 36,* 94–120.

Ployhart, R. E., Van Iddekinge, C. H., & MacKenzie, W. I. (2011). Acquiring and developing human capital in service contexts: The interconnectedness of human capital resources. *Academy of Management Journal, 54,* 353–368.

Roe, R. A. (2008). Time in applied psychology: The study of "what happens" rather than "what is." *European Psychologist, 13,* 37–52.

Ryan, A. M., & Ployhart, R. E. (2000). Applicants' perceptions of selection procedures and decisions: A critical review and agenda for the future. *Journal of Management, 26,* 565–606.

Rynes, S. L., Gerhart, B., & Parks, L. (2005). Personnel psychology: Performance evaluation and pay for performance. *Annual Review of Psychology, 56,* 571–600.

Schmidt, F. L., & Hunter, J. (2004). General mental ability in the world of work: Occupational attainment and job performance. *Journal of Personality and Social Psychology, 86*(1), 162–173.

Schneider, B. (1987). The people make the place. *Personnel Psychology, 40,* 437–454.

Schneider, B., Ehrhart, M. G., & Macey, W. H. (1990). Organizational climate and culture. *Annual Review of Psychology, 64,* 361–368.

Schuler, R. S. (1992). Strategic human resources management: Linking the people with the strategic needs of the business. *Organizational Dynamics, 21,* 18–32.

Sirmon, D. G., Hitt, M. A., & Ireland, R. D. (2007). Managing firm resources in dynamic environments to create value: Looking inside the black box. *Academy of Management Review, 32,* 273–292.

Sonnentag, S., & Frese, M. (2012). Dynamic performance. In S. W. J. Kozlowski (Ed.), *Oxford handbook of industrial and organizational psychology* (pp. 548–578). Cambridge, MA: Oxford University Press.

Van Iddekinge, C. H., Ferris, G. R., Perrewé, P. L., Perryman, A. A., Blass, F. R., & Heetderks, T. D. (2009). Effects of selection and training on unit-level performance over time: A latent growth modeling approach. *Journal of Applied Psychology, 94,* 829–843.

Wall, T. D., & Wood, S. J. (2005). The romance of human resource management and business performance and the case for big science. *Human Relations, 58,* 1–34.

Wright, P. M., & Boswell, W. R. (2002). Desegregating HRM: A review and synthesis of micro and macro human resource management. *Journal of Management, 28,* 248–276.

Wright, P. M., Dunford, B. B., & Snell, S. A. (2001). Human resources and the resource-based view of the firm. *Journal of Management, 27,* 701–721.

Wright, P. M., Dyer, L. D., & Takla, M. G. (1999). What's next? Key findings from the 1999 State-of-the-Art & Practice study. *Human Resource Planning, 22,* 12–20.

Wright, P. M., Gardner, T. M., Moynihan, L. M., & Allen, M. R. (2005). The relationship between HR practices and firm performance: Examining causal order. *Personnel Psychology, 58,* 409–446.

Wright, P. M., & Haggerty, J. J. (2005). Missing variables in theories of strategic human resource management: Time, cause, and individuals. *Management Revue, 16,* 164–173.

Wright, P. M., & McMahan, G. C. (1992). Theoretical perspectives for strategic human resource management. *Journal of Management, 18,* 295–320.

Wright, P. M., & Snell, S. A. (1998). Toward a unifying framework for exploring fit and flexibility in strategic human resource management. *Academy of Management Review, 23,* 756–772.

Zacharatos, A., Barling, J., & Iverson, R. D. (2005). High-performance work systems and occupational safety. *Journal of Applied Psychology, 90,* 77–84.

6 Conceptualizing time in entrepreneurship

Brett Anitra Gilbert

Introduction

Entrepreneurial activities generate new solutions for organizational or societal problems, and the founding of companies to support those solutions. In fact, with the introduction of a given solution to the marketplace, other solutions emerge as substitutes for initial solutions (Anderson & Tushman, 1990; Eckhardt & Shane, 2003; Tripsas, 1997; Tushman & Anderson, 1986). The substitution process places an indeterminate time limit on marketplace solutions, and with each new generation of products the cycle is repeated. Foundings also vary depending on the group of individuals considered – for example, with ethnic groups showing different propensities for entrepreneurial endeavors (Kerr, 2008). A recent Kauffman Foundation report (Fairlie, 2011) presents evidence of the constancy of new firm startups over time, and shows the process changes with the state of the economy, which has rendered foundings higher or lower during certain time periods. One important conclusion about the entrepreneurial dynamic is that it varies across time and people, and is, thus, inherently bound by time considerations.

Ancona, Goodman, Lawrence & Tushman (2001, p. 646) suggest that time is a construct that encompasses "timing, pace, cycles, rhythm, flow, temporal orientation and cultural meanings." It provides understanding of factors that influence opportunity perception, anticipation and corresponding pursuit (Bird & West, 1997). In the entrepreneurship process, time is especially important because opportunities are not constant over time – their attractiveness to the market can change on short notice (Moroz & Hindle, 2012). There is also a unique and individual timing aspect to entrepreneurship (Eckhardt & Shane, 2003), in that it requires the right people, ideas and market combining at the right time. Despite this fact, the entrepreneurship literature reflects only a limited number of studies that examine time contextual factors and their influence on entrepreneurial outcomes. For example, some research examined how entrepreneurs allocated time before founding a company (Levesque & MacCrimmon, 1997). The entrepreneurship process necessitates significant time commitment both before and after a venture is initiated. Thus, how individuals spend their time preparing to become an entrepreneur is thought to hold important implications for how the venture unfolds.

Other studies (e.g., Cooper, Ramachandran & Schoorman, 1996; McCarthy, Krueger & Schoenecker, 1990) have examined entrepreneurs' actions after the venture is founded to determine how they allocate their time to key activities involved in running a venture. They suggest that certain behavioral dynamics occur during specific points in time to influence entrepreneurial outcomes. These behaviors are understudied in extant entrepreneurship literature, likely due to the difficulties associated with chronicling all activities involved in creating a venture. Still, other strands of research argue or show that firm outcomes change depending on the environmental context that is faced (Sirmon, Hitt, Ireland & Gilbert, 2011; Yu, Gilbert & Oviatt, 2011). Context relates to relevant facts, events and points of view (Rousseau & Fried, 2001) that define the "situational opportunities and constraints" (Johns, 2006, p. 386). Environmental contexts are not constant (Haveman, Habinek & Goodman, 2012). They are dynamic with the potential to generate significant benefits or grave consequences for firms. In fact, over time, industries evolve in such a way that significant contextual shifts occur with influences on the firms operating within them (Navis & Glynn, 2010). Some (e.g., Moroz & Hindle, 2012) have even suggested that a firm can never be separated from its unique context. And yet the context surrounding entrepreneurial firms, if mentioned at all in extant research, is more often treated as a peripheral, static factor (Busenitz & Lau, 1996; Gartner, 1985) rather than a central, dynamic influence on entrepreneurial outcomes.

The purpose of this chapter is to enhance understanding of the time factors that influence entrepreneurial outcomes. Specific goals of this research include incorporating understanding of when entrepreneurial endeavors are undertaken, the activities involved, for how long they endure and how often they are experienced. The chapter primarily focuses on the entrepreneur as the catalyst for entrepreneurial change, and then addresses venture and industry creation as two key outcomes of entrepreneurial behaviors. It seeks to highlight the centrality of time – and in particular timing, pace, duration and overall flow – in entrepreneurial outcomes. Each section concludes with recommendations for future research and methodological considerations for integrating time into entrepreneurship research.

When entrepreneurship happens

Entrepreneurship is conceptualized as the discovery and exploitation of opportunities to bring new solutions to the marketplace (Shane & Venkataraman, 2000). Conversations about entrepreneurship often revolve around the question of whether entrepreneurs are made or born (e.g., Brockhaus & Horwitz, 1986; Shefsky, 1994). Many feel that entrepreneurial traits are ones you either inherently possess (i.e., are born with) or do not. Anecdotal evidence of pioneering entrepreneurs (e.g., Steve Jobs), combined with empirical work in entrepreneurship (e.g., Haveman et al., 2012, which reported on an eight-year-old founder of a magazine), illustrates why the question exists. Some individuals appear to epitomize the characteristics that are generally associated with entrepreneurs. This characterization has birthed a strand of research that seeks to delineate the individual personality traits and family characteristics that separate entrepreneurs from nonentrepreneurs (Ardichvili, Cardozo & Ray, 2003; Busenitz & Lau, 1996; Gartner, 1985; Shane, 2003).

Gartner (1985) developed a theoretical framework of individual, organizational, environmental and process factors associated with entrepreneurship. His individual factors focused on attributes such as age, education, entrepreneurial parents, job satisfaction, locus of control, need for achievement, previous work experience and risk-taking propensity. One interesting observation about these factors is that characteristics such as entrepreneurial parents may more or less remain static once an entrepreneur reaches adulthood; however, other attributes have potential to change as the individual matures and becomes positioned in new contexts that provide new opportunities (Eckhardt & Shane, 2003). New contexts present opportunities that may influence a decision to consider entrepreneurship. Moreover, many individuals first work for other companies, and essentially engage in entrepreneurship as if there is an appointed time for them to embark upon that journey. Therefore, the decision for or against becoming an entrepreneur may be fluid rather than static, such that it occurs at various points in an individual's life.

Consider for example, the remarkable story of New Jersey's Crowley family. This family documented in the movie *Extraordinary Measures*, about a father's quest to find a medical treatment for his children. In 1998, John Crowley's two youngest children were diagnosed with Pompe disease, which is an incurable neuromuscular ailment in which glycogen builds up and weakens the muscles, heart, liver and nervous system. It is almost always fatal. The children were 15 months and a few days old when diagnosed. Crowley himself was 33 at the time of the diagnosis. Crowley and his family relocated to Princeton, NJ, to be closer to specialists for Pompe treatments. Having MBA and JD degrees, he held management positions with pharmaceutical giant Bristol-Myers Squibb, but his frustrations with the slow development of treatments, and the corresponding loss of time as the disease progressed in his children, motivated Crowley to leave his position with Bristol-Myers Squibb to join Novazyme Pharmaceuticals, a biotechnology startup founded by a scientist who was developing an experimental treatment for Pompe disease. Novazyme was later acquired by Genzyme Corporation, at the time the world's third largest biotechnology company. Under Crowley's leadership of the global Genzyme Pompe disease research program, a treatment was finalized and in January of 2003 his children received the lifesaving treatment. Feeling he was better suited for the entrepreneurial lifestyle, Crowley continued on this path, becoming a serial entrepreneur, and subsequently running several biotech companies.

Another example of an individual who became an entrepreneur through perhaps an unconventional trajectory is Mayor Cory Booker of Newark, New Jersey. In 2012 at the age of 43, Mayor Booker cofounded a venture called #waywire – a video social media platform that offers the millennial generation the opportunity to voice issues of importance to them. He and cofounders Sarah Ross and Nathan Richardson recognized that the media oligarchy had shut out the voices of the upcoming generation. The #waywire platform was born with backing from prominent media personalities such as Oprah Winfrey and Gayle King. Despite being cofounder of a company, the mayor continues his full-time political pursuits, most recently announcing a prospective 2014 run for US Senate. These individuals who do not explicitly set out to become entrepreneurs, yet become motivated to pursue the lifestyle through their commitment to solving a problem, force us to consider the different flow and timing into entrepreneurship.

A limited understanding of what motivates individuals to become entrepreneurs at the time when they do restricts critical insights into the entrepreneurship cycle. Some might refer to individuals like Crowley and Booker as "accidental entrepreneurs," who enter entrepreneurship as a result of their connection to the problem and desire to identify a solution to resolve it above all else (Shah & Tripsas, 2007). These individuals achieved fit with the environment. Edwards, Cable, Williamson, Schurer Lambert and Shipp (2006) acknowledge that fit between the person and the environment and his or her perceptions of fit with the environment are important for expected outcomes to occur. The literature on person-environment fit is important for understanding entrepreneurship as it suggests that certain environments are more likely to lead to entrepreneurship, and entrepreneurs must perceive entrepreneurship as a viable and desired outcome if they will pursue it. An entrepreneurial event is unlikely to occur if an individual never enters the environment that is a fit for them. Moreover, Ancona, Goodman et al. (2001, p. 652) argue that "while the nature of work does not predict exactly when the outcomes are likely to appear, it does indicate that there will be differences across workgroups and gives us some idea of why these differences may occur." Personal work experiences likely influence the nature and form of entrepreneurship.

Corroborating this conclusion is prior entrepreneurship research which suggests that entrepreneurs perceive opportunity according to their background, skill set and personal interests (Eckhardt & Shane, 2003). For example, Mayor Booker's background in politics and personal connections with individuals in media made it possible for him and his cofounders to create a media-related venture that addressed the perceived opportunity. As Ardichvili et al. (2003) suggest, only certain individuals can pursue some opportunities because of idiosyncratic knowledge stocks, social networks and capabilities. Thus, entrepreneurial opportunities are unique because of their interrelationship with individual backgrounds and interests, and the fit between entrepreneur abilities and opportunity occurs only when the individual's abilities are in place. Therefore, every opportunity is not available to every aspiring entrepreneur (Moroz & Hindle, 2012). In fact, unique educational and social backgrounds have been found to influence the available resources and the opportunities that entrepreneurs pursued (Haveman et al., 2012).

The ever-evolving nature of the person-environment fit positions individuals in different contexts, which can influence their readiness for entrepreneurship over time. Therefore, this chapter is grounded in the premise that individual entrepreneurship is fluid, and occurs under unique timing considerations that are important for advancing understanding of entrepreneurship. By integrating the concept of time into our understanding of the emergence of entrepreneurs, their ventures and accompanying industries, this chapter explicates several additional factors that may be relevant to understanding the entrepreneurship process.

Time and entrepreneur emergence

The prior anecdotes showed how each individual's background, knowledge and connections enabled him to perceive demand for the solutions he brought to the market. It is clear their skills were well-matched to market needs (Edwards et al., 2006). However, because the fit required unique personal, educational and knowledge connections, the opportunities would not have existed until these characteristics aligned. An individual may differ as much over a period of time as two individuals might differ at the same point in time (Roe, 2008). Therefore, to understand entrepreneur emergence, it is important to address why entrepreneurs pursue ventures in the time period they do, rather than in a past or future time period (e.g., Shipp, Edwards & Lambert, 2009). Life experiences make some people more or less willing to forgo current satisfaction in exchange for future goals (Fried, Grant, Levi, Hadani & Slowik, 2007). In other words, they influence temporal focus such that events during one time period can influence an individual's intentions – the "state of mind directing a person's attention, experience and behavior toward a specific object or method of behaving" to become entrepreneurs (e.g., Bird, 1992, p. 11).

The importance of an opportunity influences how it is perceived in the present (Edwards et al., 2006), and whether an individual chooses to become an entrepreneur. For example, in the case of John Crowley, joining the biotechnology startup when he did was critical because his children's lives depended on the drug it would produce. The foray into entrepreneurship was essentially triggered by a contextual event (e.g., Johns, 2006). The intersection of intentions, importance and opportunity may yield significant understanding regarding why specific opportunities are pursued while others are not. As the Crowley example illustrates, his personal experiences due to impacted family members and his experience in the pharmaceutical industry uniquely qualified him to pursue the biotechnology opportunities that he did. Because the factors that are important to people change over time, it is necessary to assess the factors that are important to individuals during seasons of their lives.

There are clear differences in the pace and sequencing of individual forays into entrepreneurship (Ancona, Okhuysen, & Perlow, 2001). It is apparent that entrepreneurs do not follow a clear career trajectory (e.g., Super & Hall, 1978). And yet very little is known about the norms that apply to the entrepreneurial career (Fried et al., 2007). Substantial evidence corroborates that individuals become entrepreneurs at different ages. For some it happens in their teens or twenties, and others in their thirties, forties and beyond. It is important to determine the differences in the onset of entrepreneurial behaviors as well as their duration in the process (Roe, 2008). Aside from mentions in popular press and books devoted to their existence (e.g., Cathers, 2003), little scholarly attention has been devoted to understanding teen entrepreneurs. In the teen case, it is unlikely that prior work experience or potentially even knowledge drives the decision to become entrepreneurs and other factors are salient. For older ages, more attention has been given to the context surrounding the decision (e.g., Johns, 2006).

Most recent empirical studies in particular have focused on social networks as influential determinants of whether an individual becomes an entrepreneur (Busenitz & Lau, 1996). For example, Nanda and Sørensen (2010) found that having coworkers who were previously entrepreneurs influenced individual decisions to become entrepreneurs. Similarly, Obschonka, Goethner, Silbereisen and Cantner (2012) recognized that an individual's social identity, particularly with respect to colleagues, influenced his or her entrepreneurial intentions. Social networks expose individuals to new opportunities that exist, and also provide access to resources that are needed to exploit an opportunity (Zaheer & Bell, 2005). Through social networks, individuals perceive entrepreneurship as more or less viable (Eckhardt & Shane, 2003).

Knowledge, networks and capabilities are not static characteristics. Each changes over time with job changes and moves to new neighborhoods, churches, fitness centers or social clubs. New professional or social networks generate the potential for individuals to become exposed to other entrepreneurs or those who hold entrepreneurial intentions. There is also potential for one's experiences with these characteristics to affect an individual's orientation toward the past, the future or the present (Shipp et al., 2009) because networks are not emotionally neutral. They invoke positive or negative reactions in individuals that ultimately carry over into subsequent time periods (ibid.). Therefore, as individuals progress through life, their opportunities and therefore intentions to become entrepreneurs have the potential to change. These factors could explain why Brockhaus and Horwitz (1986), for example, who reviewed the psychology of the entrepreneur, suggested there are few personality traits that differentiate entrepreneurs from the general population.

Exposure to networks may be important for understanding whether an individual chooses an entrepreneurial career (Ancona, Goodman et al., 2001). This perspective may partially explain the occurrence of serial entrepreneurs, who are individuals who sometimes found several businesses – sometimes concurrently but more often subsequently in time. Little attention has been given to understanding the different opportunities that serial entrepreneurs have pursued and how those opportunities change with time. Instead, much of the work on serial entrepreneurs focuses on cognitive differences between them and novice entrepreneurs (e.g., Westhead, Ucbasaran & Wright, 2005). Cognitive processing of entrepreneurs has gained strong traction in the literature as a factor that differentiates entrepreneurs from others. As individuals gain experience their cognitive processing changes, which means that the longer an individual remains an entrepreneur, the more his or her way of thinking changes. In other words, duration matters in entrepreneurship (cf. Ancona, Goodman et al., 2001). However, we know little about how long entrepreneurs remain in a given entrepreneurial endeavor; therefore, it is unclear how long it takes this thought process to emerge.

Cognitive processes lead entrepreneurs to pursue opportunities (e.g., Gregoire & Shepherd, 2012; Pech & Cameron, 2006). Communicated information differences about technologies can influence whether an entrepreneur perceives it as an opportunity (Gregoire & Shepherd, 2012). This evidence supports the idiosyncratic nature of a given individual's opportunity recognition but also validates the influential roles of information flows and knowledge stocks in the entrepreneurship process. Individuals who increase their knowledge of markets and opportunities have greater potential to make entrepreneurial connections. Therefore, opportunities that individuals perceive are not stagnant in time. They evolve as the information an individual receives evolves, which again illustrates that timing matters for entrepreneur emergence.

An agenda for advancing research on time considerations in entrepreneur emergence

As the aforementioned discussion suggests, a given individual's knowledge levels increase, work experience deepens and social networks change. Experiences across these factors can influence a person's temporal focus (e.g., Shipp et al., 2009), and corresponding intentions for how she manages her life, and whether she chooses to become an entrepreneur. Much of prior research has been static in nature, with snapshots taken at one point in time as determinants of whether an individual possesses the criteria generally associated with entrepreneurs. Failure to account for the temporal nature of these characteristics renders a distorted view for understanding of the phenomenon (Roe, 2008). As the focus of research on entrepreneurs in recent years has moved away from examining individual traits and moved toward examining behaviors, our methodological approach must also move away from static approaches to one that accounts for the dynamic nature of individual learning, growth and behaviors.

Therefore, research must do more to explicate the context behind the development of entrepreneurial behaviors (cf. Johns, 2006) – for example, the length of time before the behaviors were engaged (cf. Ancona, Goodman et al., 2001; Ancona, Okhuysen & Perlow, 2001), how long it took and how long it lasted (cf. Roe, 2008), such that our methodological designs appropriately reflect these unique timing conditions. This approach is especially important because some entrepreneurship-associated characteristics may require accumulation, such that a threshold level is necessary before entrepreneurial intentions and corresponding behaviors emerge. Thus, the different ways that individuals become entrepreneurs merit additional attention. For some individuals, the idea for a new product or technology is conceived through work experience, which was the case for the founders of Google, who conceived of the idea during their work as research assistants to a professor at Stanford University. The field must address the question of how much work experience is required before one builds the experience that enables her to venture out on her own. For others, entrepreneurial ideas emerge through educational training, such as when Dr. William Canfield, who studied biochemistry and molecular biology at the University of Washington School of Medicine, later went on to cofound Novazyme, the company that developed early treatments for Pompe disease. We must understand how much education produces such results and for what types of firms varying levels of education matter. In other cases, companies are founded simply from personal interest in or experience with a problem, such as with John Crowley and Mayor Booker (Eckhardt & Shane, 2003). There is a need for research that explicates the drivers that elevate interests or experiences in given points in time such that individuals become motivated to build businesses around them.

The differing origins for company foundings suggest two additional implications that should be reflected in future empirical models. First, it is possible that knowledge, interests, networks and experiences have nonlinear rather than linear effects on the decision to become an entrepreneur. Developing understanding of the necessary levels of these attributes and the configurations of these attributes across groups of entrepreneurs may begin to enhance understanding of not only why some individuals elect to become entrepreneurs while others do not, but also why some entrepreneurs succeed while others fail. The second implication is the possibility that entrepreneurial intentions assume different trajectories that influence entrepreneurial outcomes. For example, ventures motivated by work experience, educational training or personal interest are likely to take on different forms. Future research on emerging entrepreneurs should give explicit attention to determining the differences in terms of when entrepreneurship is engaged and the context surrounding venture founding. These insights can provide valuable information to the field in terms of timing triggers for entrepreneurship and our ability to influence who chooses to engage in the entrepreneurial process.

Thus, the specific questions that must be addressed *are how much and what type of work experience, interests, knowledge and social networks* lead to identification of an opportunity in the marketplace? *How much and what type of education* are required for opportunity recognition? And *how much time is generally invested* before an individual has developed the necessary characteristics and is then willing to invest time and resources toward solving problems? There may also be interactions between work experience, educational and personal interest factors that lead an individual to exploit a recognized opportunity. Therefore, understanding how these factors combine would provide unique insights to the field. Addressing these questions requires specific attention to the underlying knowledge base for companies and the entrepreneur's background in order to determine when the entrepreneur's work experience, life experiences or interests drive interest in venture creation. It will also require explicit questioning with respect to the length of time that is spent acquiring education, work experience or life experience before a venture is engaged. The timing of an individual's foray into entrepreneurship may serve as a proxy for the threshold levels that determine when an individual is ready to pursue entrepreneurial ventures. Insights into what that level is hold the potential to enhance understanding of the fit of the individual with the opportunity (e.g., Edwards et al., 2006), and to provide more in-depth understanding of the flow into entrepreneurship.

These questions are important for scholarly inquiry because seldom does our research consider the possibility that an individual who is not an entrepreneur during a study's time period may become an entrepreneur before her lifetime ends. As Mitchell and James (2001) acknowledged, some predictors can require time to unfold before they are able to influence a given outcome. Extant literature often acknowledges the different motivations for venturing (e.g., Obschonka et al., 2012), yet rarely considers that timing for becoming entrepreneurs may differ. Eckhardt and Shane (2003) presented compelling arguments that different types of opportunities are available for individuals to pursue. If different motivations and timing apply, then by implication, entrepreneurship should not be viewed as a moment in time proposition, where people either are or are not entrepreneurs. Instead, our theorizing should reflect the possibility that some individuals may choose to become entrepreneurs at later points in their lives. In other words, there may be time lags to an individual's initiation of entrepreneurship (cf. Ancona, Goodman et al., 2001; Mitchell & James, 2001). Thus, in the same way that companies and industries endure life cycles, individuals may endure cycles in which they are more or less likely to become entrepreneurs. Identifying the norms (cf. Ancona, Goodman et al., 2001; Ancona, Okhuysen et al., 2001) that lead individuals to start ventures at different stages in their lives, and pursuing understanding of the type of venture chosen at each stage, would enhance overall understanding of entrepreneurship.

Another important research agenda revolves around the individual who is an entrepreneur during a study's time period but later opts for traditional employment after an unsuccessful entrepreneurship experience. We have little understanding of the factors that motivate an individual to continue attempts to initiate a venture or even several ventures if unsuccessful in her efforts, and consequently, of how much time an individual persists in her efforts to become an entrepreneur until she abandons entrepreneurship in favor of traditional employment. Such dynamics highlight the limitations associated with applying a static approach to our investigations of who is an entrepreneur and what it is that they do. Without understanding these issues, the field remains incapable of identifying the characteristics that are associated with individual decisions to enter or exit an entrepreneurial career. To begin addressing these issues, future research should explore age cohorts and the experiences that differentiate entrepreneurs from nonentrepreneurs within the cohort at various points in time. With increases in the number of colleges and universities that offer entrepreneurship programs, it may be possible to create longitudinal panel studies across ages that enhance understanding of how life changes influence the decision to venture or not, to persist or to abandon.

There is research that shows that large percentages of firms fail in the early years of operation (Watson & Everett, 1999). The presumption is often that the business operations were not successful rather than that the entrepreneur backed away from the opportunity and closed the business. How long entrepreneurs persist before determining an opportunity is no longer worth pursuing is also a matter of importance (Roe, 2008). Stronger theoretical development that explicates the contextual factors that trigger these decisions would enhance understanding of the actions that are needed to help entrepreneurs overcome obstacles they face when starting and running a venture. Without explicit attention to the motivations of individuals in similar life stages across a given period of time, and the potential timing triggers, our ability to isolate key explanatory factors of entrepreneurial behavior remains limited.

Time and new venture emergence

Entrepreneurs bring solutions to market either through a new venture that is created specifically to exploit the new solution, or through an established firm moving away from its current trajectory (Stevenson & Jarillo, 1990). For some scholars, the essence of entrepreneurship is the creation of a company to exploit a product, service or technology opportunity in the marketplace (Ardichvili et al., 2003; Gartner, 1985). Each firm is founded under unique contexts, which influences the resources the entrepreneurs can leverage to build a company around a given opportunity (Le Mens, Hannan & Polos, 2011). As a company is created, entrepreneurs must "identify, accumulate and acquire resources" that help their firms become recognized as viable entities in the marketplace (Sirmon et al., 2011, p. 1421). Creativity and business plans are useful for helping entrepreneurs consider and address the resource needs of the new venture (Spinelli & Neck, 2006). However, resources are not equivalently distributed across individuals or points in time (Haveman et al., 2012). Consequently, the resources a firm possesses at founding and the competitors that it faces hold strong implications for that firm's overall survival in the marketplace (Le Mens et al., 2011). Therefore, the founding context is especially important for entrepreneurship.

It is not difficult to imagine that firms founded during medieval times are unlike those founded during the Internet age. Values and beliefs are generally thought to remain constant over extended periods of time (Hofstede, Hofstede, & Minkov, 1991), which suggests that at macro levels, contextual understanding is needed to understand why some venture foundings occur in some cultures and time periods but not in others. There are differences across societies in terms of entrepreneurial values and cognition that influence the cognitive structure (schema) and processing (heuristics) that lead to a decision to start a venture (Busenitz & Lau, 1996), and call for greater understanding of the specific forms of entrepreneurship that different cultures and time periods proliferate. It is known that the available resources in the external environment influence the types of firms that entrepreneurs conceive. For example, Navis and Glynn (2010) found strong differences in firm structure depending on the three distinct time periods in which the firm was founded. Unique founding contexts shape a firm's choices and overall trajectory (Stinchcombe, 1965), which influence its chances for market success. For example, Baum and Haveman (1997) found that hotel entrepreneurs varied the characteristics of their hotels depending on other hotels nearby in the targeted region. Furman (2003) similarly found that different regional resources influenced the type of firms founded therein. The initial founding conditions (Bamford, Dean & McDougall, 1999), as well as the entrepreneur's efforts to acquire and deploy resources given the environmental context faced, influence new venture success (Covin & Slevin, 1991; Ireland, Hitt & Sirmon, 2003).

In the early days of existence, new ventures remain in flux with respect to key resources that are needed and available, especially for resources that are derived from stakeholders in the external environment. Their resource positions can change by the day, week, month, year or even hour (Gilbert, McDougall & Audretsch, 2006). Accounting for fluctuations in resources is important for understanding why some firms flourish while others die (Le Mens et al., 2011). Some new ventures rely on partners in order to access resources they otherwise would not be able to acquire (Eisenhardt & Schoonhoven, 1996). Research even shows that the timing for entering alliances matters for firm performance such that whether firms enter into them early or late yields more advantages than if entered at intermediate stages (Lavie, Lechner & Singh, 2007). In other words, there is heterogeneity in terms of the benefits that accrue to firms depending on when resources are acquired. Research also shows that some ties matter more at different times in the firm's life (Gulati & Higgins, 2003). In early stages of firm development, personal ties are important for venture outcomes (Hesterly & Hite, 2001). As the firm grows over time, its network ties are deliberately structured with new, often nonpersonal contacts that help it meet current and future needs. Gulati and Higgins (2003) showed that the economic cycle influences which ties benefited firm IPO success. Venture capital firms were found important during cold markets, while investment banks were important during hot markets. It is clear that the timing for how entrepreneurs structure venture operations in response to limited resources influences a venture's outcomes into the future (Sirmon et al., 2011).

The firm's use of presently available resources determines how long that firm will survive into the future. Given that the founding of a firm engages its life cycle, which is known to necessitate differing demands from the entrepreneur/managers across stages (Quinn & Cameron, 1983; Smith, Mitchell & Summer, 1985), it is important to consider a firm's founding, its current stage and the decisions that are made as the venture moves forward. These factors highlight the importance of examining both the internal and external context a firm faces and how it changes over time in order to understand new venture performance. A study from the teams literature illustrates the significance of this approach. Gersick (1988) studied individual teams completing a variety of tasks over periods of days and in some cases weeks. She recognized patterns that interrupted team performance. These punctuations changed the contexts that the teams faced by presenting new obstacles for the teams to overcome. Each team's response to the interruption was integral to their overall level of success, but would not have been recognized if the shorter time periods had not been measured.

Such insights with respect to challenges entrepreneurs face as the venture moves from startup to mature phase are an important aspect of the organizational life cycle literature (e.g., Kimberly & Miles, 1980; Koberg, Uhlenbruck & Sarason, 1996; Quinn & Cameron, 1983). However, research based on timing and sequences of actions through the life cycle has seen a precipitous decline in recent years.

Important insights such as those found in Gersick (1988) cannot be gained through cross-sectional approaches over time periods of years as is commonly done in entrepreneurship research (Gilbert et al., 2006). Static approaches to understanding how a venture is emerging into the marketplace and how it is performing against other firms ignore the inherently dynamic nature of the process for new ventures.

An agenda for advancing research on time considerations in new venture emergence

As the foregoing review shows, how a firm begins has implications for how it progresses and ends. Therefore, founding conditions are influential over the development of new ventures. It is necessary to consider how these conditions influence firm structure and ability to adapt to the external environment (Le Mens et al., 2011). The field would benefit greatly from investigations that explore the drivers of venture creation during specific historic contexts. For example, it is unlikely that entrepreneurial ventures that are founded during economic boom periods are the same as those started during times of recession. Therefore, in addition to understanding the specific founding conditions under which new ventures are formed, it is also important to highlight the overall economic climate in which new ventures are founded and performing. There is a need to compare the time intervals that are typical for venture creation activities from start to finish and how the factors vary under different environmental contexts.

Incorporating the circumstances behind the founding, such as the economic cycle, the stage of the industry or unique cultural dynamics in effect at the time the firms are founded, would greatly enhance our understanding of how different contexts influence venture foundings. A venture's growth may place strong emphasis on understanding the sequencing of actions that are undertaken to scale operations (Sirmon et al., 2011). Examining how these activities differ across economic cycles, industry stage or cultural dynamics is important for explaining differences in types and outcomes of firms at specific points in time. The attention given to the rate at which a venture is growing and how the entrepreneurs are sequencing activities could provide greater insights into the dynamics that transpire as the firm successfully or unsuccessfully grows (Gilbert et al., 2006). It would also be useful to understand the timing norms that ventures of certain forms follow and explore the possibility that these norms potentially change depending on the type of venture (e.g., lifestyle, technology, professional, medical or legal practice, etc.) Answers to questions such as how deviations from entry norms influence entrepreneurial outcomes could potentially minimize the failure levels that are so prevalent in the entrepreneurial community.

Time and industry emergence

Sometimes an entrepreneurial endeavor results only in the creation of a new product/technology and accompanying venture. Other times the endeavor brings "new-to-the-world" solutions that create opportunities for other entrepreneurs to follow with competing offerings and an entirely new industry results. For example, the emerging fuel cell technology, which is an electrochemical device for generating energy by combining hydrogen and oxygen (Srinivasan, Mosdale, Stevens & Yang, 1999), is based on a concept that was discovered over 100 years ago. Its initial commercialization occurred in the 1960s, when it was used in the US Apollo mission to go to the moon. To introduce a broader set of applications and mainstream customers, the technology requires a new industry infrastructure that includes new sources for natural gas or hydrogen. To date, the development of the infrastructure is ongoing despite the fact that the invention was conceived over a century ago, initial commercialization occurred decades later and mass market entry timing is still debatable. A significant amount of time has elapsed in bringing this technology to market. There is a unique timing window that is associated with the introduction of new technologies and industries. The length of time between invention, initial commercialization and mass market entry may provide significant information about the chances for success for the offering and industry.

Since new-to-the-world offerings commonly substitute for existing products, their successful introduction often initiates the decline of the incumbent technology and industry. Even products that are generational changes for existing products shift competitive dynamics within an industry once they are introduced by creating new markets with new life cycles (Lawless & Anderson, 1996). Industry life cycles are known to vary across industries, with some industries enduring for only a few years while others span decades and even centuries (Klepper & Graddy, 1990). Importantly, it is generally known that a firm's experiences differ depending on the stage of the industry's life cycle. As an industry emerges, there is a need for entrepreneurial actors to ensure standards, codes and regulations are enacted that permit the solution to compete in the marketplace (Aldrich, 1999). The entrepreneurial actors must agree to industry norms that define the way firms will operate (Navis & Glynn, 2010). Once these institutions are established, the industry is legitimated and subsequent entrepreneurs understand the conditions under which their firms must operate if they are to compete. Currently, it is difficult to know the time that is required for successful legitimation of new industries and products, and the associated consequences of not meeting those requirements.

The length of time required for institutions to be established has implications for whether and how the industry emerges. The longer the process takes, the greater the likelihood that new alternatives emerge and the resource availability shifts in the marketplace (Haveman et al., 2012). Such shifts make it difficult for entrepreneurial actors to acquire the resources that are needed to advance a focal industry. And yet rarely has the duration of the legitimation process been considered in extant literature. Moreover, as with other prior studies, research often reflects a bias toward the industries that successfully navigate this process, with little understanding of those that did not.

Startup levels also vary depending on product life cycle stage, with its highest levels occurring during emergence and growth stages (Klepper, 1996). When a product is new to the world and also pioneering an industry along with it, a dominant design for the industry must emerge, which initiates a shakeout and consolidation of industry players around the dominant design. The industry then moves from a fragmented state with many competitors to an oligarchic one having only a few firms. The duration of these states differs across industries. People make decisions to invest in new technologies at different times (Kauffman & Li, 2005). Entry timing and how soon the firms enter with the dominant design hold implications for firm performance (Tegarden, Hatfield & Echols, 1999). Research also shows differences between the skill and resources of pioneers, early followers and late entrants (Kerin, Varadarajan & Peterson, 1992), thus verifying that timing of entry matters for firm performance. Entering with the dominant design is more important to ensure firm survival as the industry grows than it is for driving market share performance (Tegarden et al., 1999). There is a clear need to understand how timing influences the range of firm outcomes.

The resources that are available to entrepreneurs for starting businesses are also known to differ depending on the industry life cycle (Haveman et al., 2012). They are generally highest during industry emergence and growth. Consequently, startup activity slows as an industry progresses through its life cycle stages. Thus, it appears there is a window of opportunity in which startup activity will exist at high levels, and yet the elapsed time and indicators of industry transition between stages are not well explicated in the literature. Few studies have examined how industry changes influence the perception of opportunity. One important question to address is what the indicators are that an opportunity window has closed or will be closing – or are there specific signals that show that the time for founding a specific type of venture has passed?

An agenda for advancing research on time considerations in industry emergence

Industry emergence happens with enough regularity that it is important to understand how it influences entrepreneurs and firms. Much of the research covering the phenomenon does so from either an institutional perspective that focuses on how the firms become legitimate in the external environment (e.g., Haveman et al., 2012), or an ecological point of view that emphasizes the roles of competition and resource availability for firm outcomes (e.g., Le Mens et al., 2011). These theoretical foundations give ample attention to understanding the context in which industries emerge. However, much less emphasis has been placed on understanding duration, rate of change, transition time between technological regimes, and the entrepreneurial agents driving the process. It would be useful to incorporate these perspectives into our research because they enhance understanding of the challenges entrepreneurs face as they bring new technologies to market. Furthermore, they would enable stronger cross-industry comparisons during industry emergence stages. Greater consideration of industry stage also provides understanding of the prevalence of entrepreneurship, and the types of ventures we could expect to emerge during specific stages (Klepper, 1996).

Through industry emergence, there is also the unique opportunity to examine differences in pioneering entrepreneurs relative to other types of entrepreneurs.

Indeed, those who are tasked with shaping an industry carry a greater burden than those who have the privilege of entering an industry at a time when it is legitimate and well established. Explicating these differences will provide greater understanding of who becomes an entrepreneur, when and why.

Conclusion

Entrepreneurship is important for economic growth and wealth creation (Gilbert et al., 2006). And yet there are ebbs and flows to the phenomenon that extant research neither well explains nor explores. The timing behind when people elect to pursue entrepreneurship is a matter that deserves greater exploration than it has been given in the past. As this chapter has illustrated, time clearly matters in entrepreneurial endeavors. Greater incorporation of time into studies of entrepreneurship may help us better understand the phenomenon and what needs to be done to encourage more individuals to consider engaging in the process today, as opposed to at some point in the future or never.

References

Aldrich, H. E. (1999). *Organizations evolving.* Thousand Oaks, CA: SAGE.

Alvarez, S. A., & Barney, J. B. (2007). Discovery and creation: Alternative theories of entrepreneurial action. *Strategic Entrepreneurship Journal, 1*, 11–26.

Ancona, D. G., Goodman, P. S., Lawrence, B. S., & Tushman, M. L. (2001). Time: A new research lens. *Academy of Management Review, 26*, 645–663.

Ancona, D. G., Okhuysen, G. A., & Perlow, L. A. (2001). Taking time to integrate temporal research. *Academy of Management Review, 26*, 512–529.

Anderson, P., & Tushman, M. L. (1990). Technological discontinuities and dominant designs: A cyclical model of technological change. *Administrative Science Quarterly, 35*, 604–633.

Ardichvili, A., Cardozo, R., & Ray, S. (2003). A theory of entrepreneurial opportunity identification and development. *Journal of Business Venturing, 18*, 105–123.

Bamford, C. E., Dean, T. J., & McDougall, P. P. (1999). An examination of the impact of initial founding conditions and decisions upon the performance of new bank start-ups. *Journal of Business Venturing, 15*, 253–277.

Baum, J. A., & Haveman, H. A. (1997). Love thy neighbor? Differentiation and agglomeration in the Manhattan hotel industry, 1898–1990. *Administrative Science Quarterly, 42*, 304–338.

Bird, B. (1988). Implementing entrepreneurial ideas: The case for intention. *Academy of Management Review, 13*, 442–453.

Bird, B. J. (1992). The operation of intentions in time: The emergence of the new venture. *Entrepreneurship Theory and Practice, 17*, 11.

Bird, B. J., & West, P. G. (1997). Time and entrepreneurship. *Entrepreneurship Theory & Practice, 22*, 132–136.

Brockhaus, R. H., & Horwitz, P. S. (1986). The art and science of entrepreneurship. In D.S.R. Smilor (Ed.), *The psychology of the entrepreneur* (pp. 25–48). Cambridge, MA: Ballinger.

Busenitz, L. W., & Lau, C. M. (1996). A cross-cultural cognitive model of new venture creation. *Entrepreneurship Theory and Practice, 20,* 25–40.

Cathers, B. (2003). *Conversations with teen entrepreneurs: Success secrets of the younger generation.* Lincoln, NE: iUniverse.

Cooper, A. C., Ramachandran, M., & Schoorman, F. D. (1996). Time allocation patterns of craftsmen and administrative entrepreneurs: Implications for financial performance. *Entrepreneurship Theory and Practice, 22,* 123–136.

Covin, J. G., & Slevin, D. P. (1991). A conceptual model of entrepreneurship as firm behavior. *Entrepreneurship Theory and Practice, 16,* 7–25.

Eckhardt, J. T., & Shane, S. A. (2003). Opportunities and entrepreneurship. *Journal of Management, 29,* 333–349.

Edwards, J. R., Cable, D. M., Williamson, I. O., Schurer Lambert, L., & Shipp, A. J. (2006). The phenomenology of fit: Linking the person and environment to the subjective experience of person-environment fit. *Journal of Applied Psychology, 91,* 802–827.

Eisenhardt, K. M., & Schoonhoven, C. B. (1996). Resource-based view of strategic alliance formation: Strategic and social effects in entrepreneurial firms. *Organization Science, 7,* 136–150.

Fairlie, R. W. (2011). *2010 Kauffman Index of Entrepreneurial Activity (1996–2010).* St. Louis, MO: Ewing Marion Kauffman Foundation..

Fried, Y., Grant A. M., Levi, A. S., Hadani, M., & Slowik, L. H. (2007). Job design in temporary context: A career dynamics perspective. *Journal of Organizational Behavior, 28,* 911–927.

Furman, J. L. (2003). Location and organizing strategy: exploring the influence of location on the organization of pharmaceutical research. *Advances in Strategic Management, 20,* 49–88.

Gartner, W. B. (1985). A conceptual framework for describing the phenomenon of new venture creation. *Academy of Management Review, 10,* 696–706.

Gersick, C. J. G. (1988). Time and transition in work teams: Toward a new model of group development. *Academy of Management Journal, 31,* 9–41.

Gilbert, B. A., McDougall, P. P., & Audretsch, D. B. (2006). New venture growth: A review and extension. *Journal of Management, 32,* 926–950.

Gregoire, D. A., & Shepherd, D. A. (2012). Technology-market combinations and the identification of entrepreneurial opportunities: An investigation of the opportunity-individual nexus. *Academy of Management Journal, 55,* 753–785.

Gulati, R., & Higgins, M. C. (2003). Which ties matter when? The contingent effects of interorganizational partnerships on IPO success. *Strategic Management Journal, 24,* 127–144.

Haveman, H. A., Habinek, J., & Goodman, L. A. (2012). How entrepreneurship evolves: The founders of new magazines in America, 1741–1860. *Administrative Science Quarterly, 57,* 585–624.

Hofstede, G., Hofstede, G. J., & Minkov, M. (1991). *Cultures and organizations.* London: McGraw-Hill.

Ireland, R. D., Hitt, M. A., & Sirmon, D. G. (2003). A model of strategic entrepreneurship: The construct and its dimensions. *Journal of Management, 29*(6), 963–989.

Johns, G. (2006). The essential impact of context on organizational behavior. *Academy of Management Review, 31,* 386–408.

Kauffman, R. J., & Li, X. (2005). Technology competition and optimal investment timing: A real options perspective. *IEEE Transactions on Engineering Management, 52,* 15–29.

Kerin, R. A., Varadarajan, P. R., & Peterson, R. A. (1992). First-mover advantage: Synthesis, conceptual framework, and research propositions. *Journal of Marketing, 56,* 33–52.

Kerr, W. R. (2008). Ethnic scientific communities and international technology diffusion. *Review of Economics and Statistics, 90,* 518–537.

Kimberly, J. R., & Miles, R. H. (Eds.). (1980). *The organizational life cycle: Issues in the creation, transformation and decline of organizations.* San Francisco, CA: Jossey-Bass.

Klepper, S. (1996). Entry, exit, growth and innovation over the product life cycle. *American Economic Review, 86,* 562–583.

Klepper, S., & Graddy, E. (1990). The evolution of new industries and the determinants of market structure. *RAND Journal of Economics, 21,* 27–44.

Koberg, C. S., Uhlenbruck, N., & Sarason, Y. (1996). Facilitators of organizational innovation: The role of life-cycle stage. *Journal of Business Venturing, 11,* 133–149.

Lavie, D., Lechner, C., & Singh, H. (2007). The performance implications of timing of entry and involvement in multipartner alliances. *Academy of Management Journal, 50,* 578–604.

Lawless, M. W., & Anderson, P. C. (1996). Generational technological change: Effects of innovation and local rivalry on performance. *Academy of Management Journal, 39,* 1185–1217.

Le Mens, G., Hannan, M. T., & Polos, L. (2011). Founding conditions, learning and organizational life chances: Age dependence revisited. *Administrative Science Quarterly, 56,* 95–126.

Levesque, M., & MacCrimmon, K. R. (1997). On the interaction of time and money invested in new ventures. *Entrepreneurship Theory & Practice, 22,* 89–110.

McCarthy, A. M., Krueger, D. A., & Schoenecker, T. S. (1990). Changes in the time allocation patterns of entrepreneurs. *Entrepreneurship Theory & Practice, 15,* 7–18.

Mitchell, T. R., & James, L. R. (2001). Building better theory: Time and the specification of when things happen. *Academy of Management Review, 26,* 530–547.

Moroz, P. W., & Hindle, K. (2012). Entrepreneurship as a process: Toward harmonizing multiple perspectives. *Entrepreneurship Theory and Practice, 36,* 781–818.

Nanda, R., & Sørensen, J. B. (2010). Workplace peers and entrepreneurship. *Management Science, 5,* 1116–1126.

Navis, C., & Glynn, M. A. (2010). How new market categories emerge: Temporal dynamics of legitimacy, identity, and entrepreneurship in satellite radio, 1990–2005. *Administrative Science Quarterly, 55,* 439–471.

Obschonka, M., Goethner, M., Silbereisen, R. K., & Cantner, U. (2012). Social identity and the transition to entrepreneurship: The role of group identification with workplace peers. *Journal of Vocational Behavior, 80,* 137–147.

Pech, R. J., & Cameron, A. (2006). An entrepreneurial decision process model describing opportunity recognition. *European Journal of Innovation Management, 9,* 61–78.

Quinn, J. B., & Cameron, K. (1983). Organizational life cycles and shifting criteria of effectiveness: Some preliminary evidence. *Management Science, 29,* 33–51.

Roe, R. A. (2008). Time in applied psychology: The study of "what happens" rather than "what is." *European Psychologist, 13,* 37–52.

Rousseau, D. M., & Fried, Y. (2001). Location, location, location: contextualizing organizational research. *Journal of organizational Behavior, 22,* 1–13.

Shah, S. K., & Tripsas, M. (2007). The accidental entrepreneur: The emergent and collective process of user entrepreneurship. *Strategic Entrepreneurship Journal, 1,* 123–140.

Shane, S. A. (2003). *A general theory of entrepreneurship: The individual-opportunity nexus.* Northampton: Edward Elgar.

Shane, S., & Venkataraman, S. (2000). The promise of entrepreneurship as a field of research. *Academy of Management Review, 25,* 217–226.

Shefsky, L. E. (1994). *Entrepreneurs are made not born.* New York: McGraw-Hill.

Shipp, A. J., Edwards, J. R., & Lambert, L. S. (2009). Conceptualization and measurement of temporal focus: The subjective experience of the past, present and future. *Organizational Behavior and Human Decision Processes, 110*, 1–22.

Sirmon, D. G., Hitt, M. A., Ireland, R. D., & Gilbert, B. A. (2011). Resource orchestration to create competitive advantage: Breadth, depth and life cycle effects. *Journal of Management, 37*, 1390–1412.

Smith, K. G., Mitchell, T. R., & Summer, C. E. (1985). Top-level management priorities in different stages of the organizational life cycle. *Academy of Management Journal, 28*, 799–820.

Spinelli Jr., S., & Neck, H. M. (2006). The Timmons model of the entrepreneurial process. *Entrepreneurship.* Portsmouth: Greenwood.

Srinivasan, S., Mosdale, R., Stevens, P., & Yang, C. (1999). Fuel cells: Reaching the era of clean and efficient power generation in the twenty-first century. *Annual Review of Energy Environment, 24*, 281–328.

Stevenson, H. H., & Jarillo, J. C. (1990). A paradigm of entrepreneurship: Entrepreneurial management. *Strategic Management Journal, 11*, 17–27.

Stinchcombe, A. L. (1965). Social structure and organizations. In J. March (Ed.), Handbook of organizations (pp. 142–193). Chicago: Rand McNally.

Super, D. E., & Hall, D. T. (1978). Career development: Exploration and planning. *Annual review of psychology, 29*, 333–372.

Tegarden, L. F., Hatfield, D. E., & Echols, A. E. (1999). Doomed from the start: What is the value of selecting a future dominant design? *Strategic Management Journal, 20*, 495–518.

Tripsas, M. (1997). Unraveling the process of creative destruction: Complementary assets and incumbent survival in the typesetter industry. *Strategic Management Journal, 18*, 119–142.

Tushman, M. L., & Anderson, P. (1986). Technological discontinuities and organizational environments. *Administrative Science Quarterly, 31*, 439–465.

Watson, J., & Everett, J. (1999). Small business failure rates: Choice of definition and industry effects. *International Small Business Journal, 17*, 31–48.

Westhead, P., Ucbasaran, D., & Wright, M. (2005). Experience and cognition: Do novice, serial and portfolio entrepreneurs differ? *International Small Business Journal, 23*, 72–98.

Yu, J., Gilbert, B. A., & Oviatt, B. M. (2011). Effects of alliances, time and network cohesion on the initiation of foreign sales by new ventures. *Strategic Management Journal, 32*, 424–446.

Zaheer, A., & Bell, G. G. (2005). Benefitting from network position: Firm capabilities, structural holes, and performance. *Strategic Management Journal, 26*, 809–825.

7 The temporal dimension of routines and their outcomes

Exploring the role of time in the capabilities and practice perspectives

Scott F. Turner

Routines are a central concept in strategic management and organizational theory research (Cyert & March, 1963; Hannan & Freeman, 1989; Helfat et al., 2007; March & Simon, 1958; Nelson & Winter, 1982). As repetitive patterns of interdependent actions, routines play a vital role in explaining the stable and dynamic nature of organizations' behavior, and have important implications for their efficiency and effectiveness. Examples of organizational routines are wide-ranging, including routines for hiring and training personnel (Feldman, 2000), purchasing materials and equipment (Knott, 2001), making products or performing services (Darr, Argote, & Epple, 1995; Turner & Rindova, 2012), providing technical support (Pentland & Rueter, 1994), adjusting prices (Zbaracki & Bergen, 2010), and developing new products or production processes (Howard-Grenville, 2005; Salvato, 2009). In recent years, scholars have been taking stock of what we know about organizational routines (Becker, 2004; Cohen et al., 1996; Parmigiani & Howard-Grenville, 2011; Salvato & Rerup, 2010). What is missing, though, is a review that considers the temporal dimension of routines and their outcomes.

This is an important omission because temporality is paramount for our understanding of organizational routines. Beyond playing a key role in defining and identifying routines (i.e., repetitive patterns), time is pivotal for explanations of why and how routines emerge, stabilize, vary, and change. Time is also evident in performance outcomes for routines research, such as speed of execution, and in understanding the effects of routines on performance outcomes. Despite its centrality for our understanding of routines and their outcomes, the temporal dimension has received only limited attention in existing reviews of routines scholarship. At one level, this is a function of the limited body of empirical work that has explored the temporal aspects of routines which may reflect a variety of issues, including that time is frequently taken for granted in organizations research, that collecting temporal data can be a resource-intensive process, and that researchers often have some uncertainty regarding appropriate techniques for analyzing longitudinal data (Avital, 2000; Greve & Goldeng, 2004; Ployhart & Vandenberg, 2010). At another level, the limited attention in existing reviews may reflect that we are only beginning to develop the common understandings and frameworks about time with which to compare and integrate across studies. Fortunately, though, there have been considerable developments in recent years due to heightened interest in temporality (e.g., Ancona, Okhuysen, & Perlow, 2001; Bluedorn, 2002; Jansen & Shipp, 2013; Mitchell & James, 2001). These developments enable scholars to more clearly examine organizational routines through the temporal lens, which helps to sharpen and refine our conceptual understanding.

This chapter provides a detailed review of routines research from a temporal perspective. The next section presents the concept of organizational routines, provides an introduction to the role of time in routines research, and offers an overview of the capabilities and practice perspectives (Parmigiani & Howard-Grenville, 2011) that guide this review of the literature. In reviewing the research, particular attention is given to three criteria: (1) temporal antecedents of routines (i.e., time as signal, resource, and state of mind), (2) the role of time in the performance outcomes of routines, which includes time as an outcome (e.g., the time required to perform a routine) as well as how time affects the impact of routines (e.g., how realizing value from routines can change over time), and (3) how routines evolve over time, which considers their internal and external dynamics. Consideration is also given to the methodologies by which scholars have studied temporal issues in routines. The chapter concludes with suggestions for how future research can further incorporate the temporal lens to advance our understanding of organizational routines, focusing on the need for greater breadth and conditionality in examining how time influences the performance and outcomes of routines.

A temporal review of routines research

Over the years, scholars have offered many definitions of routines that share a number of key elements, such as repetition and interdependence. Taking these points of commonality into account, Feldman and Pentland (2003, p. 96) proposed that an organizational routine is a "repetitive, recognizable pattern of interdependent actions, involving multiple actors." Scholars have emphasized that routines are organizational in the sense that the repetitive patterns involve multiple actors, as in group- or firm-level activities, while such patterns at the individual level are typically referred to as habits or skills (Becker, 2004; Cohen & Bacdayan, 1994; Hodgson, 2003). This definition makes clear that time is important for understanding organizational routines. As routines are repeated over time, they develop into recognizable patterns of actions. For any given performance of a routine, a sequence of actions takes place across time, and temporal artifacts (e.g., clocks, time-based rules) often play a prominent role in enabling and constraining routine performances. In turn, key performance outcomes of routines are based in time (e.g., task completion speed), and the effectiveness of routines can depend on time (e.g., historical specificity). Thus, time represents a central issue in the routines literature.

The scope of this review was guided by two issues. The first was to concentrate on the capabilities and practice perspectives of routines, which Parmigiani and Howard-Grenville (2011) identify as two central perspectives in the literature.[1] The capabilities perspective typically examines routines as whole entities, has

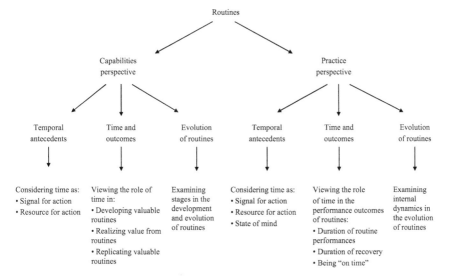

Figure 7.1 Reviewing the role of time in the capabilities and practice perspectives of routines.

roots in economics, and is prominent in strategy research. By contrast, the practice perspective focuses on the internal structure of routines, draws from sociology, and is evident in organizational theory research. The second issue focuses on how time has been incorporated in the research on routines. In this review, particular attention is given to *temporal antecedents* (i.e., time-based influences on routines), *outcomes* (i.e., the role of time in the impact of routines), and *evolution* (i.e., how routines stabilize and change over time). Figure 7.1 illustrates how these two perspectives (i.e., capabilities, practice) and three criteria (i.e., antecedents, outcomes, evolution) guide the review.

In thinking about the role of time in routines research, I revisited foundational works on routines (e.g., Stene, 1940; Nelson & Winter, 1982) and examined carefully recent reviews of the literature (Becker, 2004; Parmigiani & Howard-Grenville, 2011; Salvato & Rerup, 2010). This process helped to identify articles considering the temporal dimension of routines and their outcomes, and was augmented by searching online databases for additional articles that concentrate on the core issues. Similar to Parmigiani and Howard-Grenville (2011), I have emphasized recent empirical studies. When reviewing the works identified by this process, particular attention was given to identifying how the studies implicitly or explicitly incorporate time in their consideration of antecedents, outcomes, or evolution of routines.

The review is structured as follows. First, research by scholars working primarily from a capabilities perspective is reviewed according to the criteria of temporal antecedents, outcomes, and evolution. Second, the review examines the research from scholars working primarily from a practice perspective, focusing on the same criteria. Third, consideration is given to the set of methodologies by which capabilities- and practice-based researchers have studied temporal issues in routines. The chapter concludes by discussing similarities and complementarities between the capabilities and practice perspectives with respect to time, and by offering suggestions for ways that future research can further leverage the temporal lens to extend our understanding of organizational routines.

The capabilities perspective

The capabilities perspective focuses on the idea that routines are the building blocks of organizational capabilities. Scholars working from this perspective typically examine routines as whole entities, and are particularly interested in understanding how routines impact organizational performance (Parmigiani & Howard-Grenville, 2011; Salvato & Rerup, 2010). The capabilities perspective emphasizes the stability of routines, and tends to take a higher level of abstraction when examining them (Helfat & Winter, 2011).[2] For this perspective, scholars tend to be interested in variance in routines in terms of utilizing routines versus ad hoc problem solving, and variance across different types of routines. This review focuses on three ways in which time plays a prominent role in routines research from the capabilities perspective: how time affects the performance of routines, the role of time in the outcomes of routines, and how routines evolve over time.

Temporal antecedents

This section examines how time shapes the performance of routines, considering time as a signal for action, and as a resource for action.

Time as signal for action

This refers to the idea that time often plays a key role in initiating the performance of routines. Time can be conceptualized in multiple ways, including "clock time", which refers to the progression of time along a standard linear continuum, and "event time", which captures the progression of time as reflected in the occurrence of particular events (Ancona et al., 2001). With respect to initiating routine performances, an example of "event time" is when the completion of one routine signals the need for performing another routine, while "clock time" refers to when clocks or calendars indicate that a particular routine needs to be performed.

Clock time. For many organizations, timekeeping devices like clocks and calendars perform cueing functions for routines. In this sense, clocks provide a stimulus for initiating routines, such as performing a particular routine at the start of the workday or just prior to its conclusion (Nelson & Winter, 1982; Postrel & Rumelt, 1992). For other activities, the calendar plays a vital role. In their multicase study of innovation in the computing industry, Brown and Eisenhardt (1997) highlight that businesses have incentives to pace their introduction of innovations according to consistent time intervals, such as introducing new generations of core products every 18 or 24 months. Using the calendar in this way results in predictable patterns that facilitate planning and enable efficiencies in coordination and resource allocation, as opposed to more reactive approaches like introducing innovations in response to the arrival of new competitors in the market. In related work examining innovation in the packaged software industry, Turner, Mitchell, and Bettis (2010, 2013) found support for the idea that organizations employ routines for developing and introducing generational product innovations at consistent intervals across time. This research also considered how market and organizational conditions affect the consistency with which organizations release these innovations across time. From the market perspective, Turner et al. (2010) found evidence supporting the idea that as market concentration increases, organizations need to be more responsive to competitive events, and are less consistent in their release of innovations across time. From the organizational perspective, Turner et al. (2013) argued that accomplishing temporal consistency in innovation introduction can be challenging, and that organizations' corresponding capability is enhanced by innovation experience and diminished by organizational aging, with the empirical results providing support for these ideas. Researchers also suggest that organizational strategy and market conditions affect the span of calendar time (e.g., 12 vs. 24 months) for such time pacing of innovation (Eisenhardt & Brown, 1998).

Event time. Scholars also consider how events trigger the performance of routines. For example, routine performances are often cued by the conclusion of other routines within an organization. This may occur when one routine is sequentially dependent upon another (Thompson, 1967), in which case completing one routine makes possible the completion of the subsequent one, and can send a signal that it is now time for performing the subsequent routine (March & Simon, 1958; Nelson & Winter, 1982). As an example, in their case study of model changeover routines at the NUMMI facility, Adler, Goldoftas, & Levine (1999) described how completing a major model changeover in 1989 initiated the earliest steps of the next model changeover, and how its completion in 1993 triggered a "reflection-review" routine to document the lessons learned from the just-completed model changeover. In other instances, triggering events may lie outside organizations, such as actions taken by suppliers or competitive moves made by rival firms.

In sum, organizations structure the performance of their routines according to both clock and event time. Performing routines according to clocks and calendars reduces the need for environmental monitoring (i.e., detecting cues) and reacting to other parties, which may promote efficiencies in planning and coordination, while event-driven routines imply greater interdependence and responsiveness. In turn, whether organizations use clocks or events to guide routine performances depends upon organizational and market conditions, such as activity interdependence and market competitiveness.

Time as resource for action

Time as resource for action refers to the idea that time is a valuable asset for organizations. This is important as organizations typically employ routines in efforts to attain efficiencies in their coordination and governance of activities

(Karim & Mitchell, 2000). In this area of research, work has focused on time pressure, which can be viewed as a resource shortage (Arrow, Poole, Henry, Wheelan, & Moreland, 2004) and reflects the urgency associated with performing a task. When organizational employees face significant time pressure, they have less opportunity to consider alternative ways of performing a task, and may be less able to sacrifice the efficiencies afforded by a particular routine. By contrast, when there is less time pressure, employees have greater slack available with which to reflect on and engage in performing the task (Becker, 2004; March & Simon, 1958).

Empirical studies offer evidence that is consistent with this view of time as a resource. In their experiments involving pairs of individuals repeatedly playing a card game, Garapin and Hollard (1999) examined players' use of a learned routine based in condition-action rules (Egidi & Narduzzo, 1997). While the researchers observed greater use of the learned routine under high time pressure, the effect was not statistically significant; they did find, however, that greater time pressure resulted in significantly less time required to play hands of the game. Similar results have been shown in studies examining the effects of time pressure on routinized decision-making by individuals. In an experiment examining recurrent problem solving, Betsch, Brinkmann, Fiedler, and Breining (1999) induced learning of a "routine solution" by initially structuring payoff conditions to favor a particular solution. The researchers found that as time pressure increased, decision-makers were more likely to choose the routine solution, even when alternative solutions were preferred under subsequent payoff conditions. In a similar experiment, Betsch, Haberstroh, Molter, and Glockner (2004) examined the effect of time pressure on whether individuals favor previously learned decision rules in making a decision to solve a recurring problem. The results indicated that under high time pressure, individuals were more likely to use the learned decision rule (e.g., if facing problem A, choose solution 1), even after they had formed intentions to make an alternative decision; by contrast, under low time pressure, individuals were more likely to select their intended alternative over the choice that corresponded to the learned decision rule.

In sum, this research indicates that time pressure results in greater utilization of routines, even when alternative courses of action were intended or preferred, and in faster execution of routines.

Time and outcomes

Scholars working from the capabilities perspective are particularly interested in understanding how routines influence outcomes of interest for organizations (Parmigiani & Howard-Grenville, 2011). In this work, scholars emphasize the efficiency criterion, highlighting how routines enable efficiencies in a variety of areas, including cognition, coordination, and governance (Becker, 2004; Coriat & Dosi, 1998; Karim & Mitchell, 2000; Knott & McKelvey, 1999; Lazaric, 2008; March & Simon, 1958; Nelson & Winter, 1982). Scholars also draw from the resource-based view in considering the competitive implications of routines, involving issues like the presence of isolating mechanisms (Barney, 1991; Rumelt, 1984).

Time and developing valuable routines

This work tends to highlight how learning by doing over time contributes to the development of routines that provide value for organizations (Argote, 1999; Arrow, 1962). For example, Dutta, Zbaracki, and Bergen (2003) studied price-setting routines that enable value appropriation at a large manufacturing company. The researchers found that time compression diseconomies (Dierickx & Cool, 1989) were a key factor that decreased the risk of imitation by rivals, highlighting how it took the firm over five years to develop and refine the underlying pricing routines and systems, such that they effectively met the requirements of the firm and its customers. Similarly, in their study of strategic alliances in the biotechnology industry, Zollo, Reuer, and Singh (2002) argued that experience working with a particular alliance partner (i.e., learning by doing) enables the development of valuable interorganizational routines that facilitate coordination and cooperation. Consistent with this idea, the researchers found that the number of previous alliances with a particular partner had a positive effect on alliance performance.

While these studies have emphasized the importance of learning by doing in developing valuable routines, other work has suggested that "learning before doing" (e.g., lab experiments, simulations) can reduce the time required to develop such routines. In a study examining process development in the pharmaceuticals industry, Pisano (1994) examined how the different learning approaches (i.e., learning by doing, learning before doing) affected the time required to develop new routines in two different fields. Pisano argued that chemicals-based pharmaceuticals is a mature scientific field with developed theories available in scientific journals and textbooks, whereas biotechnology-based pharmaceuticals is a more nascent field with less established theory available to guide developers of large-scale processes. Accordingly, the results indicated that in chemicals-based pharmaceuticals, learning before doing was associated with more rapid development of routines, while it had little effect on development time in biotechnology-based pharmaceuticals. This suggests that learning before doing can be an effective way to reduce time to development when a sufficient knowledge base exists to simulate and predict effects in advance.

In sum, scholars working from the capabilities perspective are interested in the role of time in the development of valuable routines, and consider time to development as an important outcome. This work has shown that learning by doing over time is often a requirement for developing valuable routines, but under certain conditions, firms can "learn before doing" and effectively lower development time.

Time and realizing value from routines

Researchers have also considered several ways in which time contributes to realizing value from routines. One line of this work considers the counterintuitive idea that organizations benefit from enforcement mechanisms that require them to use valuable routines. In research examining routines in the franchising industry, Knott (2001, 2003) found that franchisors play an important disciplining role by requiring establishments to use valuable operating routines, and that temporal distance from such an enforcing mechanism is a key factor. In a natural experiment that compared establishments that leave a franchise with those that remain, Knott (2001) found that for those leaving the franchise, as the establishments became more temporally distant from the enforcement mechanism (i.e., the years since becoming independent of the franchisor), they were less likely to use valuable operating routines even when they had perfect incentives to do so, and the establishments experienced a corresponding decline in returns. Thus, in the absence of an enforcing mechanism, organizations can drift from valuable routines over time.

Other research examines how time can affect the value generated by a routine. For example, scholars argue that routines exhibit historical specificity, which refers to the idea that routines are shaped and supported by particular contextual features at particular points in time (Becker, 2004; Narduzzo, Rocco, & Warglien, 2000), such that as conditions change over time, organizations may no longer be able to effectively perform routines that once produced considerable value. This builds on the idea that routines are context-dependent, highlighting that routines may be effective in some contexts yet not in others (Winter in Cohen et al., 1996, p. 662). While the notion of historical specificity implicitly focuses on clock time as a proxy for changing conditions, scholars also consider how the value produced by a routine can change over time as reflected in event occurrences. In a study examining the San Francisco 49ers' West Coast Offense as an advantageous routine in professional football, Aime, Johnson, Ridge, and Hill (2010) found that the value produced by the routine dissipated over time, as knowledge of the routine diffused to rival organizations through the hiring of 49ers personnel. The researchers found that as rival organizations hired away personnel directly familiar with the routine, they became better able to implement the West Coast Offense and to defend against it.

In sum, this research suggests that realizing value from routines is a function of time in varied ways, and includes factors like temporal distance from an enforcing mechanism, how routines fit with the historical context, and how returns from an advantageous routine dissipate over time.

Time and replicating valuable routines

After developing valuable routines, firms often have incentives to replicate them in pursuit of greater profit through growth (Winter, 1995). From the perspective of the resource-based view, Winter and Szulanski (2001, pp. 740–741) highlight that resources are present in the form of the routines being replicated, and in the "capabilities for *speedy* and *precise* replication" (italics added). The *speed* of replication is important in competitive settings because of the potential to cede valuable opportunities to imitating rivals, leading to the advice of "when successful, copy yourself before others copy you" (Winter, 1995, p. 158). Winter (1995) also suggests that decisions regarding the rate of replication take into account that idiosyncratic resources are required for replication, and that those resources have opportunity costs (e.g., knowledgeable personnel from an established concern needed to facilitate the establishment of routines in a new concern). To date, though, little research has focused on the rate of replication.

Much of the research on replication has focused on the *precision* aspect. Scholars argue that replicating routines can be difficult for a variety of reasons, including challenges associated with transferring routines with tacit components. This work argues that having an established routine in operation serving as a template is important because it provides a referent for addressing problems that surface during the transfer and implementation of the routine in new locations (Nelson & Winter, 1982). Scholars further argue that precise replication (i.e., copy exactly) is important because the established routine contains considerable lessons learned from past mistakes, and that a precisely replicated routine will be better able to leverage resources from the spawning unit. In a study of the transfer of best-practice sales routines at a company in Western Europe, Jensen and Szulanski (2007) found that using a template resulted in more effective transfer of routines, particularly when recipients had little understanding of the routine and its interactions.

This line of research also examines alternative approaches to replicating routines in the context of franchising. One approach focuses on precise replication of the routine – that is, copy exactly – while the other emphasizes adaptation of the routine to fit local conditions. In one study, Winter, Szulanski, Ringov, and Jensen (2012) found that franchise outlets faced heightened risks of failure with greater departure from the franchisor template. In related work, Szulanski and Jensen (2006, 2008) found that franchisees performed better in terms of growth when they more closely replicated the franchisor's codified routine for growth, as opposed to when they sought to adapt it in light of differences in local conditions. Interestingly, the results indicated that time matters in this relationship, as there appeared to be fewer concerns from adaptation when it took place after franchisees developed greater understanding of the routine through operating experience.

In sum, scholars examining the replication of routines argue that organizations benefit from precise replication because the template represents accumulated learning and serves as a referent. Empirical work supports this idea, finding that organizations perform better following precise replication, particularly in the near term, when recipients have limited understanding of the routine.

Evolution of routines over time

Scholars working from the capabilities perspective have also given considerable attention to understanding how routines evolve over time. One of the central themes in this research is that the evolution of routines is history-dependent (Helfat, 2003), and that the paths ahead for a routine are shaped by the path along which it has traveled (Becker, 2004; Teece, Pisano, & Shuen, 1997). While capability scholars often describe the evolution of routines as path-dependent, Sydow, Schreyögg, and Koch (2009) argue that path dependence is a specific claim regarding the development of a routine: starting with a relatively open scope of action (i.e., few constraints), a path takes shape as events (e.g., decisions, accidents) begin to restrict the scope of action in which a routine can emerge as a pattern of action; this scope of action then becomes further restricted by self-reinforcing processes (e.g., learning effects), such that the path culminates in a highly restricted state that "locks in" a rigid and potentially inefficient pattern of action. In reviewing this research, I draw upon the more general ideas of history dependence and the more specific ideas of path dependence, concentrating on recent studies that capture the evolution process in stage and life-cycle models (Helfat & Peteraf, 2003; Sydow et al., 2009).

Initial stage

In these models, the initial stage focuses on the conditions for founding a routine. Scholars highlight that in the initial stage, organizations often have many options for performing a task, within the bounds of the context and involved individuals. The context encompasses various aspects, such as the physical environment in which the task is to be performed (Nelson & Winter, 1982), and the legal environment that influences what actions are permissible (Nelson, 1994). In addition, the individuals developing the routine may bring experiences from prior organizations and careers that affect the initial set of possibilities for performing the task, representing imprinting effects that influence the initial conditions (Levinthal, 2003; Sydow et al., 2009).

Self-reinforcing stage

As an organization begins to perform a task, the processes by which it is accomplished are subject to self-reinforcement, as reflected in learning, coordination, and systemic effects. Learning effects are self-reinforcing in that with repetition, an organization becomes more efficient in performing the task in particular ways – that is, learning by doing (Argote, 1999; Cohen, 1991). Coordination is also subject to self-reinforcement, in that as an organization performs a task in familiar ways, it can increasingly rely on historical precedence for coordination, which results in greater efficiencies. Systemic effects capture the idea that as an organization begins to perform a task in particular ways, it tends to invest in supporting assets and infrastructure, and may develop complementary routines; as this system develops around the focal routine, there are increasingly disruptive costs associated with changing the focal routine (Narduzzo et al., 2000; Sydow et al., 2009).

Experimental studies provide support for these ideas. In a classic experiment examining pairs of individuals playing a card game, Cohen and Bacdayan (1994) found that repetition resulted in the formation of routines that increased the efficiency with which pairs played the game. And once routines are established, studies have shown a tendency for them to persist, even when the initial conditions that led to their development are no longer in place. In an experiment involving a group writing task, Kelly and McGrath (1985) found that groups established patterns of task performance in an initial trial under particular time constraints, which persisted in a second trial even though the time constraints had changed. As another example, in an experiment building on the work by Cohen and Bacdayan (1994), Egidi and Narduzzo (1997) focused on the strategies by which actor pairs played the card game, viewing the strategies as routines based in particular sets of condition-action rules. The results showed that after being led to favor a particular strategy in an initial round, pairs were more likely to use the learned strategy in a subsequent round, even when it was less effective – and in many instances, pairs played their learned strategy exclusively, suggesting the potential for locking into a particular routine.

Maturity stage

Routines may persist for reasons beyond self-reinforcement, such as when satisficing organizations do not engage in problem-solving efforts to change a routine as long as its performance outcomes are above threshold levels (March & Simon, 1958; Nelson, 1994; Winter, 2000). Such persistence may ultimately lead to a state of lock-in, which Sydow et al. (2009) characterize by severe restriction in the scope for performing a task, which is deterministic in the extreme. However, Helfat and Peteraf (2003) highlight that routines can evolve and change when factors external to the routine intervene to change its trajectory. These forces may arise from within the organization (e.g., interventions by senior managers) or outside it (e.g., changes in demand, technological changes), and can result in a variety of changes to the routine. Helfat and Peteraf (2003) suggest several ways in which a routine might change, including enhancement (i.e., renewal), extension (i.e., replication, redeployment), innovation (i.e., recombination), and termination (i.e., retirement, retrenchment).

While research from the capabilities perspective has emphasized path-dependent evolution, scholars also argue that organizations' temporal orientation for search (i.e., backward-looking, forward-looking) can moderate the extent to which routines evolve in path-dependent ways. In routines research, much of the emphasis has been placed on a backward-looking approach, which focuses on experiential wisdom and feedback based on prior choices; in contrast, a forward-looking orientation emphasizes the idea that organizations use cognitive maps to think about how a given set of actions will influence outcomes. Studies using computational simulation have found that organizations incorporating a forward-looking orientation were less constrained by the past, and had higher fitness levels as the forward-looking orientation enabled them to find more promising regions on the landscape (Gavetti, 2005; Gavetti & Levinthal, 2000).

In sum, scholars working from the capabilities perspective argue that routines tend to evolve in path-dependent ways due to the presence of self-reinforcing processes that promote persistence and refinement in patterns of action. While routines may end in a state of "lock-in", this is not necessarily the case, as factors external to the routine may intervene and change its trajectory. Further, the extent to which routines evolve in path-dependent ways is affected by temporal orientations for search (i.e., backward-looking, forward-looking).

The practice perspective

The practice perspective concentrates on the routine itself, and its constituent parts, as the focal level of analysis. In this work, routines are viewed as comprising two aspects: the ostensive and performative. The ostensive aspects refer to the abstract pattern of actions, or the "routine in principle", while the performative aspects refer to the enactment of the pattern of actions by routine participants, or the "routine in practice" (Feldman & Pentland, 2003). These two aspects, the ostensive and the performative, are related through a process of mutual constitution (Giddens, 1984); the ostensive patterns are used to guide, account for, and refer to specific performances of the routine, and the performances of the routine serve to create, maintain, and modify the ostensive patterns (Feldman & Pentland, 2003, 2005; Pentland & Feldman, 2005). Scholars working from the practice perspective are particularly interested in the role of agency (Feldman, 2000; Pentland & Rueter, 1994). Participants in the routine take actions within the context of various enabling and constraining structures, including artifacts like standard operating procedures, and these actions can produce a variety of performances of the routine. Practice-based scholars are particularly interested in understanding the stability, variability, and change in routines.

Considered next are three areas in which time is prominent for the practice perspective: temporal influences on the performance of routines, the role of time in the performance outcomes of routines, and how routines evolve over time.

Temporal antecedents

This section focuses on three ways in which time affects how actors perform their roles in routines: time as signal for action, time as resource for action, and time as state of mind.

Time as signal for action

In this section, attention is directed to the role of time as a signal within routines (i.e., inside the black box). Both clock and event time serve as cues for actors performing their roles within routines.

Clock time. While scholars from the practice perspective have focused more on the role of preceding actions – that is, event-based cues – some recent work has been directed to the role of clocks. In a multicase study examining waste collection routines, Turner and Rindova (2012) describe how waste collection organizations have formal rules in place for customers to have their waste containers ready for service by a certain time (e.g., 7:00 a.m.); these clock-based rules are intended to create buffers between sequentially dependent actions (i.e., container preparation by customers, container emptying by waste collection crews). But given that crews tend to enact the waste collection routine similarly across performances, they frequently arrive at customer locations at about the same time on the days that service is being performed; this results in many customers developing expectations for when the crew typically arrives at their house (e.g., 11:00 a.m.), and customers evolve their role performances accordingly (i.e., "just in time" container preparation). In turn, waste collection crews feel greater pressure to perform the routine as they have in the past to ensure that their arrivals are in sync with the times at which their customers typically perform their roles.[3]

Event time. In practice-based research, the majority of attention has focused on events as cues for action. In part, this reflects scholars' examining the performance of routines in terms of sequences of actions, which emphasizes the order in which actions take place for a given routine performance (Pentland & Rueter, 1994). For actors performing their roles in a routine, completion of a particular action can serve as a signal that there is now an opportunity for the next action to be taken, particularly when the actions are sequentially dependent. For example, based on her participant observation study at McDonald's, Leidner (1993, p. 68) describes how the arrival of customers stimulates a sequence of actions for the window service routine, including greeting the customer, taking the order, assembling the order, presenting the order, receiving payment, and thanking the customer. Scholars have also argued that the completion of a preceding action can serve as a more direct stimulus for the performance of a subsequent action. This is evident in Cohen and Bacdayan's (1994, p. 554) description of routines as "interlocking, reciprocally-triggered sequences of skilled actions", such that the performance of one skilled action tends to trigger a subsequent action in the routine.

In sum, scholars working from the practice perspective have considered clock and event time as signals for action. This work considers how organizations use artifacts like clock-based rules to create buffers between actions, and how the act of performing routines in similar ways can establish expectations for when things happen, which influence subsequent performances. With respect to event time, scholars examining the internal structure of routines as sequences of actions emphasize how the occurrence of preceding actions within routines serves to stimulate subsequent actions.

Time as resource for action

Practice-based research also views time as a resource, and time pressure as a resource shortage (Arrow et al., 2004) that restricts variability in the performances of routines. As time pressure increases, actors have less time available to consider alternative avenues for performing a routine, and there may be fewer viable avenues for performing it – that is, fewer ways that can be completed within the time constraints (Becker, 2005; Turner & Fern, 2012). As indicated earlier, experimental evidence at the individual level has found that greater time pressure results in individuals being more likely to use previously learned solutions when making decisions to solve a recurring problem, even when alternative solutions are intended or desired (Betsch et al., 1999; Betsch et al., 2004). These results are consistent with the idea that greater time pressure restricts opportunities for deliberation and variability in routine performances.

In related research, Turner and Fern (2012) found consistent results, along with some nuance. The study showed that both increases and decreases in time pressure relative to typical conditions resulted in greater divergence in routine performances from the ways in which actors had previously performed the routine; the results also indicated that actors' experience in performing the routine amplified the effect of decreases in time pressure, but offered limited support for a moderating effect of experience for increases in time pressure. The idea that decreases in time pressure result in more divergent performances is consistent with time as a resource, from the view that actors have more time available for thinking about how to perform the routine, and they have more avenues available for pursuing it. That experience amplified this effect supports the notion that the time and effort that actors have previously invested in performing the routine increase their understandings of the routine, its surrounding context, and the set of possibilities for performing the routine, which heightens their capacity for recombining elements from past experience and improvising their performances. The idea that increases in time pressure result in greater divergence is less intuitive, but also appears consistent with the idea of time as a resource. Specifically, if atypically high levels of time pressure restrict the ways in which a routine can be performed, actors will be more likely to diverge from past ways of performing it, as the current performance context is more constrained relative to past conditions. The limited support for a moderating effect of experience suggests that increases in time pressure are likely to restrict actors' ability to exercise experience-based agency.

In sum, this research suggests that greater time pressure restricts the variability with which actors perform routines, and that such effects can depend upon the performance experience of actors.

Time as state of mind

Scholars have argued that actors' temporal orientation is an important element of agency (Emirbayer & Mische, 1998), which shapes the ways in which they perform routines (Howard-Grenville, 2005). This notion recognizes that actors have multiple orientations to time, which include being directed to the past, present, and/or future (Howard-Grenville, 2005; Shipp, Edwards, & Lambert, 2009).[4] These orientations have corresponding influences on actors' performances, from iterating upon past actions, to acting based upon practical evaluation of current conditions, to projecting forward and imagining novel and reconfigured ways of acting (Emirbayer & Mische, 1998). In her participant observation study of a process development routine at a semiconductor manufacturer, Howard-Grenville (2005) found that actors' primary temporal orientation affects the flexibility with which actors perform the routine, where flexibility refers to the idea that actors can perform the same routine in different ways at different times. This work indicated that the flexibility of routine performances was limited by past orientations – for example, drawing on previous experience in performing the routine – and was promoted by present and future orientations, which focus on attending to the situation at hand and imagining new possibilities for the routine.

In sum, research from the practice perspective argues that actors' orientations to the past, present, and future shape the flexibility with which they perform routines.

Time and outcomes

Practice-based research has been less focused on explaining performance outcomes, though studies have considered the role of outcomes in processes of endogenous change in routines (Feldman, 2000; Rerup & Feldman, 2011). But recent work from the practice perspective is beginning to focus more on performance outcomes in their own right. This section considers the role of time in how performances of routines impact outcomes like task efficiency and effectiveness.

Duration of routine performances

Time is often used as an indicator of the efficiency with which a routine is performed. For example, in their computational simulation study, Miller, Pentland, and Choi (2012) examined the time required to solve a problem. This is similar to Cohen and Bacdayan (1994), who focused on the amount of time required for making a move in repeated plays of a card game.

Research in this area tends to examine outcomes from a learning perspective. The work on learning by doing suggests that developing greater experience with a task results in greater efficiency in its execution, particularly under stable conditions (Argote, 1999; Arrow, 1962; Becker, 2005). Miller et al. (2012), for instance, showed gains in problem-solving efficiency across performances of the routine; specifically, the time required to solve a given problem decreased as actors developed declarative and transactive memory. Similarly, Cohen and Bacdayan (1994) argued that actors develop procedural memory as they repeatedly perform a routine, and their experiments provide evidence that as subjects gained greater experience with the routine over time, they were able to perform it more quickly. Studies also suggest necessary conditions for these effects, as Pentland, Feldman, Becker, and Liu (2012) found that selective retention of lower-cost performances was required to observe learning by doing effects in their study.

In sum, as actors gain greater experience in performing a routine for a particular task, they develop corresponding memory and discover opportunities for improvement, which enable them to perform the task more efficiently.

Duration of recovery

The work on learning effects also considers more dynamic conditions, focusing on how long it takes organizations to recover from changes that disrupt the routine. For example, Miller et al. (2012) found that organizational downsizing and introducing task novelty resulted in longer durations for performing the routine. For both types of changes, they observed that smaller organizations were able to recover more quickly due to faster experiential learning. For downsizing, the researchers observed that a higher percentage of downsized employees resulted in greater declines in problem-solving efficiency, but also led to faster recovery to efficient levels. For task novelty, they found that organizations adapt to changes faster when agents' memories are shorter and when they have greater breadth of task awareness.

In their study of waste collection routines, Turner and Rindova (2012) found that changes in the conditions for performing routines resulted in slower performances because employees had to figure out how to complete the task under different/ disrupted conditions (e.g., adverse weather conditions, equipment breakdowns), but the results also indicated two approaches that organizations used to minimize the associated recovery times. One was the use of reorganizing rules as general guidelines, which allowed actors to take into account the changing circumstances and provided them with some degree of automaticity in their responses. The other involved drawing upon established connections to reconstitute the routine, such as using team-based approaches for making sense of the modifications needed in their performances.

In sum, scholars suggest that recovery time is reduced by organizational and task conditions that enable faster learning and relearning, as well as by using artifacts like reorganizing rules and drawing upon established connections among actors.

Being "on time"

Recent work has also begun to examine time-based performance outcomes that capture the effectiveness of routine performances as reflected in customer satisfaction. Turner and Rindova (2012) found that customers of waste collection routines are more satisfied when routines are performed at typical times. When routines are performed consistently, customers tend to develop expectations for when crews typically arrive, and evolve their role performances accordingly (i.e., preparing waste containers for service in line with typical crew arrivals). As a result, when crews do not arrive at typical times, customer dissatisfaction rises markedly due to divergence with their expectations, which results in greater incidence of missed service as customers are less likely to have their containers ready in time.

In sum, research identifies that being "on time" can have important implications for the effectiveness of routine performances.

Evolution of routines over time

While the capabilities perspective emphasizes the path-dependent nature of routine evolution, the practice perspective focuses on the idea that routines exhibit elements of both path dependence and path creation (Garud, Kumaraswamy, & Karnoe, 2010; Pentland et al., 2012). According to the practice perspective, present and future routine performances build upon past performances, but practice-based researchers view routines as more variable and emergent than suggested by a strongly path-dependent model that concludes in a state of lock-in (Mahoney, 2000; Sydow et al., 2009). In this sense, the practice perspective emphasizes actors' ability to shape unfolding organizational routines, consistent with the notion of path creation (Garud et al., 2010). This work understands the evolution of routines through the recursive relationship between the ostensive and performative aspects.

When performing routines, actors may seek to reproduce past performances, or they may choose to alter how they perform the routine. In terms of incentives for reproducing past performances, scholars have offered a number of reasons, including attaining learning and coordination efficiencies (Cohen, 1991; Lazaric, 2008), steering clear of political confrontations and striving for legitimacy (Feldman, 2003; Howard-Grenville, 2005), maintaining an established truce (Turner & Rindova, 2012; Zbaracki & Bergen, 2010), and avoiding variations that could upset other interrelated routines (Howard-Grenville, 2005). Scholars also offer reasons for why actors choose to alter how they perform a routine, including adapting to organizational and environmental changes (Cohen, 2007; Turner & Fern, 2012; Turner & Rindova, 2012), and responding to problems or opportunities that were made evident from past performances (Feldman, 2000; Feldman & Pentland, 2003; Rerup & Feldman, 2011).

When actors enact routines in ways that are similar to past performances, they develop and reinforce the ostensive aspects, consistent with the idea of path dependence. But when actors perform the routine in novel ways, they alter the potential repertoire of performances, which can reshape the ostensive aspects, aligning with the idea of path creation. The ostensive aspects are modified when novel performances are taken up into the ostensive aspects (Feldman & Pentland, 2003). These modifications can take the form of changes that seek to displace existing patterns in favor of preferred ones, or extensions that result in more nuance and conditionality – for example, elaborating the ostensive aspects to reflect different variants of a routine for different conditions.

In performing routines, whether in familiar or novel ways, agency and artifacts play important roles. As such, these elements contribute to understanding the evolution of routines. From the perspective of agency, scholars have pointed to a number of factors. For example, actors' primary temporal orientation influences their likelihood of performing routines in flexible ways, with past orientations promoting stability while present and future orientations encourage variability (Howard-Grenville, 2005). Actors' experience in performing routines also affects the extent to which they diverge from past routine performances; for example, Turner and Fern (2012) found actors' performance experience had an overall stabilizing effect on routine performances, but that experience also enabled variability in response to certain contextual changes (i.e., those that provided actors with greater opportunity to exercise experience-based agency). Scholars have also highlighted how actors' understandings of the organization influence routine evolution. Feldman (2003) found that desired changes in routines were inhibited when they were perceived to run counter to actors' understandings of how the organization operated more broadly, and Rerup and Feldman (2011) explained how routines change in response to perceived inconsistencies between the routine and organizational schemata. The power of actors has also been highlighted as important for understanding when novel performances are or are not taken up in the ostensive aspects (Feldman & Pentland, 2003; Howard-Grenville, 2005).

In terms of artifacts, practice-based research has described a variety that affect the performance and evolution of routines, from formal rules and standard operating procedures to the work equipment and larger physical context (Pentland & Feldman, 2005). From the perspective of context, for example, Howard-Grenville (2005) found that the contextual embeddedness of a routine has notable implications for overlapping and interconnected structures, such that strongly embedded routines are less likely to change over time. In parallel, Turner and Fern (2012) found that changes in the context promote variability in routine performances. Scholars also highlight how artifacts serve as channels by which agency shapes interactions among actors and the evolution of routines (Bapuji, Hora, & Saeed, 2012; Cacciatori, 2008, 2012; D'Adderio, 2008, 2011; Lazaric, Mangolte, & Massue, 2003).

In sum, while actors have incentives for reproducing historical ways of performing routines, they also have incentives for novelty. When actors introduce variations while enacting routines, they increase the possible ways of performing the routine, which can result in modifications to the ostensive aspects. Accordingly, agency and artifacts play central enabling and constraining roles in the evolution of routines.

See Figure 7.2 for a summary of key findings across the two perspectives regarding temporal antecedents, outcomes, and evolution.

	Temporal antecedents	Time and outcomes	Evolution of routines
Capabilities perspective	• Signal: Organizations use clocks and events to cue routine performances, and organizational and market conditions affect their use as alternative signals for action. • Resource: Time pressure results in greater utilization and faster execution of routines.	• Developing valuable routines: Time to development is an important outcome. While learning by doing is often required, learning before doing can be effective under certain environmental conditions. • Realizing value from routines: Value realization is a function of time in varied ways, such as historical specificity in the impact of routines. • Replicating valuable routines: Organizations benefit from precise replication, particularly in the initial stages of transfer when recipients have limited understanding of the routine.	• Routines evolve in path-dependent ways due to self-reinforcing processes, but the extent of path dependence is also affected by temporal orientations for search (i.e., backward- vs. forward-looking). • Routines may end in a state of lock-in, but there is also the potential for factors external to the routine to intervene and change the trajectory of evolution.
Practice perspective	• Signal: Events and clocks serve as signals that facilitate the taking of actions within routine performances. • Resource: Time pressure reduces the variability with which actors perform routines. • State of mind: Routines are performed more flexibly when actors are oriented to the present and future, versus when they are oriented to the past.	• Duration of performance: As actors attain experience in performing a routine, they develop corresponding memory and identify improvement opportunities, which enable them to perform the routine faster. • Duration of recovery: Recovery time is reduced by conditions that enable faster learning, and by use of artifacts like re-organizing rules and drawing upon the connections among routine participants. • Being "on time": The effectiveness of routines can be a function of when activities are performed relative to the expectations of customers.	• Routine participants have incentives for both reproducing past performances and for introducing novelty. • When actors introduce novelty while performing routines, they expand the repertoire of performances, which can modify the ostensive aspects of the routine. • Agency and artifacts play key enabling and constraining roles in the evolution of routines.

Figure 7.2 Key findings regarding the role of time in the capabilities and practice perspectives.

Research methodologies

This section briefly reviews the methodologies that scholars working from the capabilities and practice perspectives have commonly used to examine temporal issues in routines, and offers some suggestions for methodology choices in future research. In considering these issues, particular attention is given to the principle of triangulation, which emphasizes how the use of multiple methodologies enables the limitations of any one method to be offset by the advantages of another. Scholars have highlighted how triangulation can enhance understanding of a phenomenon through convergence and divergence; when studies using a diversity of methodologies produce convergent findings, we have greater confidence in an explanation; by contrast, the generation of divergent findings often enables alternative and more nuanced explanations to emerge (Jick, 1979; McGrath, 1982).

Methods, time and the capabilities perspective

There is considerable variety in the methods that capabilities-based scholars have used to examine temporal issues in routines, including case studies (e.g., Dutta et al., 2003; Jensen & Szulanski, 2007) and statistical analyses of survey or archival data (e.g., Knott, 2001; Turner et al., 2010), as well as related work using lab experiments (e.g., Betsch et al., 1999; Garapin & Hollard, 1999). In this research, scholars have tended to focus on one routine or a small number of routines in a single organization, in multiple establishments within one organization, or in multiple businesses operating within one industry. The methods contribute to both theory development and theory testing, which is consistent with the moderate stage of development for capabilities-based research on routines. From a triangulation perspective, the diverse set of methodologies tend to complement one another well; for example, the strengths and weaknesses of lab experiments (i.e., high precision of control, low realism of the context for participants) are counterbalanced by the strengths and weaknesses of case studies (McGrath, 1982). And as one area of study in particular, scholars examining routine replication have effectively utilized a diverse set of methodologies to increase confidence in their arguments for the benefits of precise replication (e.g., Szulanski & Jensen, 2006; Winter et al., 2012).

Going forward, research examining temporal issues in routines from the capabilities perspective can benefit from continued diversity in methodologies, and by being more systematic in the use of multiple methods to examine particular research questions. For example, researchers can use computational simulation to elaborate theory regarding the role of time in organizational routines, particularly given the prominence of the simulation method in early work on routines (e.g., Cyert & March, 1963; Nelson & Winter, 1982). Further, scholars highlight that time structure is a core element in the design of computational simulation experiments in organizations research (Harrison, Lin, Carroll, & Carley, 2007), although time is rarely the central focus of these studies. As another example, understanding can be advanced through archival and survey-based research that spans industries, as the salience of time may differ considerably across industries. While there are increased challenges in identifying comparable routines across industries, there are a number of activities (e.g., undertaking acquisitions, introducing generational innovations) that would seem to be sufficiently comparable to facilitate investigation. Also, with a clearer and more explicit focus on particular questions that examine the role of time in routines, capabilities-based researchers can more effectively implement the principle of triangulation in their design of research programs.

Methods, time and the practice perspective

There has been less variety in the methods that practice-based researchers have used to examine temporality in routines until recently. This research has emphasized longitudinal case studies, which typically involve participant or nonparticipant observation of one or more routines within a single organization. By enabling deep examination of routines over time, this method initially helped to advance understanding of routines by revealing findings that diverged from expectations based on traditional routines research, providing the foundation for the practice-based perspective (Pentland & Feldman, 2008). The longitudinal case study method has been particularly well suited for delving into the black box of routines to explore their internal structure and dynamics, and its emphasis among practice-based scholars is consistent with the value of using case studies to provide fresh insights in established research areas and to develop theory in early stages of new research areas (Eisenhardt, 1989; Glaser & Strauss, 1967).

In more recent work focused on the microfoundations of routines (Felin, Foss, Heimeriks, & Madsen, 2012), scholars examining temporal issues in routines from the practice perspective have begun to utilize a broader array of research methodologies. In some work, scholars have expanded the breadth of field-based methodologies to include case studies examining the same routine in multiple organizations (Turner & Rindova, 2012), which helps in terms of robustness and generalizability (Eisenhardt & Graebner, 2007), and field experiments that provide greater precision in control and measurement (Bapuji et al., 2012). In other work, scholars have utilized methodologies that provide greater diversity with respect to triangulation. For example, relative to longitudinal case studies, recent simulation-based research (Miller et al., 2012; Pentland et al., 2012) provides greater precision and capacity for experimental manipulation, as well as greater generalizability with respect to populations (McGrath, 1982). This is consistent with earlier calls for using computational simulation as a way to explore the complexity and coordination of individual roles within routines (Cohen et al., 1996, p. 677), and with suggestions that simulation can be an effective method for elaborating theories that have emerged from case studies (Davis, Eisenhardt, & Bingham, 2007). As another example, recent empirical studies that use workflow data to examine the role of time in the performance of routines (Turner & Fern, 2012) provide a good avenue for theory testing. Given the early stage of development for the practice perspective, there remains considerable opportunity for developing theory regarding temporality through case studies, but to continue to advance the perspective, scholars need to increasingly focus on more diverse methods for elaborating and testing theory.

Discussion

The objective of this chapter was to examine the role of time in routines research. The review was structured according to two central perspectives that scholars in strategy and organizational theory have tended to adopt in their examination of routines: the capabilities perspective and the practice perspective (Parmigiani & Howard-Grenville, 2011). Capabilities-based research has a macro orientation that focuses on the role of routines in organizational competitiveness, views them largely as whole entities, and emphasizes their stability, while also highlighting their potential for change in relation to market and environmental conditions. Practice-based work has a micro orientation that examines the role of routines in everyday organizing, explores their constituent parts, and emphasizes their internal dynamics, particularly with regard to their potential for endogenous change. In examining the literature, attention was directed to temporal antecedents, outcomes, and evolution. In these areas, the review reveals considerable similarities and complementarities across the capabilities and practice perspectives, and points to opportunities for extending our understanding of routines through future research that provides more systematic and integrative attention to the temporal dimension.[5]

Temporal influences on the performance of routines

The review points to three categories of time-based determinants – time as signal, resource, and state of mind – that influence whether, when, why, and how routines are performed. Across the capabilities and practice perspectives are similarities, such as the attention to time as a signal and resource. The perspectives are also complementary in that capabilities-based research tends to emphasize external temporal influences (e.g., completion of other routines), while practice-based work focuses more on internal influences (e.g., temporal orientation of actors). And the perspectives tend to differ in their questions; capabilities-based scholars typically consider questions like whether and when routines are performed, while practice-based researchers concentrate more on how routines are performed. While scholars are only beginning to explore temporal influences on the performance of routines, with many questions remaining to be asked and answered, this review points to three areas in particular where future research can help to extend our understanding.

First, there are opportunities to expand the notions of time as signal, resource, and state of mind. Consider time as signal. To complement extant research that considers clock and event time in an objective way, it may help to explore the social construction of time as a signal (Ancona et al., 2001; Arrow et al., 2004).

While this can be considered at macro levels, such as the social construction of calendars (Bluedorn, 2002), for routines scholarship, concentrating at micro levels will likely provide greater value. For example, routine participants may create "times" that are seemingly unrelated to task accomplishment, but nevertheless work themselves into the routine and function as signals – for example, "banana time" as a created activity/event that breaks up repetitive work (Roy, 1960). As another example, participants in routines may develop marker events, like midpoint transitions, that serve as signals to ramp up the intensity of task performance (Gersick, 1989). Consider, also, time as state of mind. While routines scholars have developed key insights around the temporal orientation of actors, future research could explore other related aspects. For example, Ancona et al. (2001) emphasize that actors also relate to time in ways that reflect their temporal style (e.g., how predictable actors view the future) and temporal perception (e.g., whether actors perceive activities as original or unique). In addition, future research should explore how performing routines is affected by variability among routine participants with respect to time as signal, resource, and state of mind.[6]

Second, future research can extend our understanding by exploring the conditional nature of temporal influences on routines. Capabilities-based research has begun to consider how macro-level conditions, such as market concentration and organizational age, shape the degree to which routine performances are driven by calendars versus competitive events (Turner et al., 2010, 2013). And practice-based work has started to look within the routine, such as how the characteristics of individual actors (e.g., their experience, power) may condition the effects of time pressure or temporal orientation (Howard-Grenville, 2005; Turner & Fern, 2012). Scholars might also focus on characteristics at the level of the routine. For example, whether the typical performance of a routine takes place over minutes, days, weeks, or months might influence the effects of temporal orientation or time pressure.

Third, beyond the performance of established routines, the notions of time as signal, resource, and state of mind may enrich our understanding of other important activities involving routines, such as their emergence and replication. In terms of emergence, future research might focus on how time as signal, resource, or state of mind shapes the formation of new routines. From the view of time as signal, for example, research on entrainment would suggest that recurring event cycles in the surrounding environment have considerable influence on the manner and rate at which new routines emerge (Ancona & Chong, 1996; Bluedorn, 2002). In terms of replication, scholars working from the capabilities perspective may find the idea of time as resource helpful in explaining whether, when, and how routines are replicated (Winter & Szulanski, 2001). Moreover, research on replication might benefit from drawing upon ideas from the practice perspective, such as how the internal structure of routines influences the precision and rate of replication, and perhaps even conceptualizing the process of replication itself as a routine, which could be analyzed in terms of ostensive and performative parts.

How performing routines influences key outcomes

Reviewing research that examines the impact of routines also highlights similarities and complementarities across the capabilities and practice perspectives. The perspectives are similar in that both consider how routines affect outcomes of interest for organizations, and they are complementary from the view that capabilities-based research tends to focus on firm-level performance outcomes (e.g., profit, survival), while practice-based work concentrates more on routine-level outcomes like task efficiency and effectiveness. Further, while both perspectives examine how learning by doing influences outcomes (Argote, 1999), scholars working from the capabilities perspective also consider how the impact of routines is a function of their qualities as resources (Barney, 1991).

This review suggests two areas for future work on temporality that may be particularly promising for advancing our understanding of the impact of routines. First, a broader consideration of the role of time in performing routines offers potential to provide insight in areas like learning and replication. In learning-based studies, routines scholars have focused primarily on the effects of learning by doing over time, but we know relatively little about the impact of alternative investments of time, such as offline modeling (Pisano, 1994) or vicarious learning (Levitt & March, 1988); we also have limited understanding of the implications associated with different ways in which learning has taken place – exploring the effects of different patterns/sequences of learning, for example, might shed light in this area. In replication-based studies, routines scholars have focused on the benefits arising from precise replication, yet less attention has been directed to examining the impact of the rate of replication. As Winter (1995) suggests, the rate of replication should be particularly salient in competitive markets where the potential for imitation is high.

Second, our understanding of the impact of routines may be advanced by greater attention to the conditional nature of the effects by which routines influence outcomes.[7] Consider capabilities-based research that draws on the resource-based view to examine how advantageous routines impact firm performance. While this work emphasizes the importance of tacitness and firm specificity (Parmigiani & Howard-Grenville, 2011), studies also highlight how considerable differences in organizational performance can arise from advantageous routines that are explicit (Knott, 2003), and how considerable performance differences can dissipate due to the loss of a key individual (Aime et al., 2010). To advance this research, then, future work should focus on the conditions under which different types of routines are able to provide firms with competitive advantages, and for how long those advantages may be sustained.[8] Such research might draw insights from the practice perspective; for instance, scholars interested in how causal ambiguity affects the rate of routine imitation might examine the degree to which actors vary in their understandings of the routine (i.e., multiplicity in the ostensive aspects). There are also significant opportunities for practice-based research to extend our understanding of how outcomes are dependent upon the ways in which routines are performed. For instance, future research could examine when flexibility/

improvisation in the performance of routines results in beneficial versus detrimental outcomes; in exploring this question, researchers might look to work on environmental uncertainty and fit (Miller, 1992; Milliken, 1987). As another example, scholars might explore the conditions under which greater experience in performing a routine may or may not lead to heightened efficiency.

How routines evolve over time

The capabilities and practice perspectives are similar in terms of devoting attention to explaining the processes by which organizational routines evolve over time, and they are complementary with respect to emphasizing different dynamics. While capabilities scholars concentrate more on the "external dynamics" of routines, the practice perspective emphasizes their "internal dynamics". Capabilities-based research, particularly work on dynamic capabilities, focuses more on top-down processes in which higher-order routines (Winter, 2003) or managerial interventions (Teece, 2012) facilitate change in routines, whether in seeking to respond to or stimulate market and environmental changes (Barreto, 2010; Helfat et al., 2007). By contrast, researchers working from the practice perspective emphasize bottom-up processes that enable endogenous change to arise from within the routine (Feldman, 2000; Feldman, 2003).

Research on the evolution of routines emphasizes that routines are subject to self-reinforcing processes and exhibit path dependence, such that there is potential for lock-in (Sydow et al., 2009). Given this potential, future research might fruitfully explore how organizations can effectively change routines that are perceived to be detrimental. For example, we have little understanding of the conditions under which the alternative processes – "external dynamics" versus "internal dynamics" – are more likely to generate beneficial change in routines. Scholars investigating this issue might fruitfully draw from ecological research that considers the content and process effects of change (Barnett & Carroll, 1995). It could also be valuable to better understand the malleability of such processes, such as to what extent and in what ways managers can facilitate/accelerate and inhibit/decelerate these processes of change.

Along similar lines, research suggests that timing may be important, as routines are likely to be more amenable to change at particular points in time. Change may be more likely, for example, when the broader organization is undergoing pauses or transitions (Gersick & Hackman, 1990; Zellmer-Bruhn, Waller, & Ancona, 2004). Consistent with previous guidance (Cohen 1991, 2012), this may be a ripe area for drawing upon ideas from psychology, which suggest that interventions are more likely to be effective in breaking habits when they coincide with broader contextual changes. For example, Verplanken and Wood (2006) argue that informational campaigns designed to change strongly formed habits in particular areas (e.g., poor eating habits) are more likely to be successful when they occur during natural points of transition in individuals' lives, such as changing jobs or moving houses. In examining organizational routines, parallel transitions might include undergoing mergers or changing corporate headquarters.

Conclusion

The temporal dimension is central for our understanding of routines and their corresponding outcomes, but this research is still in its infancy. The aim of this review was to recognize the growing but largely fragmented work that considers the temporality of routines. By reviewing what has been done and offering some suggestions for future investigation, I hope that the research on the temporal dimension of routines will continue to grow and contribute to our broader understanding of organizational routines.

Acknowledgments

The author would like to thank coeditors Abbie Shipp and Yitzhak Fried, as well as Jennifer Howard-Grenville, Kent Miller, Anne Parmigiani, Erik Strauss, and Leona Wiegmann for their constructive comments.

Notes

1. Scholars have also put forward a view of routines as dispositions, which focuses on the idea of routines as interlocked habits or interacting action dispositions (Birnholtz, Cohen, & Hoch, 2007; Cohen, 2007; Hodgson, 2003; Knudsen, 2008). This review does not examine routines as dispositions as a separate perspective, and instead incorporates related research (e.g., Cohen & Bacdayan, 1994; Pentland et al., 2012) as it pertains to the capabilities and practice perspectives.
2. As discussed later, capabilities-based research also considers how routines evolve and change, but this work focuses on the idea that routines often change in stable ways (e.g., higher-order routines).
3. This process has interesting ties with the concept of temporal specificity, which refers to situations in which performing activities on time (e.g., according to a precise schedule) is critical because delays in key activities can be points of blockage that have system-wide disruptive effects (Masten, Meehan, & Snyder, 1991). In this case, waste collection organizations have formal rules in place for customer participation to prevent or limit temporal specificity, but by performing waste collections consistently over time, crews actually create conditions of high temporal specificity as customers establish time-based expectations and evolve their behavior accordingly, which makes subsequent collections more challenging (Turner & Rindova, 2012).
4. The idea that actors may simultaneously allocate attention to the past, present, and future is common across agency-based research on temporal orientation (Emirbayer & Mische, 1998; Howard-Grenville, 2005) and research on temporal focus (Shipp et al., 2009). In a survey, Shipp et al. (2009) found evidence consistent with this simultaneous view, with a majority of the surveyed individuals directing attention to two or three time periods; interestingly, they also found that 10% of their sample had a low focus for all three time periods (i.e., "atemporal").
5. Routines research could also benefit from greater specificity when referencing the temporal dimension. The phrase "over time" is one of the most common in the literature, yet what is meant by time is often not made clear. In many instances, for example, it is important to know whether time is being conceptualized in terms of performances/events or clocks/calendars (e.g., learning curve effects, time compression diseconomies).
6. With respect to time as state of mind, scholars might explore variability both across actors and among past, present, and future. Such work could draw upon recent research

on strategy making that explores how participants work through differences and link interpretations of the past, present, and future, which shapes the degree to which strategic decisions depart from the status quo (Kaplan & Orlikowski, 2013).

7. Scholars should also devote more attention to the temporal structure of effects; for example, theoretical arguments and empirical investigations could benefit from greater specification of the timing of effects (Mitchell & James, 2001).

8. Future research would also benefit from greater attention to potential endogeneity when examining the impact of using particular routines or replication strategies.

References

Adler, P. S., Goldoftas, B., & Levine, D. I. (1999). Flexibility versus efficiency? A case study of model changeovers in the Toyota production system. *Organization Science, 10,* 43–68.

Aime, F., Johnson, S., Ridge, J. W., & Hill, A. D. (2010). The routine may be stable but the advantage is not: Competitive implications of key employee mobility. *Strategic Management Journal, 31,* 75–87.

Ancona, D., & Chong, C. (1996). Entrainment: Pace, cycle and rhythm in organizational behavior. In B. M. Staw & L. L. Cummings (Eds.), *Research in organizational behavior* (Vol. 18, pp. 251–284). Greenwich, CT: JAI Press.

Ancona, D. G., Okhuysen, G. A., & Perlow, L. A. (2001). Taking time to integrate temporal research. *Academy of Management Review, 26,* 512–529.

Argote, L. (1999). *Organizational learning: Creating, retaining and transferring knowledge.* Norwell, MA: Kluwer Academic.

Arrow, H., Poole, M. S., Henry, K. B., Wheelan, S., & Moreland, R. (2004). Time, change, and development: The temporal perspective on groups. *Small Group Research, 35,* 73–105.

Arrow, K. J. (1962). The economic implications of learning by doing. *Review of Economic Studies, 29,* 155–173.

Avital, M. (2000). Dealing with time in social inquiry: A tension between method and lived experience. *Organization Science, 11,* 665–673.

Bapuji, H., Hora, M., & Saeed, A. M. (2012). Intentions, intermediaries, and interaction: Examining the emergence of routines. *Journal of Management Studies, 49,* 1586–1607.

Barnett, W. P., & Carroll, G. R. (1995). Modeling internal organizational change. *American Journal of Sociology, 21,* 217–236.

Barney, J. (1991). Firm resources and sustained competitive advantage. *Journal of Management, 17,* 99–120.

Barreto, I. (2010). Dynamic capabilities: A review of past research and an agenda for the future. *Journal of Management, 36,* 256–280.

Becker, M. C. (2004). Organizational routines: A review of the literature. *Industrial and Corporate Change, 13,* 643–677.

Becker, M. C. (2005). A framework for applying organizational routines in empirical research: Linking antecedents, characteristics and performance outcomes of recurrent interaction patterns. *Industrial and Corporate Change, 14,* 817–846.

Betsch, T., Brinkmann, B. J., Fiedler, K., & Breining, K. (1999). When prior knowledge overrules new evidence: Adaptive use of decision strategies and the role of behavioral routines. *Swiss Journal of Psychology, 58,* 151–160.

Betsch, T., Haberstroh, S., Molter, B., & Glockner, A. (2004). Oops, I did it again – Relapse errors in routinized decision making. *Organizational Behavior and Human Decision Processes, 93,* 62–74.

Birnholtz, J. P., Cohen, M. D., & Hoch, S. V. (2007). Organizational character: On the regeneration of Camp Popular Grove. *Organization Science, 18,* 315–332.

Bluedorn, A. C. (2002). *The human organization of time: Temporal realities and experience.* Stanford, CA: Stanford University Press.

Brown, S. L., & Eisenhardt, K. M. (1997). The art of continuous change: Linking complexity theory and time-paced evolution in relentlessly shifting organizations. *Administrative Science Quarterly, 42,* 1–34.

Cacciatori, E. (2008). Memory objects in project environments: Storing, retrieving and adapting learning in project-based firms. *Research Policy, 37,* 1591–1601.

Cacciatori, E. (2012). Resolving conflict in problem-solving: Systems of artefacts in the development of new routines. *Journal of Management Studies, 49,* 1559–1585.

Cohen, M. D. (1991). Individual learning and organizational routine. *Organization Science, 2,* 135–139.

Cohen, M. D. (2007). Reading Dewey: Reflections on the study of routine. *Organization Studies, 28,* 773–786.

Cohen, M. D. (2012). Perceiving and remembering routine action: Fundamental micro-level origins. *Journal of Management Studies, 49,* 1383–1388.

Cohen, M. D., & Bacdayan, P. (1994). Organizational routines are stored as procedural memory: Evidence from a laboratory study. *Organization Science, 5,* 554–568.

Cohen, M. D., Burkhart, R., Dosi, G., Egidi, M., Marengo, L., Warglien, M., & Winter, S. (1996). Routines and other recurring action patterns of organizations: Contemporary research issues. *Industrial and Corporate Change, 5,* 653–698.

Coriat, B., & Dosi, G. (1998). Learning how to govern and learning how to solve problems: On the co-evolution of competences, conflicts and organizational routines. In A. D. Chandler, P. Hagstrom, & O. Solvell (Eds.), *The dynamic firm: The role of technology, strategy, organization and regions* (pp. 103–133). Oxford: Oxford University Press.

Cyert, R. M., & March, J. G. (1963). *A behavioral theory of the firm.* Englewood Cliffs, NJ: Prentice-Hall.

D'Adderio, L. (2008). The performativity of routines: Theorising the influence of artefacts and distributed agencies on routines dynamics. *Research Policy, 37,* 769–789.

D'Adderio, L. (2011). Artifacts at the centre of routines: Performing the material turn in routines theory. *Journal of Institutional Economics, 7,* 197–230.

Darr, E. D., Argote, L., & Epple, D. (1995). The acquisition, transfer, and depreciation of knowledge in service organizations: Productivity in franchises. *Management Science, 41,* 1750–1762.

Davis, J. P., Eisenhardt, K. M., & Bingham, C. B. (2007). Developing theory through simulation methods. *Academy of Management Review, 32,* 480–499.

Dierickx, I., & Cool, K. (1989). Asset stock accumulation and sustainability of competitive advantage. *Management Science, 35,* 1504–1511.

Dutta, S., Zbaracki, M. J., & Bergen, M. (2003). Pricing process as a capability: A resource-based perspective. *Strategic Management Journal, 24,* 615–630.

Egidi, M., & Narduzzo, A. (1997). The emergence of path-dependent behaviors in cooperative contexts. *International Journal of Industrial Organization, 15,* 677–709.

Eisenhardt, K. M. (1989). Building theories from case study research. *Academy of Management Review, 14,* 532–550.

Eisenhardt, K. M., & Brown, S. L. (1998). Time pacing: Competing in markets that won't stand still. *Harvard Business Review, 76,* 59–69.

Eisenhardt, K. M., & Graebner, M. E. (2007). Theory building from cases: Opportunities and challenges. *Academy of Management Journal, 50,* 25–32.

Emirbayer, M., & Mische, A. (1998). What is agency? *American Journal of Sociology, 103,* 962–1023.

Feldman, M. S. (2000). Organizational routines as a source of continuous change. *Organization Science, 11,* 611–629.

Feldman, M. S. (2003). A performative perspective on stability and change in organizational routines. *Industrial and Corporate Change, 12,* 727–752.

Feldman, M. S., & Pentland, B. T. (2003). Reconceptualizing organizational routines as a source of flexibility and change. *Administrative Science Quarterly, 48,* 94–118.

Feldman, M. S, & Pentland, B. T. (2005). Organizational routines and the macro-actor. In B. Czarniawska & T. Hernes (Eds.), *Actor-network theory and organizing* (pp. 91–111). Malmö, Sweden: Copenhagen Business School Press.

Felin, T., Foss, N. J., Heimeriks, K. H., & Madsen, T. L. (2012). Microfoundations of routines and capabilities: Individuals, processes, and structure. *Journal of Management Studies, 49,* 1351–1374.

Garapin, A., & Hollard, M. (1999). Routines and incentives in group tasks. *Journal of Evolutionary Economics, 9,* 465–486.

Garud, R., Kumaraswamy, A., & Karnoe, P. (2010). Path dependence or path creation? *Journal of Management Studies, 47,* 760–774.

Gavetti, G. (2005). Cognition and hierarchy: Rethinking the microfoundations of capabilities' development. *Organization Science, 16,* 599–617.

Gavetti, G., & Levinthal, D. (2000). Looking forward and looking backward: Cognitive and experiential search. *Administrative Science Quarterly, 45,* 113–137.

Gersick, C. J. G. (1989). Marking time: Predictable transitions in task groups. *Academy of Management Journal, 32,* 274–309.

Gersick, C. J. G., & Hackman, J. R. (1990). Habitual routines in task-performing groups. *Organizational Behavior and Human Decision Processes, 47,* 65–97.

Giddens, A. (1984). *The constitution of society: Outline of the theory of structuration.* Berkeley: University of California Press.

Glaser, B. G., & Strauss, A. L. (1967). *The discovery of grounded theory: Strategies for qualitative research.* New York: Aldine de Gruyter.

Greve, H. R., & Goldeng, E. (2004). Longitudinal analysis in strategic management. *Research Methodology in Strategy and Management, 1,* 135–163.

Hannan, M. T., & Freeman, J. (1989). *Organizational ecology.* Cambridge: Harvard University Press.

Harrison, J. R., Lin, Z., Carroll, G. R., & Carley, K. M. (2007). Simulation modeling in organizational and management research. *Academy of Management Review, 32,* 1229–1245.

Helfat, C. E. (2003). Stylized facts regarding the evolution of organizational resources and capabilities. In C. E. Helfat (Ed.), *The SMS Blackwell handbook of organizational capabilities* (pp. 1–11). Malden, MA: Blackwell.

Helfat, C. E., Finkelstein, S., Mitchell, W., Peteraf, M. A., Singh, H., Teece, D. J., & Winter, S. G. (2007). *Dynamic capabilities.* Malden, MA: Blackwell.

Helfat, C. E., & Peteraf, M. A. (2003). The dynamic resource-based view: Capability life-cycles. *Strategic Management Journal, 24,* 997–1010.

Helfat, C. E., & Winter, S. G. (2011). Untangling dynamic and operational capabilities: Strategy for the (n)ever-changing world. *Strategic Management Journal, 32,* 1243–1250.

Hodgson, G. M. (2003). The mystery of the routine: The Darwinian destiny of *An Evolutionary Theory of Economic Change. Revue economique, 54,* 355–384.

Howard-Grenville, J. A. (2005). The persistence of flexible organizational routines: The role of agency and organizational context. *Organization Science, 16,* 618–636.

Jansen, K. J., & Shipp, A. J. (2013). A review and agenda for incorporating time in fit research. In A. L. Kristof-Brown & J. Billsberry (Eds.), *Organizational fit: Key issues and new directions* (pp. 195–221). Chichester, UK: Wiley.

Jensen, R. J., & Szulanski, G. (2007). Template use and the effectiveness of knowledge transfer. *Management Science, 53,* 1716–1730.

Jick, T. D. (1979). Mixing qualitative and quantitative methods: Triangulation in action. *Administrative Science Quarterly, 24,* 602–611.

Kaplan, S., & Orlikowski, W. J. (2013). Temporal work in strategy making. *Organization Science, 24,* 965–995.

Karim, S., & Mitchell, W. (2000). Path-dependent and path-breaking change: Reconfiguring business resources following acquisitions in the U.S. medical sector, 1978–1995. *Strategic Management Journal, 21,* 1061–1081.

Kelly, J. R., & McGrath, J. E. (1985). Effects of time limits and task types on task performance and interaction of four-person groups. *Journal of Personality and Social Psychology, 49,* 395–407.

Knott, A. M. (2001). The dynamic value of hierarchy. *Management Science, 47,* 430–448.

Knott, A. M. (2003). The organizational routines factor market paradox. *Strategic Management Journal, 24,* 929–943.

Knott, A. M., & McKelvey, B. (1999). Nirvana efficiency: A comparative test of residual claims and routines. *Journal of Economic Behavior and Organization, 38,* 365–383.

Knudsen, T. (2008). Organizational routines in evolutionary theory. In M. C. Becker (Ed.), *Handbook of organizational routines* (pp. 125–151). Cheltenham, UK: Edward Elgar.

Lazaric, N. (2008). Routines and routinization: An exploration of some micro-cognitive foundations. In M. C. Becker (Ed.), *Handbook of organizational routines* (pp. 205–227). Cheltenham, UK: Edward Elgar.

Lazaric, N., Mangolte, P.-A., & Massue, M.-L. (2003). Articulation and codification of collective know-how in the steel industry: Evidence from blast furnace control in France. *Research Policy, 32,* 1829–1847.

Leidner, R. (1993). *Fast food, fast talk: Service work and the routinization of everyday life.* Berkeley: University of California Press.

Levinthal, D. A. (2003). Imprinting and the evolution of firm capabilities. In C. E. Helfat (Ed.), *The SMS Blackwell handbook of organizational capabilities: Emergence, development, and change* (pp. 100–103). Malden, MA: Blackwell.

Levitt, B., & March, J. G. (1988). Organizational learning. *Annual Review of Sociology, 14,* 1319–1340.

Mahoney, J. (2000). Path dependence in historical sociology. *Theory and Society, 29,* 507–548.

March, J., & Simon, H. (1958). *Organizations.* New York: John Wiley and Sons.

Masten, S. E., Meehan, J. W., & Snyder, E. A. (1991). The costs of organization. *Journal of Law, Economics, and Organization, 7,* 1–25.

McGrath, J. E. (1982). Dilemmatics: The study of research choices and dilemmas. In J. E. McGrath, J. Martin, & R. A. Kulka (Eds.), *Judgment calls in research* (pp. 69–102). Beverly Hills: SAGE.

Miller, D. (1992). Environmental fit versus internal fit. *Organization Science, 3,* 159–178.

Miller, K. D., Pentland, B. T., & Choi, S. (2012). Dynamics of performing and remembering organizational routines. *Journal of Management Studies, 49,* 1536–1558.

Milliken, F. (1987). Three types of perceived uncertainty about the environment. *Academy of Management Review, 12*, 133–143.

Mitchell, T. R., & James, L. R. (2001). Building better theory: Time and the specification of when things happen. *Academy of Management Review, 26*, 530–547.

Narduzzo, A., Rocco, E., & Warglien, M. (2000). Talking about routines in the field: The emergence of organizational capabilities in a new cellular phone network company. In G. Dosi, R. R. Nelson, & S. G. Winter (Eds.), *The nature and dynamics of organizational capabilities* (pp. 27–50). Oxford: Oxford University Press.

Nelson, R. R. (1994). Routines. In G. M. Hodgson, W. J. Samuels, & M. R. Tool (Eds.), *Elgar companion to institutional and evolutionary economics* (Vol. 2, pp. 249–253). Brookfield, VT: Edward Elgar.

Nelson, R. R., & Winter, S. G. (1982). *An evolutionary theory of economic change.* Cambridge: Harvard University Press.

Parmigiani, A., & Howard-Grenville, J. (2011). Routines revisited: Exploring the capabilities and practice perspectives. *Academy of Management Annals, 5*, 413–453.

Pentland, B. T., & Feldman, M. S. (2005). Organizational routines as a unit of analysis. *Industrial and Corporate Change, 14*, 793–815.

Pentland, B. T., & Feldman, M. S. (2008). Issues in empirical field studies of organizational routines. In M. C. Becker (Ed.), *Handbook of organizational routines* (pp. 281–300). Cheltenham: Edward Elgar.

Pentland, B. T., Feldman, M. S., Becker, M. C., & Liu, P. (2012). Dynamics of organizational routines: A generative model. *Journal of Management Studies, 49*, 1484–1508.

Pentland, B. T., & Rueter, H. H. (1994). Organizational routines as grammars of action. *Administrative Science Quarterly, 39*, 484–510.

Pisano, G. P. (1994). Knowledge, integration, and the locus of learning: An empirical analysis of process development. *Strategic Management Journal, 15*, 85–100.

Ployhart, R. E., & Vandenberg, R. J. (2010). Longitudinal research: The theory, design, and analysis of change. *Journal of Management, 15*, 94–130.

Postrel, S., & Rumelt, R. P. (1992). Incentives, routines, and self-command. *Industrial and Corporate Change, 1*, 397–425.

Rerup, C., & Feldman, M. S. (2011). Routines as a source of change in organizational schema: The role of trial-and-error learning. *Academy of Management Journal, 54*, 577–610.

Roy, D. F. (1960). "Banana time": Job satisfaction and informal interaction. *Human Organization, 18*, 158–168.

Rumelt, R. (1984). Towards a strategic theory of the firm. In R. Lamb (Ed.), *Competitive strategic management* (pp. 556–570). Englewood Cliffs, NJ: Prentice-Hall.

Salvato, C. (2009). Capabilities unveiled. The role of ordinary activities in the evolution of product development processes. *Organization Science, 20*, 384–409.

Salvato, C., & Rerup, C. (2010). Beyond collective entities: Multilevel research on organizational routines and capabilities. *Journal of Management, 37*, 468–490.

Shipp, A. J., Edwards, J. R., & Lambert, L. S. (2009). Conceptualization and measurement of temporal focus: The subjective experience of the past, present, and future. *Organizational Behavior and Human Decision Processes, 110*, 1–22.

Stene, E. O. (1940). An approach to a science of administration. *American Political Science Review, 34*, 1124–1137.

Sydow, J., Schreyögg, G., & Koch, J. (2009). Organizational path dependence: Opening the black box. *Academy of Management Review, 34*, 689–709.

Szulanski, G., & Jensen, R. J. (2006). Presumptive adaptation and the effectiveness of knowledge transfer. *Strategic Management Journal, 27,* 937–957.

Szulanski, G., & Jensen, R. J. (2008). Growing through copying: The negative consequences of innovation on franchise network growth. *Research Policy, 37,* 1732–1741.

Teece, D. J. (2012). Dynamic capabilities: Routines versus entrepreneurial action. *Journal of Management Studies, 49,* 1395–1401.

Teece, D. J., Pisano, G., & Shuen, A. (1997). Dynamic capabilities and strategic management. *Strategic Management Journal, 18,* 509–533.

Thompson, J. D. (1967). *Organizations in action: Social science bases of administrative theory.* New York: McGraw-Hill.

Turner, S. F., & Fern, M. J. (2012). Examining the stability and variability of routine performances: The effects of experience and context change. *Journal of Management Studies, 49,* 1407–1434.

Turner, S. F., Mitchell, W., & Bettis, R. A. (2010). Responding to rivals and complements: How market concentration shapes generational product innovation strategy. *Organization Science, 21,* 854–872.

Turner, S. F., Mitchell, W., & Bettis, R. A. (2013). Strategic momentum: How experience shapes temporal consistency of ongoing innovation. *Journal of Management, 39,* 1855–1890.

Turner, S. F., & Rindova, V. (2012). A balancing act: How organizations pursue consistency in routine functioning in the face of ongoing change. *Organization Science, 23,* 24–46.

Verplanken, B., & Wood, W. (2006). Interventions to break and create habits. *Journal of Public Policy & Marketing, 25,* 90–103.

Winter, S. G. (1995). Four Rs of profitability: Rents, resources, routines, and replication. In C. A. Montgomery (Ed.), *Resource-based and evolutionary theories of the firm: Towards a synthesis* (pp. 147–178). Boston, MA: Kluwer Academic.

Winter, S. G. (2000). The satisficing principle in capability learning. *Strategic Management Journal, 21,* 981–996.

Winter, S. G. (2003). Understanding dynamic capabilities. *Strategic Management Journal, 24,* 991–995.

Winter, S. G., & Szulanski, G. (2001). Replication as strategy. *Organization Science, 12,* 730–743.

Winter, S. G., Szulanski, G., Ringov, D., & Jensen, R. J. (2012). Reproducing knowledge: Inaccurate replication and failure in franchise organizations. *Organization Science, 23,* 672–685.

Zbaracki, M. J., & Bergen, M. (2010). When truces collapse: A longitudinal study of price-adjustment routines. *Organization Science, 21,* 955–972.

Zellmer-Bruhn, M., Waller, M. J., & Ancona, D. (2004). The effect of temporal entrainment on the ability of teams to change their routines. *Research on Managing Groups and Teams, 6,* 135–158.

Zollo, M., Reuer, J. J., & Singh, H. (2002). Interorganizational routines and performance in strategic alliances. *Organization Science, 13,* 701–713.

8 Time and methodological choices

David Chan

Introduction

Studies of phenomena at the individual, group, and organizational levels can produce new insights when time is explicitly taken into account, both conceptually and methodologically. This has been shown or suggested in the various chapters in this two-volume book, as the chapter authors related their respective area of research to the concept of time – defined as either objective time (i.e., the temporal dimension of our physical universe as represented by clock time) or subjective time (i.e., the individual's psychological experience of time). Authors in this book have focused on either objective time (e.g., Ployhart & Hale) or subjective time (e.g., Fulmer, Crosby, & Gelfand), and several have considered both conceptualizations (e.g., Cojuharenco, Fortin, & German; Sonnentag, Pundt, & Albrecht). All three approaches make good sense, as evident in the new insights that the chapters have brought to the respective research area.

The incorporation of time to understand a phenomenon at work often involves complex issues that the researcher needs to consider when making decisions about methodological choices (Chan, 1998a; in press, a). These choices are concerned with the selection of study design, measurement, and data analytic techniques. It is noteworthy that the complexity of the issues increases when we apply each conceptualization of time (i.e., objective or subjective time) to new research areas and especially when we attempt to integrate both conceptualizations. The purpose of this chapter is to explicate the key issues relevant to decisions on methodological choices when time is to be incorporated in a study to examine the substantive phenomenon of interest. The focus here is on the conceptual and methodological linkages relating to both objective and subjective time. More technical treatment of specific methodological issues in the longitudinal assessment of changes over objective time is available in Chan (1998a; 2002; in press, a) and Ployhart and Vandenberg (2010).

This chapter explicates the conceptual bases for methodological choices in studies on time and discusses specific methodological issues relating to study design, measurement, and data analysis. The chapter ends with a list of strategic issues to consider for future research to advance the conceptual and methodological bases for the study on time. Throughout this chapter, the issues will be discussed with reference to the relevant literature and illustrated using the research areas presented in the various chapters in this book.

Conceptual bases for methodological choices

Substantive studies of temporal phenomena at work have benefited from several nontechnical summaries and applications of methodological advances such as unified measurement and data analytical models for assessing changes over time (e.g., Chan, 1998a; Ployhart & Vandenberg, 2010). However, technical understanding of measurement and analytical strategies for assessing time is necessary but not sufficient for advancing substantive research on temporal phenomena in specific fields of organizational research. To adequately examine temporal phenomena, empirical studies need to address complex conceptual, measurement, and data analysis issues concerning time. The methodological issues and choices concerning measurement and analysis should be grounded in the conceptual bases for the focal constructs.

In other words, when discussing methodological issues in the study of time, it is important to explicate the conceptual bases of the temporal phenomena under investigation. This is because the logical relationships linking conceptual issues and methodological decisions will determine the scientific defensibility of the various methodological choices. It is not meaningful to make general statements about the validity and usefulness of a methodological choice if we do not specify the conceptualization of the temporal phenomena in question and the substantive context of use. This section discusses several major conceptual issues including the ontological status of the time construct, the meaning and use of various temporal characteristics, and the relationships linking objective time and subjective time.

The ontological status of the time construct

The research on time or time-related issues has focused on temporal characteristics that could be objective, such as number of time points of measurement in a longitudinal study and the interval between adjacent time points, or subjective, such as an individual's time perspective (past, present, future) and experience of time urgency. Before examining these temporal characteristics, a more basic conceptual question is the ontological status of the time construct. Is the ontological status of time the same as the status of substantive constructs represented by other focal variables in the study, in that the time construct is of theoretical interest in its own right? Alternatively, is the ontological status of time simply a general notion applicable across temporal studies, in that it represents that medium of our physical universe through which the dynamics of the temporal phenomena manifest themselves?

The ontological status of time is an important basic question with conceptual and methodological implications. Specifically, if time is a substantive construct, then two things should be expected of the time construct. First, the time construct should be treated similarly as other substantive constructs in a given empirical study in terms of what is required of it, both conceptually and methodologically. The requirements of the time construct will include clarity in its conceptual definition, evidence of construct validity and other psychometric properties in its measurement, and appropriateness of statistical analysis on data representing its values. Second, the time construct should have a substantive role in a theory-based explanation of the phenomenon of interest. This role may be either the *explanadum* (i.e., the explanation of the phenomenon) or the *explanan* (i.e., the phenomenon to be explained). The explanan is the dependent variable, whereas the explanadum could be the independent variable, mediator variable, or moderator variable. In other words, for a substantive time construct, we expect it to have a specific theoretical role in the interconstruct relationships or a location in the nomological network of constructs. In contrast, if time is a temporal medium through which a substantive change occurs and not a substantive construct, then it is not meaningful to evaluate its construct validity and it should not have a specific theoretical role as an explanadum or an explanan.

To address the question of the ontological status of time, we need to specify if the time construct is about subjective time or objective time. If it is subjective time, then it is clear that the time constructs representing the temporal characteristics of interest, such as the individual's time perspective or experience of time urgency, are in fact substantive constructs. For example, in a study of the experience of time urgency, the variable representing time urgency is a theoretical variable in its own right. It is meaningful and necessary to provide a clear conceptual definition of the time construct (i.e., time urgency), examine its psychometric properties including its construct validity, and analyze data representing an individual's values on the construct. It is also meaningful to specify the theoretical role of the time construct in interconstruct relationships (e.g., time urgency as a mediator between a personality trait and task performance).

On the other hand, if the time construct is about objective time, then its ontological status is dependent on whether it is referring to (1) an objective temporal characteristic that is a focal construct with a specific theoretical role (e.g., independent variable, moderator) in a conceptual model of interconstruct relationships, or (2) the physical time period through which a substantive phenomenon of interest occurs in a longitudinal study. If it is reference (1), then the objective time construct is a substantive construct. For example, we can manipulate the objective time period allowed for completion of a task and examine this objective temporal characteristic as an independent variable that may influence creative performance on the task. Note that for an objective temporal characteristic that also has a specific theoretical role (i.e., for a substantive objective time construct), the role is not restricted to explanadums such as an independent variable, moderator variable, or a mediators; the role can also be an explanan (i.e., a dependent variable). This is because in addition to being a causal variable, objective time can also be an effect variable. For example, objective time duration such as time taken to complete a task can be an effect caused by variables such as cognitive ability and motivation.

If it is reference (2), then the objective time construct is not a substantive construct but simply a general notion of a temporal medium in the longitudinal study through which the substantive construct changes over time or the substantive process manifests itself. This latter reference deserves some elaboration ahead as it is sometimes incorrectly treated in a study as a substantive construct in conceptual analysis and methodological choices, thereby leading to incorrect data analysis and misleading interpretations.

In empirical research, the substantive variables are those focal study variables that are measures of the intended constructs of interest. In the case of a longitudinal study, the primary goal is concerned with conceptualizing and assessing the changes over time that may occur in one or more substantive variables. For example, in a longitudinal study of newcomer adaptation by Chan and Schmitt (2000), some of the substantive variables measured and tracked over time were information seeking, job performance, and social integration. As measures of the study's focal constructs, they have specific substantive content. These measures could be assessed for construct validity by obtaining relevant validity evidence. In contrast, "time" has a different ontological status from these substantive variables in the longitudinal study. This can be demonstrated in three ways.

First, when a substantive construct is tracked in a longitudinal study for changes over time, time is not a substantive measure used to represent a study construct. In the foregoing example of the newcomer adaptation study by Chan and Schmitt, it is not meaningful to assess the construct validity of time – at least not in the same way we can speak of assessing the construct validity of substantive variables such as the job performance or social integration measures.

Second, in a longitudinal study, a time point in the observation period represents one temporal instance of measurement. The time point per se, therefore, is simply the temporal marker of the state of the substantive variable at the point of measurement. The time point is not the state or value of the substantive variable that we are interested in for tracking changes over time. Changes over time occur when the state or value of substantive variables changes over different points of measurement.

Finally, in a longitudinal study of changes over time, "time" is distinct from the substantive process that underlies the substantive construct's change over time. To illustrate, consider a hypothetical study in which the levels of job performance and social integration of a group of newcomers were repeatedly measured for six time points over a six-month period, at one-month time intervals between adjacent time points. Let us suppose the study found that the observed pattern of change over time in job performance followed a functional form best described as a monotonically increasing trajectory at a decreasing rate of change. This observed functional form of the performance trajectory could serve as empirical evidence for the theory that a learning process underlies the performance level changes over time. Let us also suppose that, for the same group of newcomers, the observed pattern of change over time in their social integration levels was best described by a positive linear trajectory. This observed functional form of the social integration trajectory could serve as empirical evidence for a theory of social adjustment process that underlies the integration level changes over time. In this hypothetical study, there were two distinct substantive processes of change (learning and social adjustment) that underlie the changes in levels on the respective two study constructs (performance and social integration). There were six time points at which each substantive variable was measured over the same time period. Time, in this longitudinal study, was simply the temporal medium through which the two substantive processes occurred. Time was not an explanadum. Time did not cause the occurrence of the different substantive processes, and there was nothing in the conceptual content of the time construct that could, nor was expected to, explain the functional form or nature of the two different substantive processes. Neither was time an explanan. The substantive processes occur or unfold through time, but they did not cause time to exist.

To summarize, for subjective time, the time constructs examined in the study represent the temporal characteristics that are the focal constructs under investigation. Therefore, the ontological status of subjective time constructs is clear – they are substantive constructs in the study that are of theoretical interest in their own right. On the other hand, for objective time, its ontological status is dependent on what time is referring to. Objective time is a substantive construct if it refers to an objective temporal characteristic that is a focal construct with a specific theoretical role in a conceptual model of interconstruct relationships. Objective time is a general notion of a temporal medium, and it is not a substantive construct if it refers to the physical time period through which a substantive phenomenon of interest occurs in a longitudinal study.

Having established that subjective time is a substantive construct and objective time can be either a substantive construct or a temporal medium, we will gain more conceptual clarity when we discuss the various temporal characteristics. For ease of presentation, I will group temporal characteristics into situation temporal characteristics and person temporal characteristics, although both person and situation variables are often relevant in understanding each temporal characteristic. Although not exhaustive, the following list covers the major temporal characteristics discussed in the research on time. The next two sections explicate the conceptualization of each temporal characteristic, and subsequent sections will discuss their methodological implications.

Situation temporal characteristics: time duration, number of time points, interval between time points, event time, time lag between events

Time duration

Time duration is about the time that events last. More generally, time duration refers to the length of time of a given temporal period of interest. In a longitudinal study, the objective time period of interest is often the total length of the period of observations in which the substantive variables are repeatedly measured and tracked over time. The most common debate on the adequacy of the total time period in a longitudinal study is whether the length of the period corresponds to the duration of change in the substantive variable in a way that captures the phenomenon of interest in the research question. However, depending on the specific theoretical or methodological issue in question, the objective time duration can also refer to a subset of this total period of observation. For example, the change trajectory of a substantive variable over the total time period of study may follow a curvilinear function, and the researcher may be interested in the time duration (a subset of the total time period) it takes from the start of the time period to the first point of inflexion. In a longitudinal study, regardless of whether the objective time duration of interest is the entire time period of the observations or a subset of it, time duration is not a substantive construct per se but a temporal medium through which a substantive phenomenon occurs.

In a cross-sectional study, objective time duration may be a substantive construct. For example, the time duration taken to complete a task could be the substantive outcome of interest influenced by predictors or causal variables such as cognitive ability, motivation, or task difficulty. Alternatively, the time duration taken or allowed to complete a task could be the predictor or independent variable influencing task performance. Time duration taken to complete a task could also be a mediator variable that accounts for the indirect effect of an antecedent variable (e.g., cognitive ability) on a consequent variable (e.g., task performance).

Objective time duration of an event is unambiguous, precise, and verifiable. Subjective time duration, on the other hand, is a phenomenological experience of the individual experiencing the event and therefore dependent on the individual experiencing the event, the individual's evaluation or experience of the event, and the circumstances or context of the event or experience. Given the occurrence of an event, the subjective time duration may differ across individuals and it may be shorter, equal to, or longer than the objective time duration of the event. Studies have consistently shown that subjective time duration is shorter than objective time duration when the individual is engaged in more activities, varied activities, or challenging activities or has a pleasant experience of the activity or event. The individual's extent of underestimation of the objective time duration increases as the activity number, activity variety, activity challenge, or pleasantness of experience increases (e.g., Cahoon & Edmonds, 1980; Friedman, 1990). This underestimation may in part be due to the subjective experience of "timelessness" when the individual is involved in a highly engaging and pleasant activity, which is a critical component of the "flow" experience described by Csikszentmihalyi (1997).

Number of time points and interval between time points

In order to assess intra-individual changes over time on the substantive construct, the researcher needs to conduct a longitudinal panel study to collect repeated measures of the same substantive construct over time from the same sample of individuals in a way that can provide an accurate description of the change trajectory.[1] The first practical question on methodological choice here is the number of time points of measurement to administer in the study. It is well established that intra-individual changes cannot be adequately assessed with only two time points because (1) a two-point measurement by necessity produces a linear trajectory and therefore is unable to empirically detect the functional form of the true change trajectory and (2) time-related (random or correlated) measurement error and true change over time are confounded in the observed change in a two-point measurement (for details, see Chan, 1998a; Rogosa, 1995; Singer & Willett, 2003). Hence, the minimum number of time points for assessing intra-individual change is three, but more than three is better to obtain a more reliable and valid assessment of the change trajectory (Chan, 1998a). However, it does not mean that a larger number of time points is always better or more accurate than a smaller number of time points. Given that the total time period of study captures the change process of interest, the number of time points should be determined by the appropriate location of the time point. This brings us to the second practical question on methodological choice regarding the appropriate length of the interval between adjacent time points.

The correct length of the time interval between adjacent time points in a longitudinal study is critical because it directly affects the observed functional form of the change trajectory and in turn the inference we make about the true pattern of change over time (Chan, 1998a). For example, a change that is in fact continuous and gradual may appear in the observed results as abrupt and large in magnitude if the time interval is too large. Consider a learning situation in which, with each new day, the learner was able to acquire a new piece of information and adequately apply it to a task such that true changes in the learner's task mastery were occurring continuously and gradually. In this situation, if we use a time interval of one month instead of one day or a few days to assess changes in task mastery, the observed results will incorrectly indicate an abrupt and large change. What then should be the correct length of the time interval between adjacent time points in a longitudinal study? The answer is there is no one correct length. The correct or optimal length of the time interval will depend on the specific substantive change phenomenon of interest. This means it is dependent on the nature of the substantive construct, its underlying process of change over time, and the context in which the change process is occurring, which includes the presence of variables that influence the nature and rate of the change.

In practice, researchers determine their choice of the length of the time interval in conjunction with the choice of number of time points and the choice of the length of the total time period of study. These three choices are often influenced by the specific resource constraints and opportunities faced by the researchers when designing and conducting the longitudinal study. Deviation from the optimal time interval probably occurs frequently since decisions on time intervals are often practical and atheoretical. When the observed time interval deviates too much (i.e., too short or too long) from the optimal time interval, true patterns of change will get masked or false patterns of change will get observed. Unfortunately, we almost never know precisely what this optimal time interval is, even if we have a relatively good theory of the change phenomenon. There are two reasons. First, our theories of organizational phenomena are often static in nature. Second, even when our theories are dynamic and focus on change processes, they are almost always silent on the specific length of the temporal dimension through which the substantive processes occur over time.

Our theories of dynamic phenomena are not at the stage where we could specify the optimal time intervals. Thus, the best we could do now is to explicate the nature of the change processes and the effects of the influencing factors to serve as guides for decisions on time intervals, number of time points, and the total time period of study. Take, for example, the research on sensemaking processes in newcomer adaptation. In this area of research, the total period of study often ranged from six months to one year, with 6 to 12 time points, equally spaced at time intervals of one or two months between adjacent time points. These methodological choices are often arbitrary and convenient decisions based on logistic rather than theoretical considerations. It is noteworthy that Ashforth, Harrison, and Sluss's (Volume 1) theory of newcomer adaptation as identity formation processes provides some useful conceptual bases for using event time to guide the choice of time intervals, number of time points, and total time period of study. However, if the theoretical focus on the newcomer adaptation processes is not about identity formation, then a different time frame may be more relevant. For example, a much longer time interval and total time period, ranging from several months to several years, will be more appropriate for a change process that should take a longer time to manifest itself, such as development of cognitive processes or skill acquisition requiring extensive practice or accumulation of experiences over time. On the other extreme, if we are interested in change processes and events that occur much faster than newcomer adaptation, then a much shorter time interval and total time period, ranging from several hours to several days, will be appropriate. Examples of a change process that could take a short time to manifest itself include fairness perceptions in interactional justice situations (e.g., Sonnentag et al., Volume 1) and activation or inhibition of emotion states within a day or a week (e.g., Beal, Volume 1).

Event time and time lag between events

In the study of time, the concept of "event time" has been used in two distinct ways – one narrower and the other more general. The narrow concept of event time, pioneered by social psychologist Robert Levine, has been the focus in cross-cultural research on time, which consisted mostly of ethnographic studies (for review, see Levine, 1997; Levine & Norenzayan, 1999). Here, event time is contrasted with clock time to describe how different cultures live their lives and schedule their activities. In clock time cultures, people use clock time to schedule events and direct their activities, including how long the event or activity should last and when it should begin and end. Unless there is high importance or urgency in the event or activity, clock time will typically take precedence over events and activities, such that the event or activity will start and stop at the scheduled clock time. In event time cultures, instead of using clock time, people let the nature and ongoing experience of the event direct their activities, including how long the event or activity should last and when it should begin and end. There is some evidence that people in clock time cultures, compared to those in event time cultures, are more likely to be rigid and have higher expectations about punctuality and precision. However, it is important to avoid a simplistic classification of cultures into clock time versus event time cultures because an individual's time orientation in any given event may be influenced by a variety of situational and individual difference variables (Fulmer et al., this volume). While there is some empirical evidence of this cultural concept of event time, more research is needed to establish, with rigorous methodology, its construct validity, including its incremental predictive validity over clock time and incremental explanatory value over personality traits and general cultural differences that are not restricted to temporal orientation. This construct-oriented approach to event time is likely to advance research on the possible roles of subjective time constructs in "event-focused" areas such as creativity (e.g., Gilson, Litchfield, & Gilson, Volume 1) and stress (e.g., Sonnentag et al., Volume 1) and "stage-focused" areas such as entrepreneurship (e.g., Gilbert, this volume), newcomer socialization (e.g., Ashforth et al., Volume 1), and team development (e.g., Mathieu, Kukenberger, & Innocenzo, this volume).

The more general concept of event time simply refers to the passage of time as reflected in the occurrence of particular events (Ancona, Okhuysen, & Perlow, 2001). Although many researchers focusing on this general concept of event time would examine how the individual experiences and makes sense of the event or uses the completion of the event as a signal for action, the research is primarily interested in objective event time, which refers to the actual passage of clock time corresponding to the occurrence of the event. The focus on event time has provided new insights to several areas of research, including newcomer adaptation (Ashforth et al., Volume 1) and organizational routines (e.g., Turner, this volume). The contribution has largely been on explicating how the characteristics, duration, and sequencing of the events may affect how individuals experience and respond to the events. Ashforth et al. (Volume 1) provided a conceptual framework, based on theories of socialization and identity formation processes, to explicate how the nature and sequence of various events as experienced by organizational newcomers over the passage of clock time help them to become a part of the organization. Turner (this volume) explicated the nature of organizational routines as repetitive patterns of interdependent actions and proposed how event time contributes to the emergence and maintenance of routines, such as when the completion of an event often serves as a signal for the next action in the sequence of actions within an organizational routine.

The general concept of event time can also be construed in terms of subjective time. Here, subjective event time refers to the individual's experience or estimation of the temporal dimensions of the event. The primary focus is often the individual's feeling of how fast or slow the event has progressed or the individual's estimation of the duration of the event. As noted earlier, studies have consistently shown that when individuals experience a pleasant event, they tend to feel that the event time passed by quickly and they underestimate the objective event time. Conversely, the experience of negative events leads to the feeling that event time passed by slowly and they overestimate the objective event time.

A temporal characteristic related to the general concept of event time is the time lag between events. Time lag simply refers to the time interval between the end of an event and the start of another event that happens after it. When focusing on time lag, the researcher is typically interested in the substantive relationship between the two events (e.g., predictor and criterion, cause and effect), although sometimes the two events may be viewed as independent occurrences that have an impact on a substantive variable (e.g., two independent event stressors having an impact on an individual's health).

The methodological choice of introducing a time lag between two measurement occasions is particularly important for establishing a causal relationship between the first event (Variable X) and the second event (Variable Y). This is because one of the preconditions for causation is that the cause must temporally precede the effect. In addition, having a time lag will help address various methodological problems associated with measuring the hypothesized causal and effect events at the same time (Maxwell & Cole, 2007; Mitchell & James, 2001). The practical problem that the researcher faces when deciding to introduce a time lag between measurements of two events is that we almost always do not know, a priori, the correct length of time that constitutes the causal interval between X and Y. The causal interval is dependent on the nature of the cause and effect variables and the causal mechanism linking them. A stressor X may have short-term and long-term effects on different aspects of well-being (Y variables) (e.g., Sonnentag et al., Volume 1), a work redesign X may have short-term and long-term effects on different aspects of job performance (Y variables) (e.g., Parker, Andrei, & Li, Volume 1), and a leadership behavior X may have short-term and long-term effects on different aspects of follower perceptions (Y variables) (e.g., Day, this volume). In each of these three examples, there are different causal intervals of varying length linking the X and Y variables and therefore there will be different optimal lengths of time lag between measurements of X and Y.

Time lag has almost always been construed in objective time. The study of subjective time lag, construed in terms of individuals' estimation of the length of the time lag between two events and their perception or experience of the time lag, is likely to contribute to research in many areas. Some possible areas include research on causal attributions, perceived causal efficacy of events, and motivation mechanisms involving expectancies of effort leading to performance and instrumental beliefs of performance leading to outcome. For example, we could manipulate the time lag between an individual's action and a subsequent event to test its effects on the individual's likelihood to make an external versus internal causal attribution about the occurrence of the event. We could also test if the time lag effect on causal attribution is moderated by personality traits such as locus of control and need for closure.

Person temporal characteristics: time perspective, temporal depth, time urgency, polychronicity

Time perspective and temporal depth

When we quantify the passage of time in units (e.g., days, weeks, months, years), we can objectively specify (1) the past, present, and future, and (2) how far back into the past and how far forward into the future. Researchers on subjective time have focused on the psychological experiences of these two temporal characteristics by examining the respective subjective time constructs of (1) time perspective and (2) temporal depth.

Time perspective refers to the individual's orientation, existing at a given time, toward the past, present, and future as he or she considers events, actions, and consequences of those events and actions. The three time perspectives or orientations allow individuals to organize experiences and events into temporal categories, which help to give order, coherence, and meaning to those experiences and events (Zimbardo & Boyd, 1999). Time perspective has been found to predict a variety of beliefs, attitudes, and behaviors. For example, future orientation has been found to be positively associated with self-efficacy, proactive seeking of solutions, commitment to promises made, planning behaviors at work, preventive health behaviors, and socially desirable behaviors (Epel, Bandura, & Zimbardo, 1999; Harber, Zimbardo, & Boyd, 2003; Keough, Zimbardo, & Boyd, 1999; Orbell & Kyriakaki, 2008). Present orientation has been found to be positively associated with substance use for coping with stress (Keough et al., 1999; Wills, Sandy, & Yaeger, 2001). The research literature suggests that time perspective is both malleable and susceptible to trait influences. For example, studies have shown that time perspective can be manipulated through temporal framing and persuasion (e.g., Orbell & Kyriakaki, 2008) and induction of counterfactual thoughts (e.g., Roese, 1997) and anticipated regret (e.g., Richard, van der Pigt, & de Vries, 1996). Studies have also found trait-based influences on time perspective, such as influences from individual differences in the tendency to consider future consequences (e.g., Strathman, Gleicher, Boninger, & Edwards, 1994). More recently, Shipp, Edwards, and Lambert (2009) have clarified the concept of time perspective to take into account both person and situation variables and provided validity evidence that an individual can have multiple time perspectives or foci.

The incorporation of time perspective as a substantive variable in the study is likely to help advance many areas of research, including those examined in this book, such as newcomer socialization (Ashforth et al., Volume 1), stress (Sonnentag et al., Volume 1), team dynamics (Mathieu et al., this volume), organizational routines (Turner, this volume), work redesign (Parker et al., Volume 1), and motivation (Roe, Volume 1). Research on time perspective is more likely to provide significant contributions to these substantive research areas if the valence is taken into account since whether we think about positive or negative things in the past, present, and future should affect the direction and magnitude of effects on beliefs, attitudes, and behaviors. Most studies on time perspective incorporated valence simply by using the multidimensional scale of time perspective developed by Zimbardo and Boyd (1999). This scale incorporates valence and measures time perspective as a multidimensional construct consisting of five subconstructs, including past-positive, past-negative, present-hedonistic, present-fatalistic, and future orientation. It is noteworthy that when making the methodological choice to use this scale, a limitation is that future orientation is measured as a general orientation toward the future without distinguishing it in terms of thinking about positive versus negative things. This issue has been rectified in the Temporal Focus Scale developed by Shipp et al. (2009).

Temporal depth refers to the temporal distance into the past (i.e., how far back into the past) and the future (i.e., how far forward into the future) that an individual typically considers when thinking about events that have happened, may have happened, or may happen. That is, whereas time perspective is about the qualitative category aspect of time orientation in terms of the past, present, and future, temporal depth is about the quantitative extensions into the past and future (Bluedorn, 2002).

Early research on temporal depth focused only on future temporal depth, which was typically assessed with a single-item measure of the time horizon that respondents refer to when they think about the future (e.g., Javidan, 1984; Lindsay & Rue, 1980). More recently, temporal depth is typically measured using a six-item scale developed by Bluedorn (2002), with three items measuring past temporal depth and three items measuring future temporal depth. Respondents are asked to specify how much time they refer to when thinking about each of the phrases represented by the six items: recently, a middling time ago, a long time ago, short-term future, mid-term future, and long-term future. For each phrase, respondents select one answer from 15 choices indicating varying temporal distance ranging from one day to more than 25 years. Research has shown that future temporal depth tends to be longer than past temporal depth (ibid.). Although useful, the six-item measure by Bluedorn (2002) was designed to measure general temporal depth into the past and future and so there was no situational context or life domain specified for the respondents. An individual's temporal depth may well vary widely across contexts or domains such as family and work life. More research is needed to examine the validity, stability, and usefulness of temporal depth measures for the purpose of addressing the research questions of interest concerning temporal depth.

Time urgency

Time urgency refers to the individual's tendency to treat time as a scarce resource and plan its use carefully (Landy, Rastegary, Thayer, & Colvin, 1991). Time urgency is typically studied as a stable individual difference variable, and it is a key trait component in the Type A behavior pattern (Friedman & Rosenman, 1974; Jenkins, Zyzanski, & Rosenman, 1971). Individuals high in time urgency tend to constantly feel the pressure from the passage of time and conduct activities at high speed.

Time urgency has been found to be positively and moderately associated with task performance (e.g., Conte, Mathieu, & Landy, 1998; Greenberg, 2002). However, the association tends to exist only if time urgency is operationalized as both the feeling of urgency and time-controlling behaviors including planning and prioritizing, but not when it is operationalized as only the feeling of urgency. Thus, when making the methodological choice to incorporate and assess the time urgency construct in a study, it is important to ensure validity of its measurement given the multidimensionality of the construct. For example, Landy et al. (1991) proposed that time urgency consists of five dimensions and developed a scale to measure them – namely, eating behavior, competitiveness, general hurry, task-related hurry, and speech pattern. While potentially useful, an inspection of the items suggests that the competitiveness dimension, unlike the other four dimensions, does not appear to be an integral part of the conceptual definition of time urgency (i.e., treating time as a scarce resource and planning its use carefully) even though it may be correlated with dimensions of time urgency. In addition, it appears that the item content of the other four dimensions reflects the feeling of urgency and its behavioral manifestations rather than careful planning of time use.

Finally, although research on time urgency has almost always examined the construct as a personality trait, it should be noted that time urgency is a subjective time construct that can be induced by the situational variables. Therefore, it is possible to experimentally manipulate time urgency as an independent variable or examine it as an intervening variable that mediates the relationship between task situation demand and task performance. For example, the potential causal relationships linking the various team processes and dynamics identified by Mathieu et al. (this volume) may be directly tested by conducting experiments that manipulate team task situational variables to induce different levels of time urgency among team members and examine their effects on team functioning.

Polychronicity

Polychronicity refers to the individual's preference to perform multiple activities at the same time (Hall, 1983; Slocombe & Bluedorn, 1999). This subjective time construct has been examined as both an individual difference in preference and a collective value (e.g., Bluedorn, Kaufman, & Lance, 1992; Bluedorn, Kalliah, Strube, & Martin, 1998). Studies have found that person-job fit in polychronicity positively predicted job performance and work-relevant outcomes such as fairness perceptions, job satisfaction, and organizational commitment (e.g., Hecht & Allen, 2005; Madjar & Oldham, 2006; Slocombe & Bluedorn, 1999). There is also some evidence that organizations with a polychronic culture had higher financial performance than those with a monochronic culture (Onken, 1999).

When making a methodological choice to aggregate the individual-level measures of polychronicity to compose the higher-order organizational-level construct of polychronic culture/climate, careful attention needs to be paid to conceptual and methodological issues of aggregation and multilevel research in order to prevent fallacious inferences and obtain accurate interpretations (Chan,

1998b). For example, before using the within-organization mean polychronicity scores to represent the scores on the organizational-level construct of polychronic culture/climate, we need to test if there was in fact sufficient within-organization agreement on the individual-level measurement of polychronicity before the individual-level polychronicity scores could be aggregated to compose the mean polychronicity scores.

At the organizational level, there may be different types of organizational polychronic culture or climate constructs. When multilevel studies are properly designed and conducted, new insights on organizational polychronicity may be obtained. For example, by applying a dispersion composition model that treats within-organization variance in individual-level polychronicity scores as a theoretical variable of interest (i.e., as opposed to treating within-organization variance as a statistical hurdle to overcome in order to achieve within-organization agreement for aggregation to obtain the mean scores), it is possible to propose and validate a new polychronic construct at the organizational level called polychromic climate strength. This polychronic climate strength construct represents the extent to which individuals within the organization share the same level of polychronicity, which is conceptually distinct from the organization's level of polychronicity as indicated by the mean polychronicity score for the organization. We can then examine how this polychronic climate strength variable may affect substantive individual-level and organizational-level variables as an antecedent variable, mediator variable, or moderator variable. With a careful match of composition models and methodological choices, as well as good theory on temporal characteristics, we are likely to produce new insights on organizational culture and climate in terms of their relationships with organizational routines and work contexts (for details, see Chan, 1998b, in press, b).

Design, measurement and data analysis issues

The previous section has provided specific examples to illustrate how explicating the conceptual content of time constructs could provide the necessary conceptual bases for methodological choices. This section discusses nine key methodological issues that are common across diverse time constructs and temporal phenomena. These methodological issues, which relate to study design, measurement, and data analysis, are selected for discussion here because of their importance to the validity of inferences drawn from temporal research.

Design issues

In the research on time, issues of study design go beyond the pros and cons of selecting correlational versus experimental designs, longitudinal versus cross-sectional designs, concurrent versus predictive validation designs, or prospective versus retrospective designs, which are often discussed in many references on research methods. This section will discuss three key design issues: (1) the nature of the longitudinal change or time construct under study; (2) descriptive versus explanatory goals in the study of the temporal phenomenon; and (3) observational versus experimental intervention approaches to examine the temporal phenomenon.

Nature of longitudinal change or time construct

One of the most basic conceptual issues underlying methodological choices on study design is the nature of the temporal phenomenon under investigation. When the temporal phenomenon is about changes that occur over objective time, the basic conceptual issue is about the nature of the change process, such as the specific functional form of the change trajectory and the duration of change (Chan, 1998a; Ployhart & Vandenberg, 2010). The methodological choice of study design will depend on both theoretical and practical considerations. For example, a longitudinal panel design may be both theoretically appropriate and practically feasible for examining a change process that theoretically takes several months to manifest itself fully, such as an information-seeking process or an identity-formation process in newcomer adaptation (e.g., Chan & Schmitt, 2000; Ashforth et al., Volume 1). That is, the longitudinal panel study design tracking changes over several months makes good sense because there is sufficient opportunity provided by the time period in the study to observe the complete functional form of the trajectory over the entire duration of the change process. On the other hand, a longitudinal panel study design may be theoretically appropriate but practically nonfeasible if the change over objective time is about a gradual development process that takes several years to manifest itself fully, such as a skill acquisition process in the development of deep expertise or an aging process in the development of moral values. In such cases, the researcher may have to make do with a cross-sectional design comparing different groups of individuals who are at different ages or time points in the developmental process. Threats to validity of inferences about longitudinal changes may be mitigated to some extent with appropriate design modifications, such as using a cohort-sequential design (Duncan, Duncan, & Hops, 1996) in a theory-driven manner to model the change process.

An important issue that has not received sufficient attention in the discussion of longitudinal changes is the context sensitivity of the change process. In a study of development of social skills in children, Chan, Ramey, Ramey, and Schmitt (2000) showed that the process of changes in social skills is dependent on the context (i.e., home vs. school) in which children's social skills are exhibited and interpreted. As noted by Roe (Volume 1), the specific nature of a change process, such as those in performance and motivation changes over time, may be dependent on the work context. More generally, methodological choices of study design for a change process will need to be guided by the specification of the context of the change over time. For example, in modeling changes in job performance over time, we may need to distinguish between a typical performance change trajectory that is applicable across many task-learning situations and context-dependent performance change trajectories that are applicable to specific domains, such as changes in the development of creative performance (Gilson et al., Volume 1) and learning of organizational routines (Turner, this volume).

Issues of the nature of the temporal phenomenon and its context sensitivity are not restricted to longitudinal changes. When the temporal phenomenon is about a subjective time construct, such as time urgency, temporal depth, or polychronicity, the conceptual issue is about explicating the nature of the temporal characteristic and its context sensitivity, which in turn provide the conceptual blueprint for methodological choices of the study design. For example, if time urgency and polychronicity are conceptualized as malleable temporal characteristics similar to other task situational variables, then the researcher may choose a true experimental design to test the causal effects of time urgency and polychronicity. On the other hand, if these two subjective time constructs are conceptualized as personality traits or trait-like stable individual preferences, then a correlational design or a quasi-experimental study design may be needed to examine their potential predictive or moderating effects.

Descriptive versus explanatory goals

When assessing longitudinal changes, there are two primary sequential goals (Chan, 1998a, 2003). The first goal is descriptive, followed by the second goal, which is explanatory. The descriptive goal is to empirically represent the change process that the substantive construct is undergoing through the time period of study. The explanatory goal is to give an account of why the change process occurred the way it did by relating it to explanatory variables to be incorporated in the study.

The descriptive goal is more basic than the explanatory goal since we need to be able to first accurately describe the change process before we can adequately explain it. Two of the most important study design choices of temporal characteristics that will affect the accuracy of the description of the change process are the number of time points of measurement within the longitudinal time period of study and the length of the interval between two adjacent time points. As noted earlier in this chapter, if the number of time points or interval between time points is suboptimal, the resulting empirical description of the change process may be an inaccurate representation of the actual change process (for details, see Chan, 1998a; Ployhart & Vandenberg, 2010; Roe, Volume 1).

Depending on the theories (or educated guesses) about why the change process occurred the way it did, the researcher will need to explicitly incorporate the potential explanatory variables in the design of the study. These explanatory variables may be of different types, including group membership (i.e., experimentally manipulated or naturally occurring groups), time-invariant predictors, time-varying correlates, or the trajectories of a different substantive variable. Using latent variable modeling, Chan (1998a) provided a unified conceptual framework that could be used to guide the incorporation of these different types of explanatory variables in the study design. Of course, the identification of the substantive

variables and selection of which to include in the study will need to be guided by
the specific theories of the change phenomenon under investigation.

The descriptive-explanatory distinction also applies to the study of subjective
time constructs using cross-sectional designs. For example, in the study of time
urgency, we need to first have an explicit description of the conceptual content
of the substantive construct, followed by an explanatory account of the mean
scores or variance in the construct by relating time urgency to other substantive
constructs in a nomological network of interconstruct relationships.

Observational versus experimental intervention approaches

When the interest is in a temporal phenomenon as it "naturally" unfolds over time
under normal conditions, such as the development of social cohesion among team
members as they work as a team over time, the observational method approach is
often the appropriate design to employ to study the change process. In the observational approach, explanatory accounts of the change process are provided by
incorporating time-invariant predictors or time-varying correlates into the study
design to examine their associations with the change trajectory. The change process could also be compared across multiple naturally occurring groups (e.g.,
gender, culture) or contexts (e.g., work vs. family, school vs. home) to identify
and explain any observed differences in the change process. For example, Chan
et al. (2000) employed a multiple-context observational approach in a longitudinal
study to compare changes in social skills in the same sample of children between
their home and school contexts and found substantive differences in the functional
form of the change trajectory in social skill development. Predictors such as family background variables and child verbal skills were also included in the study to
account for the parameters of the trajectories in the two contexts.

An observational method approach may also yield insights into a change process by examining the possible impact of a naturally occurring event that happened
when the change process was in progress. This is usually accomplished by observing if there were significant changes in the magnitude or direction of the trajectory
after the occurrence of the event. The evidence is typically suggestive rather than
conclusive since the time lag of the causal interval due to the event (if the event in
fact has causal effects on the change process) is almost always not known a priori,
and also a naturally occurring event is often multivariate, making it difficult if
not impossible to disconfound the causal variables from the extraneous variables
associated with the event. Nevertheless, the observational method continues to be
a potentially useful methodological choice to examine the potential impact that a
naturally occurring event may have on the change process, especially when it is
possible to enhance the strength of the causal inference by comparing the change
trajectories of matched groups within the same duration of change where the event
occurred in only one group but not in the other.

An experimental intervention method approach is well suited when the interest
is in how a change process may be altered, either quantitatively or qualitatively,
by an experimentally manipulated intervention. For example, participants may be

randomly assigned to a treatment group or a control group to examine the effect that a training method may have on task performance changes over time. An intervention can also be experimentally manipulated by introducing the intervention when the change process is in progress (i.e., in the treatment group) and comparing the treatment group and the control group over the same duration of change.

Observational and experimental intervention approaches are also applicable in study designs used to investigate subjective time constructs. We can observe naturally occurring behaviors representing the time construct of interest (e.g., eating behaviors representing time urgency) and compare them across individuals with different levels on a personality trait. We can also test the effects of interventions on subjective time constructs, such as experimentally manipulating reward incentives, goal setting, and anticipated regret to test their effects on time urgency, polychronicity, and temporal depth.

Study designs using observation approaches have high external validity because they tend to preserve the natural settings of the temporal phenomena during the course of the study, and therefore they are more likely to obtain results that are reflective of the true nature of the change process or temporal characteristic. However, unless properly matched comparison groups are available and the isolation of effects of variables is possible in the given context of study, observational approaches are limited in terms of the strength of the causal inferences that can be made from the study findings. In contrast, when adequately implemented, study designs using intervention approaches allow strong causal inferences from the findings obtained. However, the experimental manipulation may alter the natural settings of the temporal phenomena during the course of the study through demand characteristics and reactivity effects from participants due to knowledge of or assignment to the intervention. This unintended effect will produce findings that are not reflective of the true nature of the change process or temporal characteristic. This results in substantive inferences that may be internally valid but are limited in external validity. Researchers investing in a research program to understand a temporal phenomenon should attempt to integrate the complementary strengths and weaknesses of the observational and experimental intervention approaches by adopting multiple methods or integrative methods such as quasi-experimental designs with suitably matched comparison groups.

Measurement issues

In the research on time, issues of measurement are fundamental to adequately map the conceptual content of the time constructs to their operationalizations so that adequate empirical data can be obtained. These measurement issues go beyond the traditional reliability and validity issues in developing good psychometric measures discussed in references on psychometric theory. This section will discuss three key measurement issues: (1) specification of timescales for longitudinal change and time constructs; (2) dimensionality of time constructs; and (3) measurement invariance of responses and changes in construct dimensionality over time.

Timescales

Timescales refer to the different types of time units (e.g., minutes, hours, days, weeks, months, years) that may be used to measure the passage of time. Which timescale should we use in a longitudinal study? The suitability of timescales for a study is dependent on various factors, including the nature of the temporal phenomenon and the pace of change. A timescale with years as the time units makes sense in a study of developmental changes in moral values of children. On the other hand, a timescale with weeks or months (but not hours or years) will make more sense in a study of newcomer adaptation to an organization and a timescale of minutes or hours (but not days, weeks, months, or years) will make more sense in a study of changes in emotions during a conflict resolution situation. The choice of timescale is also dependent on our linguistic conventions and the practical relevance of the level of precision. We would say an expatriate has adjusted to the new environment in the host culture after two months, rather than 61 days or 1,464 hours, even though the three different timescales refer to the same period of identical temporal length.

Although different timescales are mathematically identical when they refer to the same temporal length (e.g., 48 hours and two days are identical), the researcher's choice of a timescale is tied to his or her choice of the time period of study and the number of time points of measurement in the longitudinal study. For example, a study tracking longitudinal changes in job satisfaction over the total period of one year is more likely to use months rather than days or hours as the timescale, and the number of the time points selected for repeated measurement is unlikely to exceed 12 (corresponding to 12 months in the entire study period). However, different substantive variables may differ in their pace of change or even the nature of the change process. Thus, the use of the same single timescale for all substantive variables in a longitudinal study may pose conceptual and measurement challenges insofar as the timescale may practically constrain the number of time points and interval between adjacent time points, which in turn affect the observation of the change trajectory. In this regard, an important but neglected issue concerning the use of timescale in longitudinal studies is the use of multiple timescales in the same study to better reflect the different substantive variables under investigation. This is especially important when the study is examining multivariate changes and associations involving multiple predictors since different variables may have different paces of change or different time lags in their causal intervals. As noted by Roe (Volume 1), using multiple timescales in the same longitudinal study may also lead to more adequate inferences in multilevel research because constructs at different levels of analysis may differ in their pace of change.

In the study of subjective time constructs, the measurement issues concerning the use of timescales are different from those involving objective time in longitudinal studies. Specifically, the use of different timescales may have differential effects in the study of the same subjective time construct. For example, when experiencing a subjective temporal characteristic, it is possible that the same objective temporal length may appear to the individual as longer or shorter depending on the timescale used or time units that are made salient to the individual. The same objective time period allowed for the completion of a task may feel longer or shorter to the individual, and hence influence the sense of time urgency, depending on whether the time period is presented in days or weeks. It is also possible that the differential effects of different timescales may go beyond the estimation of temporal length to the quality of the subjective experience associated with the temporal characteristic. For example, if we induce an individual to think of a past temporal depth of either seven days or one week (which are identical in objective temporal length), the individual may recollect different memories or activate different sequences of memories depending on the timescale used for the induction (i.e., day or week). I am not aware of any studies that have directly examined the effect of different timescales on subjective time constructs. Future studies in this direction are likely to open up promising avenues for research, given the conceptual implications of how timescales may influence the content of an individual's subjective experience of time and the way the individual may process the content.

Dimensionality of time constructs

The dimensionality of time constructs is a fundamental measurement issue that needs to be addressed when investigating individuals' subjective experience of a temporal characteristic. The central measurement issue here is about construct validity in terms of the number and type of dimensions that compose the subjective time construct under study.

More attention should be given to the connection between the item content of the measure and the conceptual definition of the intended time construct. For example, polychronicity, which is conceptually defined as the individual's preference to perform multiple activities at the same time, has always been treated as a unidimensional construct reflecting a single undifferentiated subjective experience of a temporal characteristic. However, an inspection of the item content on a typical polychronicity scale (e.g., Bluedorn et al., 1992) will show that some items refer to the preference to do several things at the same time, whereas other items refer to the belief that people should not try to do many things at once. It appears that a measure as such may in fact capture at least several related but distinct dimensions, such as the preference for serial versus parallel processing, the comfort with multitasking, the ability to sustain task attention, and the belief in the value of prioritizing task activities.

As expected of good psychometric measurement of any construct, researchers should theoretically specify and empirically establish the dimensionality of a subjective time construct. The focus on the dimensionality of time constructs may lead to interesting research questions about relationships involving the subjective experience of temporal characteristics. For example, if a time construct (e.g., polychronicity) is multidimensional, then the construct may have different relationships with a given substantive construct (e.g., a personality trait) depending on the specific dimension(s) of interest. If we use polychronicity as an example, it may turn out that the polychronic dimension involving the ability to sustain task attention is better predicted by cognitive ability than conscientiousness, whereas the polychronic dimension involving the belief in the value of prioritizing task activities is better predicted by conscientiousness than cognitive ability.

In specifying and testing the dimensionality of time constructs, it is important to go beyond the number of dimensions to distinguish between two different types of hierarchical factor models representing the dimensional structure of constructs. These are the reflective model and the formative model. The reflective model is the traditional common factor variance model, where a higher-order factor underlines or accounts for the common variance among several lower-order specific factors. For example, a reflective model of time urgency may specify a higher-order factor representing a sense of time urgency that accounts for the common variance among several lower-order specific factors, such as speed of task performance, general hurry across daily activities, and careful planning of time use. In contrast, the formative model specifies the higher-order factor as a composite outcome that is made up of or "jointly caused" by the lower-order factors. For example, a formative model of polychronicity may specify a higher-order polychronicity factor that is made up of or caused by multiple lower-order domain-specific polychronicity, such as the preference for serial versus parallel processing, the comfort with multitasking, the ability to sustain task attention, and the belief in the value of prioritizing task activities. It is important to specify the correct measurement model (i.e., reflective vs. formative) to represent the hierarchical factor structure of the construct dimensions, so that fallacious inferences associated with model misspecification are avoided and the appropriate evaluation criteria are applied to assess the conceptual and measurement adequacy of the time constructs (for technical details on reflective and formative models, see Bollen & Lennox, 1991; Edwards & Bagozzi, 2000).

Measurement invariance of responses and changes in construct dimensionality over time

A critical but neglected measurement issue in the longitudinal study of temporal phenomenon concerns changes in the dimensionality of the substantive construct over time. The neglect is particularly noteworthy in the area of modeling changes in job performance dimensionality over time, given the amount of attention that researchers have focused on performance dimensionality and, separately, on performance dynamics (Chan, in press, a).

A useful way to construe change in construct dimensionality over time is in terms of differences in the factorial structure of the substantive construct between time points in the longitudinal study. These differences could be in the number and nature of the factors (where a distinct factor represents a distinct dimension) or the pattern and magnitude of the interfactor correlations. We can use longitudinal confirmatory factor analysis to compare and test alternative models specifying if and how construct dimensionality differs (i.e., changes) across time points. We can also test distinct processes of changes in dimensionality (e.g., construct differentiation, construct integration) by applying appropriate latent variable modeling approaches (for details, see Chan, 1998a, in press, a).

After addressing the descriptive question on how construct dimensionality changes over time, we could employ latent variable methods to gather further construct validity evidence and answer explanatory questions of why the construct dimensionality changes over time occurred the way they did by relating the relevant construct factors, particularly the higher-order factors, to selected external variables. These external variables could be individual difference traits (e.g., ability, personality) that predict the construct factors, perception or attitudinal variables (e.g., efficacy perceptions) that are proximal causes (and may also be mediators) that directly affect the construct factors, or criterion outcomes that are affected by the construct factors.

Changes in construct dimensionality over time are related to but distinct from the technical psychometric issues of measurement invariance of responses over time. Measurement invariance over time is a precondition for meaningful comparison of scores (i.e., construct levels) between time points. In fact, measurement invariance is fundamental for the direct application of all analytical models (e.g., latent growth modeling) to represent the intra-individual trajectory of change in the construct level because these analytical models presuppose that the scores between time points are measuring the same substantive construct and with the same precision. When the scores from different time points are in fact measuring different constructs (i.e., gamma change across time) or reflecting different subjective calibrations of the same construct (i.e., beta change across time), it is misleading to interpret the absolute difference in scores between time points as representing changes in levels on the same substantive construct (i.e., alpha change over time).

Thus, the modeling of changes in construct dimensionality over time is distinct from the issue of measurement invariance over time as a precondition for meaningful comparison of scores between time points. When studying changes in construct dimensionality over time, we have theoretical reasons to treat the changes in construct (e.g., performance) dimensionality over time as a substantive process or phenomenon that we are attempting to describe and explain. In other words, in these situations, measurement invariance over time is not treated as a statistical hurdle to be cleared. Instead, the lack of measurement invariance has theoretical meaning and the issue at hand is modeling the nature of the lack of invariance in construct dimensionality over time (Chan, 1998a).

Data analysis issues

It is beyond the scope of this chapter to discuss the various data analytical models for assessing temporal phenomena. It will suffice here to note that recent advances in data analytical models, especially in latent variable modeling, have provided unified and flexible approaches for assessing changes over time (e.g., Chan, 1998a). However, there are several important data analysis issues in the research on time that go beyond technical expertise in advanced analytical models. This section will discuss three key data analysis issues: (1) assumptions of data analytical models; (2) analysis of reliability and errors; and (3) aggregation of observations across time.

Assumptions of data analytical models

When making methodological choices regarding which data analytical model to apply to the temporal data, we need to ensure that the model assumptions are met or at least meaningful to the context of use. For example, time series, repeated measures analysis-of-variance (ANOVA), and difference scores analysis are all applied in a way that assumes, rather than empirically tests for, the measurement invariance of responses over time. If the assumption of measurement invariance is in fact not met, results from the observed trajectory will lead to erroneous inferences about the temporal phenomenon.

The technical treatments of statistical assumptions of the different data analytical models are readily available in references on analytical techniques. A good grasp of the technical knowledge of these statistical assumptions will allow the researcher to choose the appropriate data analytical models. However, what is less well known is that sometimes the nature of an analytical model's statistical assumption per se, regardless of whether the assumption is empirically met by the dataset, renders the application of the model meaningless for the purpose of modeling the temporal phenomenon. This may be illustrated using the example of the attempt to use repeated measures ANOVA to model interindividual differences in intra-individual changes over time.

In using repeated measures ANOVA to analyze longitudinal data, time serves as a repeated measures (i.e., within-subjects) factor (independent variable) in the analysis and the substantive variable being analyzed for changes over time is treated as the dependent variable. The goal of the analysis becomes testing the difference in means across the different time points. The repeated measures ANOVA analysis does not allow us to model the variance in the individual slopes representing interindividual differences in intra-individual differences over time.

More fundamentally, it is not logically meaningful to apply the repeated measures ANOVA technique to analyze these individual changes. Repeated measures ANOVA assumes that the common, orthonormalized variance-covariance matrix of the "time observations" is spherical – that is, the matrix demonstrates constant variance across time observations and constant covariance between time observations. However, there will be many instances of true patterns of intra-individual change that would lead to a lack of constant variance across time observations (Chan, 1998a). For example, all individuals may share a positive (increasing) linear trajectory and are very similar in initial status (at Time 1) but differ in their rate of change (slope), thereby producing a lack of constant variance across time. But this lack of constant variance (i.e., violation of sphericity) is substantively meaningful because it reflects systematic interindividual differences in intra-individual change over time. Repeated measures ANOVA fails to structure these meaningful differences in intra-individual change patterns. In fact, the very existence of these true differences violates the statistical assumption of the technique, and it makes no sense to correct for departure from sphericity. Hence, repeated measures ANOVA is inherently deficient for examining individual differences in intra-individual changes over time.

Reliability and errors

Reliable measurement is necessary for establishing the validity of measures intended to assess time constructs or other substantive constructs in the temporal phenomenon. Detailed discussions of reliability concepts are readily available in textbooks on psychometrics and research methodology. However, there are several specific issues involving reliability and errors that are pertinent to the study of time but have not received sufficient attention.

In the study of changes over time, the first basic question about reliability and measurement errors is whether the observed change over time (and observed between-group differences in change over time) is due to meaningful systematic differences or random fluctuations resulting from measurement error. Inaccurate or incorrect inferences about the true changes over time, or the lack thereof, are likely to result if measurement error is not adequately taken into account when specifying the data analysis model and estimating the parameters. It is noteworthy that the assumption of independence of errors, which is common among many traditional data analysis procedures, may be violated when assessing change over time in longitudinal study designs, particularly when the longitudinal data are collected on measurement occasions closely spaced together using identical measures. Failing to adequately account for the error covariance structure in the longitudinal data could result in, at best, biased estimates of the magnitude of the true change or, at worst, misspecification of the true change patterns. Chan (1998a) showed how a unified analytical framework that incorporates different latent variable modeling techniques can be used to decompose a measure's observed variance into true construct variance, nonrandom (systematic) measurement error variance, and random measurement error variance, as well as model different patterns of systematic measurement error covariance and assess their impact on estimates of true change over time. This variance decomposition is important as it allows us to better capture true change by providing accurate estimates of the change parameters.

The estimation of correlated errors in a model of longitudinal change needs to be based in theoretical foundations or at least be guided by a priori reasons for selecting which time points to specify the error covariance. This is especially so in latent variable modeling as it is easy to obtain empirically good-fitting models to the data simply by increasing the fit of the model through increasing the number of freely estimated parameters in the error covariance matrix. The issue here is similar to the abuse of the flexibility of structural equation modeling by increasing model fit to the data through specifying increasingly complex but atheoretical models.

Aggregation of observations across time

In some longitudinal panel studies, the researcher may end up with a relatively long series of observations. The researcher may need to decide whether to aggregate across time some (and if so, which) or all of the observations in the series.

The researcher's primary reason for aggregation of observations across time may be either practical or theoretical.

An example of a practical reason for aggregation across time is when the researcher has intended to apply a latent growth model to assess and predict intra-individual changes in sales performance over a one-year period and the available longitudinal dataset has too many time points of measurement for applying the modeling technique (e.g., an archival longitudinal dataset with weekly sales performance). In this case, the researcher may aggregate the actual observations (e.g., weekly performance) to derive fewer and equally spaced time points (e.g., monthly). When motivated by practical reasons as such, it is important for the researcher to guard against the unintended consequence that the aggregation across time produces a time interval that is inappropriate for assessing the true pattern of the change process.

An example of a theoretical reason for aggregation across time is when a researcher is interested in testing a hypothesis of a specific cyclical pattern of emotional fluctuation over the particular structure of the individual's work life such as the workweek or the work shift's activities (e.g., Beal & Ghandour, 2011; Beal, Trougakos, Weiss, & Dalal, 2013), using an available longitudinal dataset containing multiple measurements of emotions assessed at different times within the workday collected over many workdays using an experience sampling method. In this case, the researcher may aggregate the actual observations across time in various ways so that the time points for the derived (i.e., aggregated across time) observations correspond to the theoretical time point and time frame (e.g., five time points corresponding to the five days of the workweek to test the workweek cyclical fluctuation hypothesis). In many areas of longitudinal research, the time points of actual measurement existed due to logistic and other practical considerations, and they may not represent the time points of interest according to the theory of change in the substantive construct. When the practically observed time interval between adjacent time points is shorter than the theoretical effective time interval for true change to occur in the substantive construct, aggregation of observations across time should be considered and carefully implemented in a theory-driven manner.

More generally, issues of aggregation of observations across time should always be discussed and evaluated within the larger research context of the conceptual questions about the underlying substantive constructs and change processes that may account for patterns of responses over time. Many of these conceptual questions are likely to relate to construct-oriented issues, such as the location of the substantive construct on the state-trait continuum and the time frame through which short-term or long-term effects on the temporal changes in the substantive construct are likely to be manifested (e.g., effects of stressors on changes in health).

Finally, there are situations where the issue of aggregation of observations across time may in fact be part of a more basic question about whether an individual's subjective experience on a substantive construct (e.g., emotional well-being) should be assessed using momentary measures (e.g., assessing the individual's current emotional state, measured daily over the past one week) or retrospective global reports (e.g., asking the individual to report an overall assessment of his or her emotional state over the past one week). Each of the two measurement perspectives (i.e., momentary and global retrospective) has both strengths and limitations. For example, momentary measures are less prone to recall biases compared to global retrospective measures (Kahneman, 1999). Global retrospective measures, on the other hand, are widely used in diverse studies for the assessment of many subjective experience constructs with a large database of evidence concerning the measure's reliability and validity evidence (Diener, Inglehart, & Tay, 2013). Tay, Chan, and Diener (in press) reviewed the conceptual, methodological, and practical issues in the debate between the momentary and global retrospective perspectives as applied to the research on subjective well-being. They concluded that both perspectives, when adequately applied, could offer useful insights for understanding subjective well-being and related substantive constructs. They suggested a multiple-method approach that is sensitive to the nature of the substantive construct and specific context of use, but also called for more research on the use of momentary measures to obtain more evidence for their psychometric properties and practical value.

Strategic issues for future research

In the preceding sections on design, measurement, and data analysis issues, specific implications for methodological choices were discussed. This last section of the chapter will explicate several general but strategic issues to consider for future research to advance the conceptual and methodological bases for the study on time. Although not an exhaustive list, a careful consideration of at least some of the following strategic issues prior to the research is likely to enhance the scientific rigor and defensibility of the methodological choices made, as well as the theoretical and practical relevance of the findings obtained in the study.

Theoretical role of the substantive constructs

When examining a temporal phenomenon, whether it is about a substantive subjective time construct (e.g., time urgency) or tracking some other substantive construct (e.g., job performance) as it changes over time, the theoretical role of substantive construct(s) needs to be clearly specified. The possible roles of the construct include being a predictor or independent variable, a moderator or interacting variable, a mediator, and an outcome or dependent variable. The search for the role of the substantive construct should be driven by theoretical considerations. A clear specification of the construct's role will help provide the necessary conceptual linkages between methodological choices (i.e., in design, measurement, and analysis) on one hand and the theory of the construct and the nomological network of interconstruct relationships on the other.

Malleability of the substantive constructs

In longitudinal studies tracking changes in a substantive construct over time, the malleability of the substantive construct is a given. That is, the logical assumption in such studies is that the construct is malleable, and hence it may change as the underlying process naturally unfolds over time or it may change because of the impact of an intervention. On the other hand, in studies of subjective time constructs, the malleability of the construct is not a given. In fact, the conceptual definitions for many subjective time constructs (e.g., time urgency, polychronicity) are either silent about the malleability of the construct or they can be readily interpreted and operationalized as either a stable individual difference variable or a malleable variable that is susceptible to change. Thus, the degree of malleability of the subjective time construct under study should be explicated in the theory of the construct. Whether a substantive construct's malleability is a given or has been specified, the precise nature of the malleability mechanism will depend on the theory of the specific change process involving the construct and the context or other associated constructs.

Levels of analysis issues

Organizational phenomena are inherently multilevel in nature. Thus, the study of temporal phenomena at work needs to identify and address the conceptual and methodological issues involving multiple levels of analysis. The change process in a temporal phenomenon may occur at the individual, group, or organizational level, and changes may also be occurring simultaneously at multiple levels. This raises basic composition model and construct validity issues, such as whether the same or different constructs are being conceptualized and assessed at different levels, what is the nature of the functional relationships linking the constructs at the different levels, and whether the same or different processes of changes over time or interconstruct relationships are occurring at different levels (for details, see Chan, 1998b). Changes over time may also exist in complex ways in cross-levels situations. Chan (in press, b) provided two such examples. One example is when changes over time at one level (e.g., subcultures) affect the changes over time or eventual outcome at another level (e.g., organizational culture). Another example concerns changes over time in an inherently cross-levels construct such as person-organization fit in culture dimensions. Person-organization fit constructs are composite constructs consisting of the lower-level person component and the higher-level organization component. The cross-levels nature of the construct raises issues of how different rates of change or different types of change occurring at different levels (or components) impact on the cross-levels (composite) construct.

Integrating the temporal phenomenon with other change processes

While the researcher may be interested in a focal construct undergoing changes over time, it is highly unlikely that all other variables relevant to the temporal phenomenon of interest are remaining static over the duration of change in the focal construct. A change process may affect or be affected by another change process. For example, the occurrence of a performance change process may affect or be affected by the occurrence of a motivation change process in ways such that each process would have turned out differently had the other process not occurred. It is therefore theoretically and practically important to consider how the temporal phenomenon of interest may be integrated with or at least related to other change processes. These other change processes may have occurred prior to, may be occurring in parallel with, or may occur after the occurrence of the focal change process. Advances in multivariate latent growth modeling allow us to specify and test, in a single unified analytic model, multiple change processes with varying duration of change, number of time points, or length of time interval. Time-invariant predictors and multiple groups (either observed or unobserved groups) can also be incorporated to examine different explanatory accounts of these multiple change processes and how and why they are related to each other (for technical details and examples of modeling of multiple change processes, see Chan, 2011; Chan et al., 2000).

Conclusion

Theories of time provide the substantive bases for specifying the conceptual issues that should guide the evaluation and selection of methodological choices. It is apt to end this chapter with two concluding remarks. First, advances in both theories and methods often proceed concurrently and they can complement and inform each other. When we approach theories and methods in an integrative manner, we will be able to design and conduct more rigorous and relevant studies of time that will lead to a better understanding of temporal phenomena. Second, the scientific defensibility of methodological choices in the study of time is dependent on the logical relationships between methodological decisions and the conceptual bases of the temporal phenomena under investigation. Hence, the adequacy of the methodological choice is evaluated based on the extent to which it allows us to make more direct and better connections linking theory, measurement, data, and interpretation concerning the temporal constructs or processes. This chapter has explicated these linkages and suggested future research directions related to integrating conceptual and methodological issues. It is hoped that, in doing so, the chapter has provided a springboard for researchers to advance their research programs on time.

Note

1. Two issues are noteworthy here for assessing intra-individual change. First, the individual is the most common unit of measurement in longitudinal panel studies in organizational research, but the unit of observation may also be the work team, department, organization, or other higher-level unit. Second, the same substantive construct needs to be repeatedly measured over time because measuring different substantive constructs at different time points (e.g., predictor at Time 1 and criterion at Time 2) is still a cross-sectional design (even when there is a time lag between the predictor measurement and the criterion measurement) and not a longitudinal design (Chan, 1998a).

References

Ancona, D. G., Okhuysen, G. A., & Perlow, L. A. (2001). Taking time to integrate temporal research. *Academy of Management Review, 26,* 512–529.

Beal, D. J., & Ghandour, L. (2011). Stability, change, and the stability of change in daily workplace affect. *Journal of Organizational Behavior, 32,* 526–546.

Beal, D. J., Trougakos, J. P., Weiss, H. M., & Dalal, R. S. (2013). Affect spin and the emotion regulation process at work. *Journal of Applied Psychology, 98,* 593–605.

Bluedorn, A. C. (2002). *The human organization of time: Temporal realities and experience.* Stanford: Stanford University Press.

Bluedorn, A. C., Kalliah, T. J., Strube, M. J., & Martin, G. D. (1998). Polychronicity and the inventory polychronic values (IPV). *Journal of Managerial Psychology, 14,* 205–230.

Bluedorn, A. C., Kaufman, C. F., & Lance, P. M. (1992). How many things do you like to do at once? An introduction to monochromic and polychromic time. *Academy of Management Executive, 6,* 17–26.

Bollen, K., & Lennox, R. (1991). Conventional wisdom on measurement: A structural equation perspective. *Psychological Bulletin, 110,* 305–314.

Cahoon, D., & Edmonds, E. M. (1980). The watched pot still won't boil: Expectancy as a variable in estimating the passage of time. *Bulleting of the Psychonomic Society, 16,* 115–116.

Chan, D. (1998a). The conceptualization of change over time: An integrative approach incorporating longitudinal means and covariance structures analysis (LMACS) and multiple indicator latent growth modeling (MLGM). *Organizational Research Methods, 1,* 421–483.

Chan, D. (1998b). Functional relations among constructs in the same content domain at different levels of analysis: A typology of composition models. *Journal of Applied Psychology, 83,* 234–246.

Chan, D. (2002). Longitudinal modeling. In S. Rogelberg (Ed.), *Handbook of research methods in industrial and organizational psychology* (pp. 412–430). Malden, MA: Blackwell.

Chan, D. (2003). Data analysis and modeling longitudinal processes. *Group and Organization Management, 28,* 341–365.

Chan, D. (2011). Longitudinal assessment of changes in job performance and work attitudes: Conceptual and methodological issues. *International Review of Industrial and Organizational Psychology, 26,* 93–117.

Chan, D. (in press, a). Advances in modeling dimensionality and dynamics of job performance. In K. J. Ford, J. Hollenbeck, & A. M. Ryan (Eds.), *The psychology of work.* Washington, DC: American Psychological Association.

Chan, D. (in press, b). Multilevel and aggregation issues in climate and culture research. In B. Schneider and K. M. Barbera (Eds.), *Oxford handbook of organizational climate and culture.* New York: Oxford University Press.

Chan, D. Ramey, S., Ramey, C., & Schmitt, N. (2000). Modeling intraindividual changes in children's social skills at home and at school: A multivariate latent growth approach to understanding between-settings differences in children's social skills development. *Multivariate Behavioral Research, 35,* 365–396.

Chan, D., & Schmitt, N. (2000). Interindividual differences in intraindividual changes in proactivity during organizational entry: A latent growth modeling approach to understanding newcomer adaptation. *Journal of Applied Psychology, 85,* 190–210.

Conte, J. M., Mathieu, J. E., & Landy, F. J. (1998). The nomological and predictive validity of time urgency. *Journal of Organizational Behavior, 19,* 1–13.

Csikszentmihalyi, M. (1997). *Creativity: Flow and the psychology of discovery and invention.* New York: HarperCollins.

Diener, E., Inglehart, R., & Tay, L. (2013). Theory and validity of life satisfaction scales. *Social Indicators Research, 112,* 497–527.

Duncan, S. C., Duncan, T. E., & Hops, H. (1996). Analysis of longitudinal data within accelerated longitudinal designs. *Psychological Methods, 1,* 236–248.

Edwards, J. R., & Bagozzi, R. P. (2000). On the nature and direction of relationships between constructs and measures. *Psychological Methods, 5,* 155–174.

Epel, E. S., Bandura, A., & Zimbardo, P. G. (1999). Escaping homelessness: The influence of self-efficacy and time perspective on coping with homelessness. *Journal of Applied Social Psychology, 29,* 575–596.

Friedman, M., & Rosenman, R. (1974). *Type A behavior and your heart.* New York: Knopf.

Friedman, W. (1990). *About time: Inventing the fourth dimension.* Cambridge: MIT Press.

Greenberg, J. (2002). Time urgency and job performance: Field evidence of an interactionist perspective. *Journal of Applied Social Psychology, 32,* 1964–1973.

Hall, E. T. (1983). *The dance of life.* New York: Doubleday.

Harber, K. D., Zimbardo, P. G., & Boyd, J. N. (2003). Participant self-selection biases as a function of individual differences in time perspective. *Basic and Applied Social Psychology, 25,* 255–264.

Hecht, T. D., & Allen, N. J. (2005). Exploring links between polychronicity and well-being from the perspective of person-job fit: Does it matter if you prefer to do only one thing at a time? *Organizational Behavior and Human Decision Processes, 98,* 155–178.

Javidan, M. (1984). The impact of environmental uncertainty on long-range planning practices of the U.S. savings and loan industry. *Strategic Management Journal, 5,* 381–392.

Jenkins, C. D., Zyzanski, S. J., & Rosenman, R. H. (1971). Progress toward validation of a computer-scored test for the Type A coronary-prone behavior pattern. *Psychosomatic Medicine, 33,* 193–202.

Kahneman, D. (1999). Objective happiness. In D. Kahneman, E. Diener, & N. Schwarz (Eds.), *Well-being: The foundations of hedonic psychology* (pp. 3–25). New York: Russell Sage Foundation.

Keough, K. A., Zimbardo, P. G., & Boyd, J. N. (1999). Who's smoking, drinking, and using drugs? Time perspective as a predictor of substance use. *Basic and Applied Social Psychology, 21,* 149–164.

Landy, F. J., Rastegary, H., Thayer, J., & Colvin, C. (1991). Time urgency: The construct and its measurement. *Journal of Applied Psychology, 76,* 644–657.

Levine, R. (1997). *A geography of time: The temporal misadventures of a social psychologist.* New York: Basic.

Levine, R. V., & Norenzayan, A. (1999). The pace of life in 31 countries. *Journal of Cross-Cultural Psychology, 30,* 178–205.

Lindsay, W. M., & Rue, L. W. (1980). Impact of organization environment on the long-range planning process: A contingency view. *Academy of Management Journal, 23,* 385–404.

Madjar, N., & Oldham, G. R. (2006). Task rotation and polychronicity: Effects on individuals' creativity. *Human Performance, 19,* 117–131.

Maxwell, S. E., & Cole, D. A. (2007). Bias in cross-sectional analyses of longitudinal mediation. *Psychological Methods, 12,* 23–44.

Mitchell, T. R., & James, L. R. (2001). Building better theory: Time and the specification of when things happen. *Academy of Management Review, 26,* 530–547.

Onken, M. H. (1999). Temporal elements of organizational culture and impact on firm performance. *Journal of Managerial Psychology, 14,* 231–244.

Orbell, S., & Kyriakaki, M. (2008). Temporal framing and persuasion to adopt preventive health behavior: Moderating effects of individual differences in consideration of future consequences on sunscreen use. *Health Psychology, 27,* 770–779.

Ployhart, R. E., & Vandenberg, R. J. (2010). Longitudinal research: The theory, design, and analysis of change. *Journal of Management, 36,* 94–120.

Richard, R., van der Pigt, J., & de Vries, N. K. (1996). Anticipated regret and time perspective: Changing sexual risk-taking behavior. *Journal of Behavioral Decision Making, 9,* 185–199.

Roese, N. J. (1997). Counterfactual thinking. *Psychological Bulletin, 121,* 133–148.

Rogosa, D. R. (1995). Myths and methods: "Myths about longitudinal research" plus supplemental questions. In J. M. Gottman (Ed.), *The analysis of change* (pp. 3–66). Mahwah, NJ: Lawrence Erlbaum.

Shipp, A. J., Edwards, J. R., & Lambert, L. S. (2009). Conceptualization and measurement of temporal focus: The subjective experience of the past, present, and future. *Organizational Behavior and Human Decision Processes, 110,* 1–22.

Singer, J. D., & Willett, J. B. (2003). *Applied longitudinal data analysis.* New York: Oxford University Press.

Slocombe, T. E., & Bluedorn, A. C. (1999). Organizational behavior implications of the congruence between preferred polychronicity and experienced work-unit polychronicity. *Journal of Organizational Behavior, 20,* 75–99.

Strathman, A., Gleicher, F., Boninger, D. S., & Edwards, C. S. (1994). The consideration of future consequences: Weighing immediate and distant outcomes of behavior. *Journal of Personality and Social Psychology, 66,* 742–752.

Tay, L., Chan, D., & Diener, E. (in press). The metrics of societal happiness. *Social Indicators Research.*

Wills, T. A., Sandy, J. M., & Yaeger, A. M. (2001). Time perspective and early-onset substance use: A model based on stress-coping theory. *Psychology of Addictive Behaviors, 15,* 118–125.

Zimbardo, P. G., & Boyd, J. N. (1999). Putting time in perspective: A valid, reliable individual differences metric. *Journal of Personality and Social Psychology, 77,* 1271–1288.

Index

Note: page numbers followed by f or t denote figures and tables respectively

selection, of personnel 88–9
self-reinforcing stage, of routines 124–5
Servant Leadership Scale (SLS) 32–3
short-term orientation 64
Silent Language, The (Hall) 55
Singapore, temporal orientation in 60, 68
skill acquisition 41
social capital 81
social conditions, and temporal orientation 60
social influence, and leadership 36
social media 86, 99
social networks: and entrepreneurship 102; and leadership 37
social skills, development of 160
social structure, and temporal orientation 58–9
sociotechnical systems 8–9
South Asia, temporal orientation in 55
Spanish language 59
stranger stage, of leadership making 39
strategic human resource management (SHRM) 79; *see also* human resource management (HRM)
strategic planning, corporate 63
stress 2, 154, 156
stressors 155, 170
subjective time 146–8, 150–1, 154–6, 158, 161–5, 171–2
surveys: diagnostic 22; on leader behavior 32–3

Taiwan: language and time in 59; pace of life in 56
task novelty 129
team analysis, psycho-physiological measures 22
team debriefs 18, 22
team design 9–10
team development 13; action processes 15–16; adjourning stage 12; conflict stage 11–12; contingency model 12; coordination 16; cyclical models of 18; effect of studies on 22–3; effect of temporal dynamics on 22; episodic theories of 15–19; forming stage 11–12; historical viewpoint of 8–11, 18–19; interpersonal processes 16–17; linear group 11; longitudinal models 11; maturation process 24; models of 11–14; multiple-sequence model 13; norming stage 12, 62; patterns of 22; and recurrent periodicity 15; repeated activity mapping 15; stages of 6–7, 11–14, 18–19; storming stage 12–13; TEAM model 13;

temporal 6; and training 22–3; transition processes 15, 17–18; transition stage 18; transition-action periods 18; *see also* team dynamics; team members; team outcomes; teams
team dynamics, temporal 6, 24
team effectiveness framework 7
Team Evolution and Maturation (TEAM) developmental model 13
team functioning, temporal influences on 3
team mediators 19–20
team members: backup behaviors of 9; competencies of 9; cross-training of 9; monitoring of 22, 24; *see also* team development; teamwork
team outcomes 7, 19–20
team processes, measurement of 17
team research 8; temporal issues in 23f
team theories, cyclical 7
teams: backup behaviors of 15–16; coordination of 18; diversity in 10; effectiveness of 14; effect of temporal orientation on 62; effectiveness of 7–8, 13–14, 18–24; empowerment of 9–10; influences on 7; life cycle of 23; monitoring of 15; multiteam systems 10; research on 9; virtual 21; *see also* team development
teamwork 9, 24; *see also* team members
technology: human interface with 9; interaction through 10; and interpersonal teamwork 9; small teams operating with 8; and team analysis 24; and team functioning 21; work-related 24
temporal antecedents, of routines 117, 132f, 136
temporal characteristics, of HR policies 2
temporal constructs *see* time constructs
temporal context: analysis of 1–2; cross-cultural 1, 3
temporal depth 5, 156–7
temporal dynamics, and team efficiency 18–19
temporal focus 4–5, 20, 33, 55–60, 62–4, 68, 101, 103, 128, 131, 156–7
temporal framing 156
temporal influences, on team functioning 3
temporal orientation 55–60, 62–4; antecedents of cultural differences in 57–60; consequences of cultural differences in 60–4; cultural differences in 54–7, 67–8; and cultural metaphors 57; cultural perspectives 53; and language 59–60; long-term vs. short-term 64; measurement challenges 64–6;

Lightning Source UK Ltd.
Milton Keynes UK
UKHW021535040922
408155UK00017B/293